SALMAGUNDI

SALMAGUNDI

A Celebration of Salads from around the World

Sally Butcher

Photography by Yuki Sugiura

Interlink Books

An imprint of Interlink Publishing Group, Inc.
Northampton, Massachusetts

CONTENTS

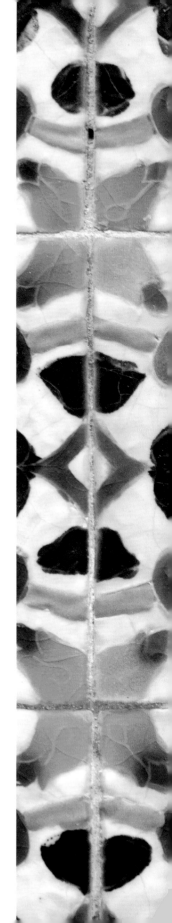

INTRODUCTION

A question. If someone tells you that it's salad for dinner, isn't there a teensy petulant you inside that stomps their foot a little at the prospect of being fed rabbit food as a repast? Be honest now. You are not alone: back in the (seventeenth century) day one Robert Burton wrote: "Some are of the opinion that all raw herbs and sallets breed melancholy blood." We have all had luscious salads full of melty cheese, naughty croutons, and sizzled meat or fish, but still the initial mention of salad immediately conjures visions of floppy lettuce, diet clubs, detoxing, and virtuosity. Or very sad garnishes composed of wilted round lettuce leaves and slightly sweaty tomatoes.

What are your first salad day memories? Apart from my grandfather's wonderful (basic) coleslaw (see p.62), my childhood resonates with the clickety-clack of mid-air salads being cobbled together on melamine plates. My dreamer of a father believed that life was for living, and was quite happy to make sacrifices (sell my grandmother, send the cat out on a paper route, you know, that sort of thing) so that we could have adventures (this gave my mother a lot of headaches and me the best childhood imaginable). So first there was a trailer, then a boat. And anyone who has ever camped or boated will know that one of the best sounds of the day is that special noise that plastic camping "crockery" makes as it is readied for lunch/the evening meal. My mother would produce an astonishing variety of meals out of a tiny galley, but the lettuce, tomato, cucumber, scallion salads were always snipped and shredded mid-air with a weensy knife and tumbled onto a plate with salad cream. (My mother-in-law still prepares salads this way, and looks at me with amusement as I sharpen my knife, get out a chopping board, and start assembling ingredients.) The point is, for many of us, being allowed to "help" make a salad rates among one of our first experiences in the kitchen.

Thing is, you can make anything into a salad. There are no rules. If you want steak and fries in your salad, or fruit and nuts, or 10 types of cheese, well, there's nothing stopping you. Salads can be hot, cold, or somewhere in between. (They may comprise cooked ingredients, but unless you are cooking everything up together, the combo is a salad, not a stew.)

Furthermore, you don't have to go out and buy special materials for a salad: you can always find things in your fridge, your pantry, or your veggie drawer that can be pressed into service. Go with the seasons, the weather, or circumstance.

Salad, you see, is a state of mind. It's all about finding ingredients that will play nicely together in one bowl. It's about having a feel for things that work, and the willingness to let your imagination travel.

Salmagundi, for those of you who have not yet encountered it on a trivia night somewhere, is a seventeenth-century English expression denoting a salad dish comprising, well, everything. The term is derived from the French word *salmigondis*, but the first recorded mention of it in English comes in an eighteenth-century tome by well-known plagiarist Hannah Glasse. I include here the recipe in full for your culinary delight, wonderfully random CAPITAL LETTERS and all:

To Make Salamongundy
Take two or three Roman or Cabbage Lettice, and when you have washed them clean,
swing them pretty dry in a Cloth; then beginning at the open End, cut them cross-
ways, as fine as a good big Thread, and lay the Lettices so cut, about an Inch thick all
over the Bottom of the Dish. When you have thus garnished your Dish, take a Couple
of cold roasted Pullets, or Chickens, and cut the Flesh off the Breasts and Wings into
Slices, about three Inches long, a Quarter of an Inch broad, and as thin as a Shilling;
lay them upon the Lettice round the End to the Middle of the Dish and the other
towards the Brim; then having boned and cut six Anchovies each into eight Pieces, lay
them all between each Slice of the Fowls, then cut the lean Meat of the Legs into Dice,
and cut a Lemon into small Dice; then mince the Yolks of four Eggs, three or four
Anchovies, and a little Parsley, and make a round Heap of these in your Dish, piling it
up in the Form of a Sugar-loaf, and garnish it with Onions, as big as the Yolk of Eggs,
boiled in a good deal of Water very tender and white. Put the largest of the Onions in
the Middle on the Top of the Salamongundy, and lay the rest all round the Brim of the
Dish, as thick as you can lay them; then beat some Sallat-Oil up with Vinegar, Salt
and Pepper and pour over it all. Garnish with Grapes just scalded, or French beans
blanched, or Station [nasturtium] Flowers, and serve it up for a first Course.

She mentions two other salmagundis, both comprising multiple minced ingredients
layered with salad greens and garnished with lemon, barberries (interestingly enough),
and astertion (probably nasturtium) flowers. In the third recipe she somehow captures the
very essence of this book when she writes: "This is a fine middle-dish for supper; but you
may always make salamongundy of such things as you have, according to your fancy."

Salmagundi is not in any obvious way related to the children's rhyme, Solomon
Grundy, but it may have given rise to the Caribbean dish Solomon Gundy: a paste
comprising all sorts of stuff. The nearest modern equivalent is perhaps *Fiambre* (see
p.189), a Guatemalan salad containing in excess of 20 ingredients.

A Potted History of Salletting
Yup, salletting is a thing, a real verb, albeit a somewhat archaic one, meaning "to make
salads." But who are the salad heroes of yesteryear?

The practice started with the Romans. Now I am no fan of the Romans, as I generally
regard them as copycats rather than innovators, the Borg of antiquity—although for the
most part they managed to assimilate without destroying stuff. But when it comes to
gastronomy, I am in awe of their achievements. Their understanding of subtle flavors and
balance, and their sheer delight in food was something new in the ancient world. They, via
the medium that is mostly known as Apicius and his book *De Re Coqinaria*, recorded the
first instances of herbs and other ingredients being prepared as *salata* (from the Latin
word *sal*, or salt). Simple leaf salads were eaten as part of the *gustatio* (the Romans' first
course of appetizers). There are various (and frankly fairly bizarre) recipes for composed,
layered, potted salads as well (see p.61).

There is not much salad action thereafter until the Middle Ages. Impressive works that reference salads were brought out in Italy and France, but the first one in English was a fourteenth-century book called *Forme of Cury* (as in the French verb *cuire*, "to cook," as opposed to an early work on curries). The unknown author suggests that we:

> *Take persel, sawge, garlec, chibolles, oynouns, leek, borage, myntes,*
> *porrectes, fenel and ton tressis, rew, rosemarye, purslarye, laue and waische hem clene,*
> *pike hem, pluk hem small wi yn honde and myng hem wel with rawe oile.*
> *lay on vynegur and salt, and serue it forth.*

Which after a lot of humming and hah-ing I reckon probably transcribes as:

Take parsley, sage, spring garlic, shallots, onions, leeks, borage, mint, scallions, fennel, cress, rue, rosemary, and purslane. Rinse and wash them clean, pick through them and pluck them into small pieces by hand, and mix them well with extra-virgin oil, then add vinegar and salt and serve.

By the sixteenth century there were quite a number of foodie manuscripts in circulation: produced mostly by country squires, they offer a valuable, albeit sexist, complicated, and often hysterically funny view of rural life at the time. My favorite is a guy called Thomas Tusser who wrote *A Hundreth Good Poyntes of Husbandrie*: his poem is brilliant in its apportion of farm household tasks and for all of the husbandrie in the title, seems mostly to focus on good wiferie. This is not a book for Liberated Twenty-first Century Woman. Anyway, he mentions no fewer than 70 different herbs, salad greens, and edible blooms including many which we sadly no longer play with in the kitchen: skirrets (which yield a root a bit like Jerusalem artichoke), Alexanders (posh word for horse parsley), rampions (a type of campanula, cultivated for its spinach-like leaves and edible roots), a number of worts, and orach (a kind of spinach).

But it was in the seventeenth century that salads came to prominence, and this was mostly the work of John Evelyn, prolific diarist, curious gardener, passionate ecologist, and founder of the Royal Society. His work *Acetaria: A Discourse of Sallets* is the first book uniquely dedicated to salads… although he shoots off at all sorts of tangents from decrying "modern" obesity, to imprecating that we all eschew meat (he quotes another author who reckons flesh-devourers are "heavy, dull, unactive and much more stupid"), to an astonishing tirade against forced vegetables and the artifice of urban market gardening.

His treatise is most fascinating for me in that it ties in with my previous playing around in the Middle Eastern kitchen, as every ingredient mentioned is assigned one of the four humors: still to this day in most of Iran and Afghanistan meals are planned according to their "hot" (*garm*) or "cold" (*sard*) properties. Medieval dietetics followed this ancient system, as interpreted by Avicenna; thus each fruit, vegetable, herb, or spice in *Acetaria* is ascribed a "character," from "hot and dry" through to "cold and moist." Furthermore, we all have different temperaments, which affect our digestion of food. An imbalance of hot foods was thought to induce giddiness and fever, while overly cold consumption was thought to make the body sluggish. Hot, dry foods include things like garlic, hot pepper, artichoke, mint, mustard, and fennel; cold, moist foods include lettuce, beets, spinach, cucumber, and barberries. It has partly been my aim in assembling this "gallimaufry" of recipes old and new to follow Evelyn's example, offering food that is balanced, and including nutritional snippets where I have found them interesting. Even in his day it was believed that you are what you eat, as Cowley wrote in his poem The Garden:

> *If thro the stong and beauteous fence*
> *Of Temperance and Innocence*
> *And wholsome Labours, and a quiet Mind*
> *Diseases passage find;*
> *They must not think here to assail*
> *A Land unarm'd or without Guard*
> *They must fight for it, and dispute it hard,*
> *Before they can prevail;*
> *Scarce any Plant is used here,*
> *Which 'gainst some Aile a Weapon does not bear.*

Salmagundi looks at salad bowls across the world. The recipes feature a number of archaic, traditional, and staple dishes—and a whole lot of funky new stuff as well. Evelyn would, in truth, be horrified by the vast array of ingredients that creep onto the following pages. But as the world has gotten smaller, inevitably ingredients from the New World (grains and exotic fruit, tomatoes, potatoes, and peppers), Africa (many grains and vegetables) and the Far East (spices and rice) have crept into our salad bowls.

Salletting has lost its way a bit here at least; in Roman times and in Evelyn's day, it was regarded as an appetizer (see Chapter 1, p.11 on the effect of herbs on the digestion). In France and much of the Mediterranean sallet is regarded as a course between courses, a palate cleanser. In the Middle East salad is either part of a *mezze*, or again is eaten as an appetizer before the main meal. In the US and UK it has been somewhat relegated to a desultory side dish for far too long. It is time for it to shine again.

Once again I have been interrogating and badgering my customers for tales of their back-home salads. The fact that I now have a salad bar in my shop means that this book has been a pleasure to put together; I have also had no shortage of guinea pigs. I would hope that you will use it to reboot your perception of salads and turn them into something fun, a dish to which you look forward. To quote from satirist Sydney Smith's famous rhyming salad dressing:

> *Oh, green and glorious! Oh, herbaceous treat!*
> *'Twould tempt the dying anchorite to eat;*
> *Back to the world he'd turn his fleeting soul,*
> *And plunge his fingers in the salad bowl!*
> *Serenely full the epicure would say,*
> *"Fate cannot harm me, I have dined today."*

CHAPTER ONE
Herbs and leaves

For many salad = lettuce. Well, to be precise, lettuce, tomato, and cucumber.
But for years the lettuce leaf has been used as the padding of the salad bowl,
a prop in other dishes, a last minute garnish, or the mousey extra in a cast of
super-glam ingredients all jostling for stardom. This is a shame, as lettuce and
salad greens in general offer a world of flavor and texture: sweet, bitter,
nutty, fresh, crispy, floppy, wispy, pert… take your pick. Add their even
more exotic cousins, the herb family, and you have an exciting range of
produce to play with indeed.

In Iran, herbs (*sabzi khordan*) are eaten as a dish all by themselves. Great handfuls of them are eaten at the beginning of a meal to whet the appetite and aid digestion, incorporated into sandwiches, or used as a side. Although they remain "undressed" they do form a salad of sorts, and in this the Iranians have much to teach us. We should all keep fresh herbs in the fridge (ideally sourced from our own gardens: see p.28–9).

If you want to develop a herb habit (if you see what I mean), look for pert, green herbs. Farmer's markets are good places to buy. When you get them home remove the stalks (keep these for stock if you are of thrifty bent), pick out any mangy bits and plunge the herbs into a bowl of cold water (see the guide to salad washing on p.21). After 10 minutes scoop the herbs out, tip the water away, and repeat: most herbs need two washes at least. Drain the herbs thoroughly in a colander, invert a plate on top, then store in the fridge until needed; they also keep well in a plastic bag if fridge space is at a premium. Try serving a plate of fresh herbs with raw onion, radishes, raw garlic, and scallions as an appetizer with some warm bread, feta, and walnuts. Chop handfuls of herbs as a garnish or to throw into salads. And as mentioned above they are great wrapped into sandwiches.

What herbs should you be buying? Well here's a brief list of the basics.

BASIL: sweet or lemon basil are both lovely eaten raw. And they both contain lots of good stuff: basil is anti-inflammatory, laden with flavonoids, and full of vitamin K. Basil leaves are the most delicate of the leaves mentioned here so treat it with care and consume within a day or so.

CHIVES: a junior member of the garlic family, and imbued with most of the properties thereof. Useful in cooking/salads, and also great eaten just as they are.

CILANTRO: improves the appetite and aids digestion/reduces nausea (seriously: try chewing on a small handful of cilantro next time you feel queasy—it works). It too is a powerful anti-inflammatory agent, and eaten over a long time works as a chelation agent (getting rid of heavy metals and other nasty stuff from your system). Most excitingly, it enhances your good cholesterol uptake and suppresses the bad stuff. Cilantro, like basil, needs looking after—check your herb basket on a daily basis to pick out any bits that have gone bad.

DILL: famously good at ridding one of hiccups. Dill is also very good for the digestive system, and sweetens the breath. Most importantly it works in a mysterious (very complicated scientific) way to neutralize toxins in the body and prevent certain bacteria from growing.

MINT: famously good for the digestive system—mint tea after a meal works wonders. But let me try and tell you something you didn't know… one good thing about it is that mice hate it. Growing mint near your house will keep the little rascals out. It is also very good for the skin: if you pound it to a pulp and mix it with yogurt it makes a soothing face mask. Add some coarse salt and it then becomes a very effective foot scrub. As someone with an expensive spa habit, I tried the latter out and thoroughly endorse it.

PARSLEY: used everywhere to freshen the breath after a night drinking or too much garlic, parsley has a host of other attributes worth bragging about. It is full of vitamins A and C, and potassium. And it generally seems to be good for, er, things below the waist (although pregnant ladies should beware—it was used historically to procure abortion). It is especially touted as a tonic for the kidneys: juice it and consume thrice daily. Pounding a few sprigs of parsley and warming them through will give you a (pretty, green) poultice, which you can apply as a zit zapper.

TARRAGON: is known to stimulate the appetite and aid digestion. Of all the common or garden herbs, it has the highest quantity of antioxidants, and a fair serving of trace minerals and vitamins to boot. It's mildly anaesthetic quality makes it quite good for treating mild toothache.

LETTUCE SALAD BITES WITH AVGOLEMONO DRESSING

This is a great way to use up that less-than pert-lettuce lurking in the hydrator drawer of your fridge. Round (butterhead or Boston) lettuce works best with this as it is already soft, but any lettuce can be rendered pliable by the process of blanching. Salad bites are perfect for finger buffets, since the whole salad thing is wrapped up in the lettuce leaf. No mess. No dish washing. Rather clever really.

MAKES 12
FOR THE BITES:

12 lettuce leaves
4 firm tomatoes, diced
6 pickled baby cucumbers, finely diced
1 small onion, diced
12 pitted green olives, sliced
6 anchovies, chopped (optional)
salt (if necessary) and
　　freshly ground black pepper

FOR THE EGGY LEMON SAUCE:

4 eggs
5 tbsp nice olive oil
juice and grated zest of 1 lemon
2 tsp English mustard
½ tsp cayenne pepper
½ tsp paprika

This is simple stuff and then some, but they are best prepared as last minute as possible. If your lettuce leaves are drooping, then just skip to the second paragraph. If not... fill a bowl with really cold water and park it near your oven. Next, bring a pan of water to a boil and blanch the lettuce leaves: they only need around 45 seconds. Remove them from the pan and plunge them into the cold water—this will stop them from becoming completely mushy and unworkable—before leaving them to drain thoroughly in a colander. Better still, pat them dry with paper towel.

Next, hard-boil the eggs (10 minutes from cold normally works for me) then plunge them into cold water to cool.

Mix the rest of the ingredients for the bites together in a bowl and season to taste. Take a lettuce leaf and put it on the surface in front of you, stalky-end pointing away from you. Place about 2 tablespoons of salad mixture at the end of the leaf nearest you and roll the leaf away from you, tucking the side bit in as you roll so that the filling ends up completely encased in lettuce. Repeat with the other leaves.

Set aside while you whisk up the lemon sauce. Carefully peel and then cut through the eggs and extract the yolks.* Press the yolks through a sieve (or just mash them thoroughly) and put them in a bowl with all the other dressing ingredients. Beat well to form a thick sauce, and pour into a little serving bowl. Arrange the salad wraps on a plate with the dressing in the middle and dig in.

✳ A note on leftover egg whites

Well, they're pretty good chopped into an omelette, or you could stuff them with cheese or the Marmite dip on p.250—they would make good lunchbox fare. Just don't throw them away, OK?

Broken eggshells are also pretty handy: scatter them around your favorite garden plants to deter slugs from feasting on them. Not that I'm good at gardening or anything...

MEET MIN, THE GOD OF LETTUCE AND SEX

If you dig hard enough you will find that everything has a god or a patron saint. And lettuce is no exception. The salad vegetable was famously regarded as an aphrodisiac in ancient Egypt: this originally had a lot to do with the fact that if you crush lettuce it secretes a milky white substance (ahem), but it has indeed been shown to boost the libido.

For this reason rituals associated with the worship of the Egyptian fertility deity Min had much to do with the consumption and sowing of Romaine. Being a sex god in the literal sense, Min's image is traditionally, er, graphic: he's usually depicted with arms (and everything else) raised as a sign of his supremacy. He's often associated with Set and Horus: I am too prudish to elaborate on these latters' adventures with lettuce, but suffice it to say that you should always wash the stuff thoroughly. Those ancient Egyptian immortals were naughty, naughty boys, I tell you.

CAHOO VA SEKANJEBIN: LETTUCE STEAKS WITH MINT SYRUP

This is eaten as a dish all on its own in hot weather in Iran—it is incredibly refreshing. Traditionally it is made with romaine lettuce, but I happily substitute iceberg, which can be cut into neat "steaks." The syrup featured here, *sekanjebin*, is quite versatile—I add it to all sorts of dishes. It was devised originally as a *shabat* (sherbet)—a syrup to have over ice in the summer, but its culinary applications are far more interesting to me.

generous 1 cup/250ml water
1¾ cups/¾lb/350g sugar
4 tbsp white vinegar
dozen sprigs of fresh mint
1 lettuce of your choosing

Place the water in a pan; add the sugar and bring to a boil. Bubble for 10 minutes, remove from the heat, and add the vinegar. When it is a bit cooler, add the mint, pour into a sterilized bottle, and chill.

To serve, wash the lettuce of your choice, and dissect leaf by leaf. Arrange the leaves like a flower on a plate around a bowl of the *sekanjabin*. If you are using something like iceberg lettuce, you can cut it into "steaks" and drizzle the syrup over each portion.

JEWELED (LITTLE) GEM SALAD WITH POMEGRANATE

A good salad should suck you in visually before you even consider raising a fork and digging in. This little number certainly does that: it is about as flirtatious as food can get. Add some seared tuna or a little duck breast and you have an elegant appetizer.

A DAINTY LITTLE SIDE FOR 2

½ small pomegranate
1 little gem lettuce, roughly shredded
1 clementine, carefully peeled, segmented
   and seeded
⅓ cup/1¾oz/50g slivered pistachios
1 small carrot, grated
½ red onion, finely sliced
big handful of watercress
big handful of fresh mint, finely chopped

FOR THE DRESSING:

⅛ tsp ground saffron, steeped in a splash
   of boiling water
3 tbsp extra-virgin olive oil
juice of ½ small lime
1 tbsp orange juice
1 tsp honey
1 level tsp mustard
freshly ground black pepper
salt

First prepare your pomegranate. Change into your reddest outfit, then don an apron for good measure. Now you could just cut the pomegranate open and pry out the seeds. But the Persian pro way to do it is to pummel the fruit all around with your thumbs, thus loosening the seeds nearest the skin. Once it starts to feel quite soggy, make a small incision in the flesh of the fruit, hold the hole over a glass or jug, and squeeze very gently so that the juice released trickles out (you may drink this—it will put hairs on your chest). Now that the pressure has been released, it should be easy to pry the pomegranate open and release the rest of the (intact) seeds: make sure you discard the white pith, as it is bitter (although it is very good for you, especially when consumed as a tea). Throw the pomegranate seeds into a bowl and mix gently with all the other salad ingredients.

   Add the steeped saffron to the olive oil, fruit juices, honey, and mustard and whisk into an emulsion. Season to taste and drizzle across the salad. Pretty pretty, no?

HAIL, CAESAR

Is Caesar salad the most famous salad in the world? And has ever a salad recipe been so abused? The term is used indiscriminately to describe more or less any salad containing romaine lettuce and cheese, and is featured as the token salad/diet option on many an ill-thought-out menu. The attention it gets is ironic in view of the fact that it was created (like so many great dishes) when a Tijuana restaurant catering mostly for Prohibition-weary Americans in the 1920s ran out of regular salad ingredients. Owner Caesar Cardini did what any experienced restaurateur would do: he improvised with such bluff and bravado that whatever the customers had originally ordered was quite forgotten. He grabbed a few bits and pieces, prepared what we now know as a Caesar salad at the table right in front of his guests, and the rest is salad history...

There has been much ferocious debate about what should and shouldn't go into this emperor of salads (and no: anchovies are not authentic). I will not enter the fray, but have chosen merely to replicate the original recipe, as related by Julia Childs (who had actually visited Cardini's establishment). "Cause if something ain't broke, it doesn't really need fixing."

A CLASSIC APPETIZER FOR 4

2 garlic cloves, minced
¾ cup/175ml olive oil
3 slices stale bread, crusts off and cubed
1 head of romaine lettuce

1 large egg
juice of ½ lemon
1 tsp Worcestershire sauce
sea salt and freshly ground black pepper
scant ¼ cup/1oz/25g freshly grated Parmesan

Mix the garlic with the olive oil and leave to macerate for at least 6 hours, preferably overnight.

When you are ready to think about your salad, preheat the oven to 340°F/170°C. Brush the bread croutons with some of the garlic oil and bake for about 30 minutes. Set aside to cool.

Wash the romaine and dry it thoroughly: there are few crimes in the salad world as heinous as watery lettuce leaves. Bring a small pan of water to just under boiling point and cook the egg for exactly 1 minute (i.e. coddle it); remove it from the pan and set aside.

I will leave it to you as to whether you want to do this tableside or hidden in the kitchen, but when you are ready to assemble the Caesar, rip the lettuce leaves into small chunks with your hands and arrange them in a big bowl.* Crack the egg into a small bowl and whisk it with the rest of the garlic olive oil, the lemon juice, Worcestershire sauce, and pepper, and pour this dressing over the lettuce. Throw in the cheese and croutons, and toss well. Serve with sea salt on the side.

* Note

Some reports suggest that the original dish was served with whole romaine leaves, which diners then used as scoops for the rest of the ingredients, but this seems mighty impractical to me.

PROPER TABOULEH

Because proper tabouleh is a herb salad with wheat, not a wheat salad with herbs. But y'all knew that, right? This version is based on the lovely Anissa Helou's recipe, because she is an authority on Levantine food. And learning a cuisine is a bit like learning to be a clown: you need to grasp how to do it properly before you can start playing around with it. But the truth is that you can throw more or less anything at bulgar and make a serviceable salad (see the brown bulgar salad on p.126).

FOR 4–6 PEOPLE

⅓ cup/1¾oz/50g fine bulgar
1lb 2oz/500g very best tomatoes
3 scallions
2 bunches of fresh parsley
1 bunch of fresh mint
½ tsp ground cinnamon

½ tsp *baharat* (Iraqi 7 spice mix), or use ground allspice
¼ tsp ground black pepper
sea salt
juice of 1 lemon
⅔ cup/150ml extra-virgin olive oil
romaine lettuce leaves (optional)

* Handy hint
Cosmetically speaking, any grain-based salad is best dressed at the last minute as the grain subsequently sucks up the dressing and ends up looking rather tired.

Wash the bulgar several times, drain it well, then spoon it into a large-ish bowl. Continue to fluff it occasionally with a fork as you get the rest of the dish ready.

Finely dice the tomatoes and scallions, setting the former in a colander to drain. Discard the woodier parts of the parsley and chop the rest finely with a knife; do the same with the mint. Add the tomatoes, scallions, and herbs to the bulgar together with the spice and black pepper and mix well before sprinkling in salt to taste.

Pour the lemon juice and olive oil over the tabouleh and stir one more time before serving. It is traditionally piled into the middle of an array of lettuce leaves, which are in turn used as scoops.

ON URBAN FORAGING

Salad leaves, right. They're getting just so very posh. Little bags of silly expensive arugula and mizuna and tatsoi and other things that sound like the roll call at a private girls' preparatory school. It can verge on the pretentious: I once worked with a (stuck-up pain of a) restaurant manager who nearly fired me for mistreating his radicchio…

"It needs to be pulled, darling, not cut: you just aren't listening to the leaves now are you?"*

"Um, no: it's a lettuce."

Anyway, the point is that we don't need to buy this stuff at all. With some knowledge (and time) we can forage for it. There is an astonishing amount of free stuff out there just waiting to be plucked by plucky pluckers, especially when it comes to salad material.

In the interests of research I walked out one midsummer morning with Penny Pickle, a knowledgeable (and very funny) urban forager. I learned more about botany during my one hour Peckham perambulation with her than I have in years of watching nature documentaries and quaint gardening shows on tv.

I expected a special camouflage outfit, a secret handshake, and a 6am start. Instead we set off at 9am on a Monday morning dressed in civvies and armed with nothing more than some plastic bags for collecting stuff. Foraging has, of course, become more or less mainstream now: this probably has much to do with the economic climate, staying in being the new going out and thrift replacing ostentation as a social virtue.

On our little urban adventure we traversed a public garden, peeked over the fences of some private ones, and meandered along the course of an old canal.

We saw cardoons, wild carrots, plums, damsons, crab apples, sweet chestnuts, filberts, and medlars growing: Penny also told us of quince, barberry, raspberries, cherry, and loquats all in the vicinity.

Of more relevance to my salad, I picked hedge garlic leaves, fat hen (nope, I'd never heard of it either), dandelion, fennel, and arugula, together with sage and rosemary for flavor, and some linden flowers for color. This did produce a salad fit for kings (albeit ones of the South London variety). Other edible wild plants that are easy to find here are chickweed, wild violets, sorrel, and elderflower, but you're sure to find many others in your particular region. Spring is the best time for all types of foraging but there is produce to be had throughout the year for the determined and the sharp-eyed.

There are guided foraging walks all over the place now, but allow me to summarize the golden rules that I have learned thus far.

1. It is not for you if you don't like creepy crawlies.
2. Go with an experienced forager: there's a lot of stuff out there that is at best inedible, and potentially poisonous.
3. You will need a plastic bag and a Swiss army knife at the very least: garden gloves are also useful.
4. Never take too much from one source: foraging and sustainability are completely intertwined.
5. Always remove fruit and leaves with care so as not to damage the plant.
6. Respect the needs of other wildlife sharing the same habitat.
7. Pretty obvious this one, but always ask before picking stuff on private land.
8. Pick away from roadsides and above the, um, dog-pee-line….

* Note

Just for the record, he was, irritatingly, right: radicchio (and many other leaves) should always be shredded with the hands.

PENNY PICKLES'
PECKHAM SALAD

So you've been and gone and gotten yourself some fancy free salad stuff (see p.19). Here's what to do with it...

A SIDE DISH FOR 4
5½oz/150g fine foraged leaves
    (see p.19 for commonly found varieties)
3–4 tbsp extra-virgin olive oil
2 tbsp balsamic vinegar
1–2 garlic cloves, minced
sea salt and freshly ground black pepper

Now the thing with foraged leaves is to wash them well. Generally speaking all salad leaves should be plunged into a bowl of cold water, allowed to soak for around 10 minutes, then removed from the water and put in a colander to drain. The really dirty straight-from-Farmer-Giles'-field stuff is probably much healthier, but you will almost certainly need to wash it thoroughly in 2 bowls of water: you will know when it is clean when there is no sediment left at the bottom of the bowl. Rinsing leaves and vegetables quickly under a tap is not really "washing" it: what it is is that you are just paying lip service to something your mother once told you (although it is better than not washing it at all).

    Foraged leaves need a bit of extra help. Putting salt in the water in which you are washing them is the best thing (most salad-dwelling wildlife doesn't like salt), although if you are really fastidious you could invest in a simple old-fashioned sterilizing liquid such as Milton.

    While your salad is soaking and draining, whisk the rest of the ingredients together: any dressing containing garlic benefits from extra "mingling" time. Foraged and wild leaves are usually very flavorsome (or maybe it just seems that way because you've worked up such a big appetite while you've been out gathering the stuff in the great outdoors), so you don't want to douse them with a heavily flavored dressing. But they are also often bitter and earthy in flavor, and so a good sweet vinegar is required to counteract this.

    To serve this salad the proper John Evelyn way (he'd have loved the idea of foraging, see p.19), you should tip your dressing into a non-metallic bowl, and then add your drained leaves, tossing with your hands. It would also be a good idea to leave your pruning shears (scissors) and muddied walking boots (sneakers) lying around as testimony to your magnificent foraging skills.

TARRAGON SALAD WITH SOUTHERN FRIED CHICKEN

Those that know me will possibly brand me a hypocrite over this salad. I have a theory that fried chicken is one of the greatest evils facing modern society today. That is… if you buy it dripping in fat and swamped in salt from a greasy fast food joint (you'll find one located outside your nearest high school). But there's a vast difference between that and this home-seasoned, pan-fried recipe.

A SPRING SALAD FOR 4
FOR THE CHICKEN:

4 skinless, boneless chicken breasts

2 tbsp tarragon vinegar (see p.255 or just use white wine vinegar and tarragon)

3 tbsp buttermilk

2–3 garlic cloves, finely minced

1 tsp salt

oil, for frying (peanut would be nice here)

4 slices Canadian (back) bacon, diced

½ tsp cayenne pepper

scant 1 cup/¼lb/120g polenta (aka cornmeal)

FOR THE SALAD:

1 lettuce, washed (or a mix of soft bitter, such as batavia, and crisp sweet, such as romaine)

2–3 sprigs of fresh tarragon, chopped (or use 2 tsp dried French tarragon)

1 large red onion, sliced

12 cherry tomatoes

7oz/200g cooked corn kernels (optional)

3 tbsp buttermilk

1 tbsp olive oil

2 tbsp tarragon vinegar

1 tsp Dijon-style mustard

salt and freshly ground black pepper

* A note on tarragon

Tarragon (from the Farsi word *tarkhoun*) is an outstanding herb. In Iran it is one of the most coveted stars of the sabzi basket (see p.11), consumed for its ability to aid the digestion and sweeten the breath.

There are two basic varieties of the herb, and while I am of course paid to suggest that the Persians are better at everything, in this instance the French variety is greatly superior. Tarragon's pungent flavor is the perfect foil to fish and chicken.

First cut each chicken breast into 4–5 strips lengthways, then halve each strip crossways. Whisk the vinegar, buttermilk, garlic, and salt together in a bowl and lower the chicken pieces in, turning them over so that they all get thoroughly coated. Cover the bowl and refrigerate it for around an hour or until you're ready to cook: if you need to cook sooner, leave the chicken somewhere at room temperature for around 20–30 minutes.

Next, heat a splash of oil in a frying pan and fry the diced bacon until it is crispy. Remove it with a slotted spoon and set aside. Mix the cayenne with the polenta on a plate. Now take the chicken pieces one at a time, shake them to get rid of any surplus marinade, and roll them in the polenta mix before frying them in the hot bacony oil until the outside is crisp and no pink remains inside (a few minutes per piece should be enough, but cut one open to check). Set the chicken aside to cool slightly while you assemble the salad.

Shred the leaves roughly with your hands and mix them with the tarragon and sliced onion in your prettiest bowl. Sprinkle the tomatoes, corn, and bacon on top, followed by the still-warm fried chicken. Whisk the buttermilk, oil, vinegar, mustard, and seasoning together and pour it over the top of your creation. Serve immediately with crusty bread and homemade lemonade…

RADICCHIO, LIVER, AND SAGE SALAD

This is a take on the classic Italian dish *fegato alla salvia*, which Mr. Shopkeeper and I eat at our favorite classic Italian restaurant nearly every time we go.* You know how it is when you have a pet restaurant: on each visit you peruse the specials board, even ask the chef for his recommendations, consult with your dining companion… and then order exactly the same as you always order. It's part of the comforting ritual.

This is a healthy salad: liver is full of iron and other trace minerals, while both sage and radicchio contain compounds that may combat memory loss and high blood pressure. It is a very bitter combo, but the soused onion and cucumber offer a pleasing counterpoint.

SUPPER FOR 2

2–3 baby cucumbers (or ⅓ of a regular one)
1 small red onion, finely sliced
2 tbsp sherry (or cider) vinegar
1 tbsp water
½ tsp sugar
12 black peppercorns, crushed
½ tsp dill (fresh or dried)
¼ tsp ground saffron
9oz/250g lambs' liver (or calves'—but lamb
    is more delicate/less bitter), peeled
knob of butter

about 12 fresh sage leaves (grows everywhere—
    check your neighbor's garden),
    chiffonaded (i.e. shredded into ribbons)
salt and freshly ground black pepper
1 pert-looking head radicchio
2 tbsp pumpkin seed oil (if you can get it:
    it is not cheap, so feel free to use
    extra-virgin olive oil)
1 tbsp balsamic vinegar
6–7 frisée leaves (curly endive)
    or just use iceberg

Peel and deseed the cucumber, then cut it in half lengthways, and slice it thinly. Place it in a shallow bowl together with the onion. Next, pour the vinegar into a saucepan along with the water, add the sugar, and bring to a boil. Take the pan off the heat, add the pepper, dill, and saffron, and pour the hot liquid over the cucumber and onion. Leave to stand for 2–3 hours (or more, if time permits).

When you are ready to cook, finely slice the liver. Melt the butter in a frying pan; when it is hot, fry the liver (around 1½ minutes per side should do) together with around half the sage, and season lightly. Remove the meat with a slotted spoon and set aside. Pull the radicchio apart, and with your hands shred around half of it into the pan in which you have just cooked the liver, turning it over so that it gets coated: cook for a minute or so (you want it to wilt, not dissolve); then take off the heat.

Whisk the pumpkin seed oil, vinegar, and salt and pepper together. Shred the frisée lettuce together with the remaining sage and radicchio. Strew it prettily on a platter and drizzle it with the dressing. Spoon the sautéed liver and radicchio over the dressed leaves, and arrange the soused vegetables around the edge. Some top-notch rye bread would be good with this, but anything interestingly wholegrainy and/or nutty will do.

* Il Giardino in Peckham
Confusingly, it is actually Sardinian, and run by Peruvians. Peckham is that sort of place.

CHINESE CABBAGE WITH SPICED TOFU

Nice and simple, this. Just one ingredient smothered in a yippee-ki-yay kind of dressing. Just in case you live somewhere more exotic than London's home counties, Chinese cabbage is also known as Napa cabbage or Chinese leaves.

A SIDE DISH FOR 6 OR SO

1 pert-looking head Chinese (Napa) cabbage

4 tbsp silken tofu

1 large carrot, grated

2 tbsp peanut oil (or use oil mixed with
   1 tsp peanut butter)

1 tbsp white miso

1 tbsp rice vinegar

1 tbsp mirin (or other strong sweet wine)

4 garlic cloves, crushed

¾ in/2cm knob fresh ginger, peeled
   and minced

big handful of fresh sweet basil

salt

Shred the Chinese cabbage leaves on to your finest willow pattern platter.

Blend the rest of the ingredients, seasoning to taste, and serve in a bowl in the middle of the leaves. Regale your guests with the tale of the plate's star-crossed lovers as they emerge from beneath the salad...

THE STORY BEHIND WILLOW PATTERN

Many years ago, when the moon was still young and made of silken tofu, the lands to the north of the Yangtze River were ruled by a wealthy, despotic mandarin. Like many tyrants in fairy stories, he had a daughter, Koong-se, who was as fair and gentle as he was evil. And she, again somewhat predictably, had fallen for her father's gardener, who was called Chang. Every night they would meet by the garden wall: so strong and pure was their love that even the nightingales sang to them as they walked and talked in the moonlight.

Unbeknown to Koong-se, her father had arranged for her to be married to a malodorous rich merchant. This latter had offered a treasure

trunkful of golden *zhu* (coins) for her hand. When she found out, she was devastated, and so she and Chang snatched the treasure and fled by boat in the middle of the night.

Their escape was successful... at least for a few years, and they lived happily on a little island in the Yellow Sea. But eventually the usurped merchant tracked them down and had them killed. The gods were enraged, and turned the tragic pair into lovebirds, forever to fly together across the crockery of the world...

A friend of ours actually wooed his wife by charming her with this tale. Stories are powerful things, I tell you.

A WINTER HERB SALAD:
CARROT AND CRISPY KALE

Gaia, Demeter, Ceres (whatever your pet name for Mother Earth) is really quite a clever divine entity. She sends fruit to cool the febrile in summer and veggies to soothe the flu-ridden in winter. And even when the fields are apparently barren and there is frost on the ground she sends us stuff to use for salads. It may not be the pert lettuces and juicy tomatoes of summer, but it is still saladable.

If you have a herb patch, frankly there is no excuse for it to lie fallow when the temperature drops. Cilantro, parsley, mint, salad burnet, fennel, chervil, sorrel, and dill enjoy the cooler months, and then there are winter varieties of purslane and savory. Kale too is happiest sprouting in colder months. Check out Dan Pearson's guide on pp.28–9 for a few handy hints.

If you don't grow your own (and I have to admit that while I sing her praises, it is likely that Mother Earth shudders at my clumsy attempts at horticulture) then these leafy goodies are available to buy at good grocery stores and farmers' markets. Better still, befriend a neighbor with a garden…

TO PERK UP A LUNCH FOR 4
1 fat head of curly or lacinato kale
3 medium carrots, peeled
2 tbsp pure olive oil
salt and freshly ground black pepper
½ tsp caraway seeds
½ tsp fennel seeds
⅔ cup/2¾oz/75g pumpkin seeds
1 nice apple, cored
1¾oz/50g smoked cheese, diced

1 very big handful of mixed fresh winter herbs:
    your choice of parsley, chervil, cilantro,
    sorrel, and dill, roughly chopped

FOR THE DRESSING:
4 tbsp extra-virgin olive oil
1 tbsp apple cider vinegar
1 tbsp pomegranate molasses
sea salt and freshly ground black pepper

Preheat the oven to 350°F/180°C.

Chop the kale into 1 in/ 2.5cm wide strips and place it in a bowl. Cut the carrot into matchsticks and add it to the kale. Mix the pure olive oil with a sprinkling of salt and pepper together with the caraway and fennel seeds, and pour the mixture over the kale/ carrot combo, rubbing it in with your hands to ensure that the strips are all coated. Then spread the veggies out on a baking tray and roast them for around 10 minutes: you are aiming for a crispy rather than cremated effect. Set aside but keep warmish.

Turn the oven down to 300°F/150°C, throw the pumpkin seeds into an oven dish, and roast for about 6 minutes, or until crisp, before adding them to the hot veggies.

Next, cut the apple into matchsticks and mix together in a bowl along with the cheese and chopped herbs. Add the warm vegetables and pumpkin seeds, then whisk the dressing ingredients together, and pour them over the salad.

Serve as a delish side for your roast dinner: it works well with pork or lamb.

DAN PEARSON'S GUIDE TO GROWING HERBS

If you are going to tarry a while in these pages, you'll need fresh herbs. If you live in a big city, then you will have no trouble buying them; but if you live halfway up Mount Snowdon, then clearly your best bet is to grow them yourself.

A confession. I'm rubbish at gardening—brown fingers, that's me. I'm also pretty ignorant (although if I don't know what something is called, I tend to inform everyone in my most authoritative voice that it is a lobelia). And I'm a chronic arachnophobe, which tends to keep me out of much of the garden at the best of times. But even I have had some success at growing herbs. And there is nothing quite as satisfying as heading outside to harvest herbs that you are just about to use in the kitchen…

Below is my brief guide to the most useful herbs you can grow. So you don't have to replicate my method, which consists largely of keeping my fingers crossed, I got one of Britain's nicest gardeners (who happens to be a former Peckham resident) to jot down a few handy herby hints…

Dan Pearson is the gardening columnist for the *Observer* newspaper and the author of a number of beautiful books on garden projects, which have been known to inspire even horticultural eejits such as myself to Google chichi wellies and dust off their trowels.

Anyway, now we must cultivate our garden. I have but taken the Big Six: basil, cilantro, dill, mint, parsley, and tarragon.

GENERAL ADVICE

Dan says: most herbs like plenty of light and air with well-drained soil. That said, if you are growing them in pots or window boxes try and use a loam rather than a peat-based compost as it is easier to re-wet if it dries. It also has more long-term stamina.

BASIL: likes pots (remember Isabella and her pot of basil?). This is good as it means that you can plant it in pots indoors to germinate and take it outside once it's sprouting. You can also bring it back inside for the winter (which it doesn't like). You should plant seedlings about 6–8in/15–20cm apart, then water them sparingly but regularly (preferably at midday).

Dan says: basil is an annual and is easily grown from seed. Basil likes good living, and all the warmth it can get to do well. It will rapidly run to seed if it gets dry. Pinch out the growing tips when you harvest to encouraging branching and new foliage.

CILANTRO: needs a fair bit of soil, as it has a long taproot (hark at me using the lingo). If you are growing it in a pot, choose a deep one. It likes sunshine, and doesn't like too much water.

Dan says: cilantro is also an annual and shares many of the same requirements and foibles as basil. Where basil will happily transplant as seedlings, cilantro must be sown direct and allowed to run its life cycle in the same position. Re-sow every six weeks during the growing season for a crop of new plants.

DILL: doesn't like it too hot. It grows well in the spring. Harvesting the green bits is easy, but if you want to harvest the seeds (which are also good for cooking) you should wait until the heads have gone brown, wrap them in a paper bag and hang them up upside down so that the seeds drop out.

Dan says: dill is also an annual and like cilantro must be sown direct and left where it is. Dill does not share the same requirement as basil for good living and can cope with cooler temperatures. Easy, but re-sow monthly to keep you in a succession of young foliage, since it runs to seed rapidly.

PARSLEY: soaking parsley seeds in warm water gets them off to a good start in life. They too can be started indoors then kicked outside when the weather gets warmer. They like to be around 8in/20cm apart. If you are leaving parsley plants outside in the colder months, snuggle them up under a cloche.

Dan says: parsley is a biennial, forming a good crop of foliage in the first year and bolting to seed the next. Flat-leaf parsley is superior to curly. Best sown in rows and avoid drying out to prevent bolting.

MINT: is rather hard to grow from seed, so best use cuttings. Look out for "rust": if your mint gets rusty, destroy the crop as this is what gardeners call a bad thing. It is quite hardy, and you can plant a batch in fall.

TARRAGON: is also best grown from cuttings. It's a sensitive soul, and quite likes living indoors.

Dan says: tarragon and mint are best grown in pots as they are both prone to running. Both are perennial and will come back year after year but divide and replant biennially in spring to ensure the healthiest plants as they are hungry and will rapidly outstrip their resources. Pinch out tips to harvest and cut to the base if the plant gets tired to encourage a fresh new crop of leaves.

Off you go then. You don't have to take it as seriously as our somewhat misogynistic friend Thomas Tusser:

In March and in April from morning till night
In sowing and seeding good housewives delight.

But get in there and have a little play around.

SUMMER HERB SALAD WITH LAVENDER, NECTARINE, AND CAERPHILLY

Gee this is a bling recipe, a ditsy young girl of a salad, guaranteed to skip across your taste buds and transport you to those halcyon days of long picnics and overhead larks and sand between the toes and the plop of water against the dock and the sigh of wind in the reeds, and poppies peeping out of the hedgerows, and the far away cry of plaintive gulls, and the knowledge of the whole summer yawning ahead. Of course, the truth is that this showy-but-delectable salad is full of new-fangled floral swagger, and the salads of one's youth were much simpler affairs. But it is undeniably full of zing and joie de vivre—one to pull out when you are really trying to impress.

SERVES 4
FOR THE DRESSING:
1 heaped tsp dried organic lavender
4 tbsp extra-virgin olive oil
1–2 tbsp red wine vinegar
1 heaped tsp creamed horseradish
2–3 garlic cloves, minced
salt and freshly ground black pepper

FOR THE SALAD:
4–5 leaves of romaine lettuce,
    roughly shredded
big handful of watercress
12 cherry tomatoes, halved

2 fat nectarines (or peach, mango, or plum),
    pitted
1 small zucchini
1 red onion, finely sliced
½ cup/3½oz/100g plump black olives
4½oz/125g Caerphilly cheese (or any salty,
    tangy, crumbly cheese), roughly cubed
3–4 sprigs of fresh lemon verbena, crushed
1 big handful of edible flowers (see pp.262–4)
1 big handful of mixed aromatic summer
    herbs: red amaranth, chickweed, dill,
    fennel leaf, nasturtium leaves, anise hyssop,
    purple basil, tarragon, oregano,
    summer purslane…

Whisk the ingredients for the dressing together and leave to mingle for at least 30 minutes. Mix the lettuce, watercress, and tomatoes in a shallow dish. Slice the nectarines and cut the zucchini lengthways before slicing it thinly into half moons. Stir these into the salad along with the onion, olives, cheese, and verbena. Scatter the flowers and remaining herbs gaily over the top and drizzle with the dressing. Swoon at the prettiness and fragrance of it all.

GREEN PEA AND SORREL SALAD

In theory, just as you really only need two people to make a party, you really only need one choice ingredient and a pot of salt to make a salad. This is pretty close to that: just three ingredients and a bit of sauce (that's just about as minimalist as I get before I start feeling insecure).

Sorrel grows wild all over the place and is one to look out for on your next foraging walk (see p.19). Evelyn rated it very highly, writing that he found it "abstersive,* acid, sharpening appetite, asswages heat, cools the liver, strengthens the heart, antiscorbutic,** resisting putrefaction, and imparting so grateful a quickness to the rest... as never to be excluded." Better plant some pronto, eh?

By the way, the name "sorrel" is often applied to drinks and products made from hibiscus, but they are not the same plant at all: they both have attractive red flowers, but that is all they have in common.

*

Yes—I didn't know what that meant either. It means "cleansing."

**

Prevents scurvy.

***

Or use watercress—but if so, add the juice of ½ lime to the dressing. Sorrel is naturally sharp, whereas cress is not.

A SUPER-SIMPLE SIDE SALAD FOR 4

5½oz/150g fresh, pert-looking podded peas

big bunch of fresh sorrel (about 2¾oz/75g), roughly torn ***

small bunch of scallions, chopped

1½ tbsp crème fraîche

1 tsp honey

3 tbsp walnut oil (or extra-virgin olive oil)

salt and freshly ground black pepper

Mix the first 3 ingredients in a bowl. Whisk the other 4 ingredients together and pour over the salad. Couldn't be much easier.

A WATER THEMED SALAD: WATERMELON WATER ICE, WATERCRESS TARATOR, WATER CHESTNUTS

Playtime in the kitchen. This looks tricky but really isn't, since a) I'm a clumsy so and so and so incapable of doing "tricky," and b) you can do most of it in advance. It is so worth the effort—a salad of contrasts in temperature and texture and color. It would make a good appetizer, or better still an impressive salad to serve alongside a simple cut of meat or piece of fish.

A BIT OF OSTENTATION
FOR 4–6
FOR THE SORBET:
1lb 2oz/500g skinned watermelon, deseeded
juice of 1 small lime
handful of fresh basil, shredded
½ tsp cayenne pepper

FOR THE SALAD:
½ cup/3oz/80g toasted hazelnut halves*
1¾oz/50g canned water chestnuts, sliced
1 bunch of watercress, pulled apart roughly
3oz/80g oakleaf lettuce, shredded by hand

1 bunch of scallions, chopped
⅓ cucumber, thinly sliced

FOR THE TARATOR:
1 small onion, chopped
dash of oil, for frying
2 garlic cloves, minced
1 bunch of watercress, chopped
2 tbsp lemon juice
1 level tbsp tahina
salt and ground white pepper

First the sorbet, which clearly needs time to set. Blend the watermelon with the other ingredients, pour it into a mold, and place it in the freezer to set. After an hour give it a quick churn and leave it for another 2–3 hours to set firm.

Get the salad ready by mixing all the ingredients on a platter. About 10 minutes before you want to serve, remove the sorbet from the freezer to soften slightly.

Make the tarator by frying the onion in a little oil: once it starts to brown, add the garlic and the watercress, stirring well. After a couple of minutes add the lemon juice and the tahina together with enough water to make the sauce pourable (around ½ cup/100ml). Season to taste and keep warm until needed.

Right at the last moment, scoop pretty little balls of sorbet on to the salad platter, and spoon the warm tahini sauce over the sorbet. Serve immediately. Some suitably elegant brown bread on the side would be an appropriate extra.

* Or use cobnuts
Cobnuts are just a cultivar of the hazelnut family, after all. But they are a bit like the forgotten cousin these days, which is a shame as they have a stronger flavor. Random cobnut fact: like chestnuts, whole cobnuts used to be used in children's games.

WILD RICE WITH "WILD" GREENS AND NETTLE PESTO *SUPER-HEALTHY*

I once made the mistake of serving wild rice to my Iranian family-in-law. Now Iranians probably make the finest range of rice dishes in the world, but they are all based on cousins of basmati type rice. Wild rice isn't even a rice—it's a type of water-loving grass and from the expression on the faces of the aforementioned in-laws, I may as well have been serving, well, grass, as in the sort you find in your backyard. This was a shame, as wild rice is a gourmet carb and a tad pricier than your average box of Uncle Ben's.

Extra-curricular wild rice activity: you can pop it like popcorn by heating it with a little oil in a sealed pan…

You could source the "wild" greens used in this salad by foraging (see p.19), but in this context any nutty and bitter mixture of herbs will do. And if you cannot find pert baby nettles to make the pesto, just use watercress (although it is somewhat satisfying telling people that they are eating stinging nettles). Because *Salmagundi* is all about fun, and no recipe should send you into an ingredient-related tizzy.

* Nettles

They're everywhere. They are always especially dense when you're wearing shorts and the dog dives off into the bushes. So it only seems fair to get your own back and cook the little devils, especially as they are super-nutritious (good for allergies, asthma, and the kidneys). You should only use the tops of young nettles, and make sure you gather those that grow above the dog-pee line and away from main roads. A pair of thick gloves is essential for harvesting them. To render them usable (sting-free) blanch them in boiling salted water for just a minute before draining and plunging them into iced water (to arrest the cooking process). Drain and use as required.

** Adding salt

If you want to preserve the life of your saucepans always add salt to water after it has come to a boil, since at lower temperatures the salt merely serves to scour and erode the pan. When one's mother works in the homeware department of a big store one gets bombarded with useful stuff like this…

A SIDE FOR 4
scant 1 cup/6oz/175g wild rice, washed
salt
1 small red onion, finely sliced
12 radishes, finely sliced
3oz/80g wild greens, julienned (radish or beet tops, purslane, sorrel, spinach, fennel fronds, watercress, arugula… the list is endless, so you choose)

FOR THE PESTO:
3oz/80g (raw weight) nettle tops, blanched*
generous 1/3 cup/1¾oz/50g pine nuts, toasted (or use the significantly cheaper sunflower seed kernels)
2–3 garlic cloves
¼ cup/1oz/30g grated Parmesan (or halloumi or just omit if cooking for vegans)
¼ tsp sugar
scant ½ cup/100ml extra-virgin olive oil
salt and freshly ground black pepper

Place the wild rice in a saucepan containing about 2½ cups/600ml salted water. Bring to a boil, add salt,** cover, and set to simmer for around 40 minutes, or until the rice puffs up and is soft when you bite it. Drain if necessary. Fluff with a fork and allow to cool.

Next, make the pesto. Using a food processor or knife/mortar and pestle, blend the nettles, pine nuts, garlic, cheese, and sugar together, then trickle in the oil to make a pleasing green emulsion. Season to taste.

We'll make this the way old Oscar of the Waldorf made his salads—it works well for thick dressings. Scrape the pesto into a salad bowl and toss in the rice, onion, radishes, and greens, stirring well from the bottom up until everything is coated.

CHAPTER TWO
Vegetables

So when we first started walking out together, me and the man, we did this crazy romantic Breakfast at Tiffany's thing where we tried to spend a day doing things neither of us had done before. All good until the end of the day when we both realized that neither of us had ever been brave enough to eat in a certain London-based chain of steak houses. And that was where the romance stopped. Without going off into one of my rants, let me just tell you about the house salad, which was very "special." It comprised warm, overcooked vegetables and a cold sliced tomato. When I mentioned the fact that it was warm in all the wrong ways, the waiter removed the offending dish and reappeared, Basil Fawlty style, with the vegetables now suspended in a dripping colander. "I cooled it down a bit more for you," he informed us… really, you couldn't make that up, now could you?

Fortunately the salad genre has come on in leaps and bounds, not to mention our general understanding of how (and whether) to cook vegetables. And restaurant standards have improved (although there are still branches of the aforementioned and now more or less iconic steak house chain which look untouched by the hand of culinary progress). Vegetables, whether salad veggies or otherwise, have come of age. And salads are important: gone is the time when a salad was often added to the menu as an afterthought or extra.

MAURITIAN PALM HEART SALAD

Let's be honest here—palm hearts are just bling artichoke hearts. I mean, they're not—they are the heart of the trunk of the palm tree—it's just that they taste similar, and to all intents and purposes behave the same way.

Now stealing the heart of a palm may seem a little callous—and in the case of wild palms it is, as the action of removing the core of the trunk kills the tree. But fear not—by some quirk of nature, the "peach palm" produces several trunks, which enables this delicacy to be harvested without any harm to the tree.

Anyway, here at least we are largely limited to canned palm hearts, which are available in some supermarkets and most Afro-Caribbean–South American grocery stores.

FOR A GENEROUS SALAD FOR 6

1 romaine lettuce, roughly shredded
1 can (16oz/450g or thereabouts) palm hearts
2 medium avocados, cut into rough chunks
1 small can anchovy fillets (about 8–10),
    roughly chopped
scant ½ cup/1¾oz/50g grated Parmesan
3–4 hard-boiled eggs, peeled and quartered
generous ¼ cup/1¾oz/50g (or so—does
    anyone actually weigh olives?) black olives
3–4 lovely tomatoes, halved and sliced

2 handfuls (about ½ bunch) of fresh cilantro,
    chopped

FOR THE DRESSING:

2 garlic cloves, minced
4–5 tbsp olive oil
2–2½ tbsp white wine vinegar
1 good tsp grainy mustard
2 shakes of Worcestershire sauce
2 sprinkles of Tabasco
(a little) salt and freshly ground black pepper

Ok, so you mix up the dressing and let it sit around and mingle for 30 minutes or so to let the flavors get to know each other.

Layer the lettuce over a large platter or in a pretty bowl, halve the palm hearts, and mix them with all the other ingredients; then pile the mix on top of the lettuce. Finally, drizzle on the dressing.

BONUS RECIPE

You could also make this fruitier salsa-type salad—the contrast of textures and flavors is nothing short of stunning:

2 small green chilies, chopped
4 tbsp olive oil
juice of 2 limes and the grated zest of 1
salt and freshly ground black pepper
1 can (1lb/450g or thereabouts) palm hearts

1 small papaya (or ¼ melon), cut into
    ½in/1cm cubes
2 avocados, cut into ½in/1cm cubes
½ cucumber, cut into ½in/1cm cubes
1 medium red onion, chopped

Whisk together the first 4 ingredients on the list. Quarter the pieces of palm heart, and mix with the rest of the ingredients before tossing in the dressing.

RETRO AVOCADO SALAD TWO WAYS

The 1970s. Platform shoes! The Osmonds! Hot pants! Glam rock! Lava lamps! Tank tops! Snowballs! Need I go on? No other decade is quite so well viewed from the "retro" angle: from an eyewitness' point of view, the decade was truly the 10 years that taste forgot. It is only now, 30 years on, that we can look back at it with a degree of affection, from a warm, fuzzy Instagrammed perspective.

The height of exotic food at the time was cheese fondue, spaghetti Bolognese, or Black Forest cake... or avocado and shrimp. It was only during the 70s that the avocado pear was launched on the general public you see, and that was largely thanks to a very clever viral marketing campaign by Carmel (coffee mornings and Tupperware parties being early forms of viral marketing, yes? Because if your neighbor is going to an event, you most certainly have to go too...). Anyway, as a child of the 70s, I cannot, even now, look at an avocado without a teensy David Cassidy riff running through my head...

AVOCADO AND CITRUS SALAD

A confession: this is based on something I once saw on TV by a portly guy known as the Cooking Canon. Oh for the luxury of being able to watch lunchtime TV once more...

AN APPETIZER FOR 4
2 perfectly ripe avocados
splash of lemon juice
1 orange
1 small grapefruit
1 head of chicory, divided into leaves
2 tbsp olive oil

2 tbsp walnut oil (or just use 4 tbsp olive oil)
1 tsp Dijon mustard
1½ tbsp red wine vinegar
½ tsp brown sugar
salt and freshly ground black pepper
few sprigs of fresh curly parsley

Halve the avocados carefully, removing and discarding the pits, then scoop out the fruit with a spoon (keeping the skin intact) before cutting it into small cubes. Sprinkle the flesh (of the fruit, that is—although rubbing used lemon halves on one's elbows and knees does keep them looking pert and youthful) with a little lemon juice to prevent discoloration.

Remove the peel and pith of the citrus fruits with a sharp knife, and cube them, discarding any seeds, before adding them to the avocado. Retaining at least 8 larger leaves, chop the smaller chicory leaves and add them to the salad.

Next, whisk the oils, mustard, vinegar, sugar, and seasoning together and pour it over the salad. Arrange the reserved chicory leaves on side plates and nestle the empty avocado shells on top. Spoon the dressed fruit and veggies into the avocado hollows, and garnish with parsley. Serve with wheat bread and butter and some nice Liebfraumilch.

AVOCADO SHRIMP JELLO SALAD

Once upon a time all housewives had jelly molds, knew how to use aspic, polished all their silverware once a week, went to the hairdresser at least every other week, and had dinner parties at least once a month. No, not Stepford. The US. Circa 1975. Jello was very big in the 70s. Not just sweet, but savory and all sorts of crossovers, some of them quite vile. This, however, is just plain fun, and a little bit fabulous.

KLINGON PARTY FOOD FOR 6

1 pack (3oz/85g) lime jello (enough to make
  generous 2 cups/500ml)
scant ½ cup/100ml vodka
  (optional, just use water if you like)
½ tsp Tabasco
1 bunch of fresh chives, chopped
4½oz/125g nice peeled shrimp

1 avocado, peeled, pitted, and cut into
  elegant slices
12 fat olives stuffed with pimento, sliced
3 tbsp mayonnaise
2 tbsp ketchup
juice and grated zest of 1 lime
1 small head of frisée (curly endive)

Make up the jello according to the directions on the pack, replacing scant ½ cup/100ml of the water required with vodka, if using. Add the Tabasco and the chives to the jello mixture, and pour it into a ring mold or bundt pan. (If you don't have a one just use any mold and scoop out some of the jelly in the middle to make a well.) Place in the fridge to set (or freezer if your time or patience is limited).

When the jello is lightly set, take it out of the fridge. Arrange the shrimp, avocado, and olive slices at regular intervals in the jello all around the mold so that when the thing is turned out it looks real pretty. Put it back in the fridge to set firm. Meanwhile, mix the mayonnaise, ketchup, and lime juice together.

When you are ready to amaze your guests, turn the jello out onto a plate and surround it with frisée leavs. Pile some of the leaves into the middle of the jello, and top them with the sauce "Marie Rose" (pink mayo). Serve with crispbreads, and you may as well make use of the rest of that bottle of "voddie."

FAVA BEAN SALAD WITH SESAME

The beginning of the fava bean season is an ugly time in our household. We buy them by the case, you see, and then fight over the last portion. Traditional Iranian *taruf*, or politeness, does not apply here.

This salad sees them teamed and steamed with their early summer chum, asparagus, and then drizzled with a lemony sesame dressing. If you happen to be reading this in mid-winter all is not lost: canned or jarred asparagus and frozen beans work pretty well too.

SERVES 4 AS AN APPETIZER OR SIDE

2 tbsp sesame seeds

9oz/250g fresh fava beans (podded weight)

1 bunch of asparagus (or 1 can, or 1 jar)

4 garlic cloves, smashed

2 tbsp chopped fresh chervil, if available (if not use the poor cousin, parsley)

4 perfectly hard-boiled eggs

2 tbsp water

2 tsp tahina

¼ cup/1¾oz/50g clarified butter (melt butter; then strain it)

2 tbsp olive oil

½ tsp ground cumin

juice of 1 lemon

salt and coarsely ground black pepper

Dry-fry (well, toast) the sesame seeds in a little pan and set them aside.

Shuck the beans (best done while watching something inane on TV). If they are anything other than early summer babies, then trim the woody end bits from the asparagus (usually up to where the whitish part starts to merge into the green). Put the vegetables and the garlic in a steamer (or a colander suspended over boiling water) and steam for about 6 minutes, or until both beans and tips are tender. If you are using canned asparagus, just drain it.

Allow the beans and asparagus to cool a little and place them in a bowl; roughly chop the garlic and stir it back into the salad with the chervil. Quarter the eggs and arrange them prettily over the top.

Now for the dressing. Beat the water and tahina together, then whisk in the butter, olive oil, and cumin, followed by the lemon juice.* Season to taste. Pour the dressing over the salad, and sprinkle the sesame seeds on top.

* Note

If you are cooking ahead, or wish to chill the salad before use, add a little more water to the dressing as it will set in the fridge.

GAZPACHO SALAD

I invented this by accident when I was cooking for xenophobic ex-pats out in Spain. You know the kind: they want to live in abroad-shire, but only as long as it tastes and smells like home. I took puerile delight in feeding them local delicacies disguised as, well, "safe food." Thus a classic chilled soup with croutons becomes a crouton salad with a soup dressing.

My parents lived in Spain for quite a few years, and this is based on their neighbor's recipe. My mother (who learned to speak fluent Spanish minus all the verbs) often wonders if they still make as much use of her Aunty Norah's recipe for banana cake as she does on some of their shared recipes. Cross culturalism: it's everywhere you know.

A SIDE DISH FOR 4–6
FOR THE "SOUP DRESSING":

6 garlic cloves, minced

2 tbsp/25ml red wine vinegar

scant ¼ cup/50ml extra-virgin
    olive oil

14oz/400g fresh plum tomatoes, peeled and
    chopped (canned will not do here)

1 tsp paprika

salt and ground white pepper

1–2 tbsp cold water

FOR THE CROUTON SALAD:

oil, for frying

2 slices stale bread, crusts removed and cubed

1 level tsp dried marjoram

½ cucumber, peeled and diced

1 red onion, finely diced

2 tomatoes, finely diced

1 green bell pepper, finely diced

1 red bell pepper, finely diced

1 avocado, peeled, pitted, and diced

½ bunch of fresh parsley, finely chopped

¿Vamos? Start by pounding (or blending) the garlic with the vinegar, then add the olive oil to make a paste. Beat in the peeled tomatoes and seasoning, then add just enough water to make it pourable. Refrigerate for around 6 hours (or overnight).

Ready to serve? Heat a little oil in a frying pan and fry the bread cubes until golden, adding the marjoram right at the end. Drain the croutons on paper towel. Mix all the vegetables together; stir the "dressing" and then pour it over the salad. Strew with the croutons and the parsley. *Muy bueno*.

GADO GADO: INDONESIAN PEANUT SALAD

This salad is so popular in our household that when a certain small person started calling it "Good-oh Good-oh salad" no one corrected him. Well, it has got peanut butter in it, and peanut butter makes everything good, yes?

Gado Gado just means "mixed" in Indonesian, and this is indeed a sort of Asian salmagundi. The vegetable and carb contents can be varied according to season/availability, but the sauce is practically incommutable. Don't be put off by the number of ingredients: it all comes together pretty easily, as it happens.

A HEALTHY LUNCH FOR 6

¾lb/350g firm potatoes, peeled and cut
　　into thick slices
salt
¼ tsp ground turmeric
2 medium carrots, cut into matchsticks
7oz/200g green beans, cut into short lengths
¼ white cabbage, finely shredded
1⅔ cups/7oz/200g beansprouts, rinsed
a little sesame oil, for frying
9oz/250g firm tofu, cut into ¾in/2cm cubes
3 hard-boiled eggs, peeled and quartered
3 tomatoes, quartered
around 4in/10cm piece cucumber, sliced
big handful of fresh cilantro, chopped

2½–2¾oz/60–75g shrimp crackers, optional,
　　but authentic
scant ⅓–½ cup/2½–2¾oz/60–75g shelled
　　roasted peanuts, lightly chopped

FOR THE MAGIC SAUCE:

1 medium onion, finely diced
3 garlic cloves, minced
¾in/2cm knob fresh ginger, minced
1–2 bird's eye chilies, finely chopped
2 sticks of lemongrass, finely chopped
1 cup/9oz/250g crunchy peanut butter
juice and grated zest of 1 lime
1 tbsp kecap manis*
generous ¾ cup/200ml coconut milk
salt

Put the potatoes in a pan of cold water along with salt and turmeric. Bring to a boil; then simmer for 15 minutes, or until the potatoes are cooked but firm. Remove the potato slices, (leave the water in the pan), dunk them into cold water to stop them cooking, drain, and set aside. Drop the carrots and green beans into the still-simmering water, and cook for 6 minutes, or until they too are cooked but firm. At the last minute add the cabbage and sprouts, bubble for just 30 seconds, then drain the pan and refresh the contents under cold water.

Next, heat the oil in a frying pan or wok and fry the tofu cubes until they are just starting to brown. Remove with a slotted spoon and drain on paper towel.

Now for the sauce. Fry the onion, garlic, ginger, chilies, and lemongrass in the leftover oil in the pan (adding more oil if necessary). When the onions have softened, take off the heat and beat in the peanut butter, lime juice, and kecap manis (you can do it in a blender if you like). Stir in the coconut milk and enough water to make the sauce, well, just saucy enough to pour. Check the seasoning and add salt if you require.

There are two schools of thought on presentation: one has the ingredients grouped together tidily like an edible Mondrian; the other is more Picasso or Pollock—an abstract but undeniably pleasing jumble. Gently mix the veggies, tofu, egg, tomato, cucumber, and cilantro together on a platter. Drizzle with the magic sauce and garnish with crackers and peanuts.

∗ Note

Kecap manis is basically Indonesian sweet soy sauce. It is readily available online and in larger Asian supermarkets, but you can replicate it either by boiling regular soy sauce and brown sugar (in equal measures, volume wise) gently for around 20 minutes until the mixture is thick and ketchupy, or if you're in a real hurry just whisk soy sauce and honey together.

TOMATOES AND CUCUMBERS

To quite a lot of my Iranian family-in-law, salad is just tomato and cucumber with seasoning. Anything else comprises saladic heresy. Some of the salads I lovingly used to create for them had them at best chortling in disbelief, and I did overhear one or two conversations to Iran along the lines of, "You'll never guess what she did last night…." (yes, I speak Farsi, paranoia being the best teacher of any foreign language).

So this section is dedicated to these most elemental of Middle Eastern salads. *Salad-e-shirazi, fatoush,* *salata duco, salaata*—these are all, basically, the same salad—tiny-diced tomato, cucumber, onion, and herbs, with salt and lemon juice and maybe some pepper.

To get the best out of these classic dishes, you need the very best ingredients. Heritage or home-grown tomatoes (fancy cherry tomatoes will also do), and knobbly, wibbly-wobbly cucumbers: organic or home-grown, or baby Middle Eastern-style ones.

SALAD-E-SHIRAZI

Salad-e-Shirazi is THE classic Iranian salad. *Salaata* is the Central European equivalent—it is pretty much the same but with added chilies—while *salata duco* is the Saudi version and uses peeled tomatoes (but no cucumber), lime instead of lemon, cilantro, chili, and garlic.

This is a fantastic accompaniment to just about any savory dish you can think of. Husband often makes it for his lunch and adds nice tuna for protein. I personally love it with a light crumbling of labneh or goat's cheese—although I am not allowed to make this salad at home as apparently I "don't understand it" (this is, of course, fine, as it allows me to sit back and let other people prepare it).

FOR A BIG BOWLFUL
6 baby Middle Eastern-style cucumbers
   (or 1 regular one)
6–8 large and wonderful tomatoes
2 medium onions
big handful of fresh parsley and/or cilantro,
   chopped
juice of 1–2 lemons
sea salt

OPTIONAL (LESS AUTHENTIC)
EXTRAS:
freshly ground black pepper
drizzle of olive oil
shredded fresh mint leaves

Peel the cucumbers. Yes—I know this goes against everything that one is taught about stuff with the skin being better for you and so on—but it just gives a much better flavor. Next, chop the cucumber, tomatoes, and onions into chunks bigger than a salsa but smaller than your average salad chunk (let's say ½in/1cm cubes or less). Add the herbs, lemon juice, and salt to taste together with any optional extras. Serve with kebab/barbecued meats, grilled fish, in sandwiches, as part of a buffet spread, in your lunchbox…

PROPER FATOUSH

Fatoush is the Levantine version of *Salad-e-Shirazi* (see opposite), although I do not wish to hazard a guess as to which came first. What makes *fatoush* interesting is the inclusion of croutons. Croutons instantly add a frisson of naughtiness to a salad, not to mention crunch. This is, in fact, one of a range of dishes known as *fatta* (literally: crushed bread or crumbs), which evolved to use up stale bread. So it's a thrifty little number, and you earn extra points for it if you do actually use leftover crusts.

A SIDE SALAD FOR 4

1½ pieces pita bread, preferably whole-wheat, since it is better for you (or, to be more authentic, the equivalent in stale bread)

little non-virgin olive oil, for frying

2 tsp sumac

4 tasty tomatoes (not the supermarket ones that taste of water)

2 baby cucumbers, scraped (or ½ regular one, peeled)

4 scallions

1 green bell pepper

1 little gem lettuce

around 20 black olives (choose ones with character)

1 handful of fresh mint, chopped

1 handful of fresh parsley, chopped

1 handful of fresh cilantro, chopped

6 tbsp olive oil

juice of 1½ lemons

2 garlic cloves, minced (optional)

salt and freshly ground black pepper

Toast the pita bread until it just puffs up, split it, and then cut it into 2in/3cm chunks. Heat a little oil in a frying pan, tip in the bread, and cook it for a couple of minutes, turning it over halfway through, before lifting it out on to a piece of paper towel to drain (don't worry if the bread still seems soft—it will become crunchier as it cools). Put the sumac in a paper bag (or shallow tray), add the croutons, and shake the bag to ensure that they get coated evenly before setting them aside.

Cube the tomatoes and cucumbers (⅝–¾in/1.5–2cm chunks are good). This should be a salad with texture, not a salsa. Chop the scallions, green pepper, and lettuce to match, and then add the olives and herbs. Whisk the olive oil with the lemon juice, garlic, and seasoning, and stir it over the salad ingredients. Toss in the croutons and voila.

蒜泥拍黄瓜 *(SUÀNNÍ PAI HUÁNGGU)* OR WAI YEE HONG'S SMACKED CUCUMBER SALAD

The world is getting smaller. Modern technology means that you can, at the click of a socially connected button, be friends with someone you've never met. It has also enabled my emporium to make friends/swap gossip with other shops. True words: the bricks and mortar that comprise my shop have a better social life than I do. One of its best Twitter friends is a jolly, well-stocked Chinese Cash and Carry in Bristol. Owner Joe-Wah and Mom Wai Yee Hong are very fond of food, so it seemed natural to ask them to provide an authentic Chinese salad for this book.

Joe-Wah writes thus: "Growing up in a Cantonese family, I never really ate much in the way of salads. Vegetables were usually cooked and served hot in our household. It wasn't until later in life I discovered the great variety of Chinese 'cold-plates' (涼菜—*Liáng cài*) enjoyed by our northern countrymen. Since discovering these wonderful chilled dishes, I have sought them out in every restaurant and experimented in making my own at home."

A garlicky, cooling dish. It may be simple to put together, but it is just as easy to consume a whole dish on your own. I like to use white vinegar, so that the dish looks clean and bright, but black rice vinegar would work just as well.

Investing in a pure sesame oil will mean that you can use less, as it has not been diluted with vegetable oil.

AN UNUSUAL TREAT FOR 2

1 large cucumber
1 tsp salt
2 tsp light soy sauce
small chunk of brown sugar slice (片糖—*Piàn táng*) equivalent to 1 tsp brown sugar

5 tbsp white rice vinegar
1 tbsp pure sesame oil
4–5 garlic cloves, smashed and roughly chopped
sliced red chili
chopped fresh cilantro

Optional Extras
* Add pieces of double-fried *youtiew* (Chinese savory doughnuts) to the salad just before serving for contrasting crunch.
* Add a little spice with a pinch of Sichuan peppercorn powder or 1 teaspoon chili oil in the dressing.
* Add a pinch of chicken bouillon powder to up the umami savory flavor in this dish.

As you might imagine, one of the important parts to this recipe is the smacking. Smacking the cucumber loosens the flesh and leaves lots of lovely jaggedy edges that the dressing clings to. Don't get too enthusiastic though; you do not want cucumber mush.

Place the cucumber on your chopping board, then "smack" it with the flat of a Chinese cleaver or other broad-bladed knife (a rolling pin would do). Do this a couple of times up and down the cucumber just enough to make the cucumber split and crack.

Once it has split, pull the cucumber open and scrape out the main bulk of seeds. Next, slice the cucumber into batons or chunks and place in a bowl. Salt and mix well to ensure even coverage. Cover and leave to chill in the fridge for 15 minutes.

While the cucumber is chilling, warm the soy sauce with the sugar and vinegar gently until the sugar is dissolved, then take off the heat. Add the sesame oil and garlic to infuse into the dressing while it cools.

Finally, drain the cucumber. Mix well with the dressing, garnish with a little sliced chili and fresh cilantro, and it is ready to serve.

YUKI'S JAPANESE SALAD BAR

A book might initially be the product of the lady/gent what wrote it, but there is a lot more to a finished tome than the words, the spaces between the words, and the commas and dots and dashes. Recipes need to be tested, cooked, styled, tweaked, photographed—and the book itself needs to be designed, proofread, type-set... Anyway, as this is the third book I have written with the same team, I decided it was only fair to bring them on to the pages of the book.

Yuki is from Japan, and loves cooking, so that makes her my pet expert on Japanese salads already (although what she is really, really good at is taking photos—but you can see that on the other pages of the book). Here is what I have learned from her thus far...

The main word for Japanese salads is *aemono* which literally means "mixed (or coated) things"—it is a very loose term but usually refers to stuff—veggies, meat, fish—dressed in other stuff—Yuki mentions mustard soy, shira-ae (mashed tofu), and sweet miso as being among the most popular dressings.

Other notable sub-categories of salad include *sunomono*, which means "things dressed in vinegar" and *gomaaee*, which means "things dressed with sesame." For the former rice vinegar is used to dress anything from cucumber or daikon to fish—but as we have already had a vinegary cucumber salad on the previous page, I thought we'd take the sesame route for the first of our Japanese recipes...

DEEP-FRIED EGGPLANT *GOMAAEE* WITH BLACK SESAME DRESSING

A SIDE SALAD FOR 4

6 tbsp black sesame seeds

3 tsp maple or agave syrup

1½ tbsp dark soy sauce

1½ tbsp sake (use water if you prefer)

vegetable or sunflower oil, for deep-frying

2 big firm eggplants (or even better, 8 firm baby eggplants), cut into chunks (or quartered lengthways if using baby ones)

pickled or fresh sliced ginger, to garnish (optional)

This is a naughty but nice recipe—although as Yuki says the weight-conscious among you could always steam the eggplants instead of frying them. Black sesame has a more intense flavor, but you could use easier-to-find white sesame.

To get the best flavor and max the nutritious value of the dish, great care needs to be taken when grinding the sesame. Now I am rarely prone to gadget envy, even of the kitchen variety. But when Yuki showed me her grandmother's special sesame grinding bowl, I was a little in awe. And struck yet again by how much I have to learn about world cuisine. If you don't happen to have a Japanese sesame grinder, a mortar and pestle makes a fine substitute.

Toast the sesame seeds gently until they smell nutty, but be careful not to let them catch (they will taste bitter if they are even a teensy bit burnt). Tip them into a mortar and pestle and grind the still-warm seeds to a rough paste until they look a bit oily. Add the syrup, soy sauce, and sake and mix well.

Heat around 1in/3cm of oil in a pan and bring it to about 350°F/180°C. It needs to be hot otherwise the eggplant will suck up the oil and become soggy. Fry the eggplant until golden: do this in small batches and allow the oil to recover in between each batch.

Drain the eggplant on paper towel and while it is still warm coat it in the sesame dressing. Serve warm or at room temperature with some ginger on top. Yuki says this dressing also works well with broccoli, sweet potatoes, green beans, and tomatoes, i.e. vegetables with their own fairly robust flavor.

ASPARAGUS *SHIRA AE*: MORE SESAME!

FOR 4 AS A SMALL
SIDE DISH
FOR THE SAUCE:

9oz/250g silken or medium
   firm tofu
4 tbsp white sesame seeds
1 tsp light soy sauce
½ tsp fish sauce (optional, if not
   using add extra salt)
1 tbsp maple syrup/agave
   syrup/sugar
½ tsp salt

FOR THE SALAD:

1 bunch of asparagus
1 small carrot, cut in half
   lengthways
1¼ cups/300ml vegetable
   stock (or water)

This is another sesame dish, this time using white seeds blended with tofu.

Put the tofu in a sieve and leave for 15–30 minutes to get rid of the excess water.

Next, gently toast the sesame seeds in a frying pan until golden but not burned. While still warm, grind them in a mortar and pestle until you achieve a smooth and oily paste. Mix in the drained tofu and other sauce ingredients and work the paste until it becomes the consistency of hummus (add some water if necessary).

Now boil the asparagus and carrot in the stock until they are just cooked. Drain and pat them dry with paper towel before cutting them into 1¼in/3cm strips on the bias. Mix into the *Shira Ae* sauce, check the seasoning (it should be both sweet and salty), and serve immediately.

ASAZUKE: QUICK PICKLED SALAD WITH CABBAGE

A SUPER-QUICK
SALT-SOUR SIDE
SALAD FOR 4

1¼in/3cm knob fresh ginger,
   peeled and shredded
2 tbsp rice vinegar
1½ tsp sugar
½ green cabbage (Chinese
   is best), shredded into
   ½in/1cm strips
3 sticks of celery, finely sliced
2 tsp salt (authentically around
   2 percent of the weight of the
   vegetables used in the recipe)

This recipe may come from the other side of the globe, but is as close to the original Roman concept of salads (as in vegetables with salt) as any in this book.

Place the ginger, vinegar, and sugar in a small pan and bring it to a boil. Take it off the heat and leave to cool.

Rub the cabbage and celery thoroughly with the salt and set it aside for around 30 minutes. After this time, crush them gently in both hands to soften a little, tip off any excess water, pour the spiced vinegar over the vegetables, and enjoy.

FRIED OKRA SALAD WITH HARISSA MAYO

Okra belongs to a school of vegetables known to traumatize some consumers: along with rhubarb, marrow, and *molokhia*. It is famed for its slime, you see, and slime doesn't meet with everybody's favor. With this salad, however, you can expunge all thoughts of the mucilaginous: it is crispy-crunchy-okra-makeover time.

This is a particularly good salad to have with sautéed shrimp—there's a kind of gumbo vibe running through it.

AN ELEGANT APPETIZER OR
SIDE DISH FOR 4
FOR THE MAYO:
1 egg yolk
1 tsp harissa paste
2 garlic cloves, peeled
1 tbsp lime juice
1 tsp orange flower water
roughly ½ cup/125ml canola oil
salt

FOR THE SALAD:
1oz/25g dried sour orange peel (or use
    the pared zest of 2 fresh oranges)
1½lb/600g baby okra
splash of peanut or sesame oil
1 tsp cumin seeds
1 red onion, finely sliced
3oz/80g snow peas,
    julienned
3oz/80g baby spinach leaves
handful of fresh cilantro sprigs

First make the mayo. You can do this by hand but using a blender is much easier. Whisk the egg yolk, harissa, garlic, lime, and flower water together, then trickle in the oil ever-so ever-so slowly until you end up with a fairly thick orange emulsion—it should be just about pourable. Check the seasoning and chill until needed.

Bring a pan of water to a boil and blanch the orange peel for around a minute before draining and refreshing it. Next for the okra: remove the calyces (tops) and cut the rest into julienne strips.

Now heat the oil in a skillet (such a nice word compared with "frying pan") and toss in the cumin seeds, followed by the orange peel and the okra: fry for 2–3 minutes then take off the heat.

Toss the red onion, snow peas, spinach, and cilantro sprigs together. Add the warm orange and okra, then spoon a little of the harissa mayo over it. Serve the rest of the mayo in a bowl on the side.

A TRIO OF PICKLED SALADS

In theory this could be a huge section. All manner of stuff can be pickled and eaten with salads. So I have narrowed it down to dishes that are designated salads first and foremost, with the fact of their being pickled remaining quite secondary.

SOUSED LETTUCE, CUCUMBER, AND TOMATO SALAD

I had the privilege of growing up in a *close* (houses built around a central courtyard)—a mixed *close* full of children from all backgrounds. We all used to meet on the grass in the middle for generally-good-natured-but-occasionally-spiteful play. This ragtag bunch also got to enjoy that strange childhood ritual of visiting each other's houses for tea. And it was thus that I got introduced to a wonderful range of kosher foods, the like of which I have long sought to re-create. This soused salad is one such attempt. I cannot guarantee its authenticity, as I grew up a while ago now (well, kind of), and it's been a long time since anyone asked me over for tea, but it is a pleasant and unusual dish nevertheless.

A SIDE DISH FOR 4

scant ½ cup/100ml white wine vinegar

scant ¼ cup/50ml sweet-ish
    white wine

1 tbsp sugar

2 tsp dried dill

5 tbsp/75ml extra-virgin olive oil

salt and freshly ground black pepper

2 baby gem lettuces

6 baby cucumbers (or ⅔ regular one)

6 tomatoes

handful of fresh chives

Put the vinegar, wine, sugar, and dill in a pan and bring to a boil. Turn down the heat and simmer for 5–6 minutes; then take off the heat. Allow to cool to more or less room temperature, then whisk in the oil, and season to taste.

Halve the lettuces and arrange them in a shallow dish. Cut the cucumbers on the bias into very thin strips (a mandolin would help here) and the tomatoes into equally thin slices. Arrange these over the lettuces, then pour the cooled syrup over the top, turning the vegetables over so they all get coated. Cover and chill the dish: this benefits from a good 6 hours of souse activity.

Serve garnished with snipped chives.

KIMKRAUT: ON FERMENTED CABBAGE SALAD

Fermented food is very good for you: sauerkraut in particular is credited with all sorts of medical applications, packing an antioxidant, antibacterial, probiotic, vitamin-stuffed punch. We've all eaten it, but making at home is different: it feels all odd setting out to ferment stuff deliberately.

Kimchi, for the uninitiated, is Korean sauerkraut: fermented, spiced cabbage. Equally good for you, although we will take the story about it being a possible remedy for bird flu with a (literal and metaphorical) big pinch of salt.

This recipe takes a bit from both classic dishes and owes a lot to the lovely lady who runs the new Asian deli opposite us. Is it salad? Well, it can be eaten as such, especially if you use a mixture of veggies. It is, it has to be said, a bit "strong" to eat all on its ownio.

TO MAKE 2 BIG JARS
(2 X 24OZ–32OZ/800G–1KG
JARS, TO BE PRECISE-ISH)
1 small head of Chinese cabbage (also known as Napa cabbage)
2 medium carrots, peeled
1 small daikon (white radish), peeled
1 level tbsp sea salt
1 or 2 small apples, cored

1 small bunch of scallions, chopped
¾ in/2cm knob fresh ginger, peeled and minced
1 bulb garlic, minced
1 tbsp coriander seeds, cracked
2 tsp good chili powder
2 tbsp fish sauce

Pull off any ugly outer bits then finely shred the rest of the Chinese cabbage leaves. Coarsely grate the carrots and daikon, and place the vegetables in a shallow dish. Sprinkle the salt over them, then add just enough water to cover. Turn it all over, cover the dish, and rest a weight on top so that the contents are firmly pressed down. Leave for about 2 hours, then drain.

Coarsely grate the apple and place it in a bowl with the scallions, ginger, garlic, spices, and fish sauce, mixing well. Add the drained vegetables and mix again: you want every bit of everything to be coated, so to that effect I use my hands to mix it. Pile the kimkraut into sterilized jars, seal, and leave it somewhere at room temperature for a day or two. After this time, open the jars to see if the fermentation process has started: if it has, then place the jars in the fridge; if it hasn't, then just leave them for a day or two more. Kimchi keeps in the fridge for a week or so.

ACAR: INDONESIAN PICKLED
PEANUTTED SALAD

Well here's an embarrassing-drool-inducing little number. It's got all the cheek-suckingly addictive qualities of proper pickle, with added sweetness and crunchy nuttiness (that last sentence is best imagined in a breathless, faux mid-Atlantic made-for-TV accent).

The word *acar* crops up in many Indo-European languages and is used to denote a number of varieties of spicy pickle: many of my Afghan customers use it in reference to curry paste as well. This particular salad is to be found all over Southeast Asia, but I like the Indonesian one best as it has added fruity bits. And we could all do with more fruity bits in our lives, no?

A SHOW-STEALING SIDE FOR 4
around ⅔ regular cucumber
2 medium carrots, peeled
generous ¾ cup/200ml rice vinegar
3½oz/100g green beans, topped and tailed
3½oz/100g cabbage cut into ¾in/2cm chunks
6–8 small florets cauliflower
3½oz/100g fresh pineapple, cut into
  ½in/1.5cm cubes

FOR THE SECRET SAUCE:
scant ¼ cup/50ml peanut
  (or sunflower) oil
1 large onion, very finely diced
1 tsp red pepper flakes

¾in/2cm knob fresh ginger, peeled
  and minced
6 garlic cloves, minced
½ cup/2¾oz/75g macadamia nuts, crushed
  (authentically, this would be the candlenut
  or kukui, but I'd hazard a guess that you're
  all out of those)
1 tsp ground turmeric
⅔ cup/3½oz/100g peanuts, crushed
sugar and salt, to taste

TO FINISH:
⅓ cup/1¾oz/50g sesame seeds, toasted
2–3 fresh green chilies, chopped (optional)
handful of fresh cilantro, chopped

Ready? Preheat the oven to 275°F/140°C. Cut the cucumber into 2in/5cm strips about ¼in/5mm thick; then do the same with the carrot. Bring a pan of salted water to a boil, add around half of the vinegar, and blanch the vegetables in batches: the cucumbers need 30 seconds, the carrot and green beans around 2 minutes, and the cabbage and cauli around 1 minute. Drain, then spread them out on an oven tray along with the pineapple and throw them in the oven for around 15 minutes to "dry out."

Heat the oil in a wok/frying pan and add the onion, red pepper flakes, ginger, and garlic. Cook for around a minute before adding the macadamia nuts and turmeric; simmer for 30 seconds or so, stirring well, before adding the peanuts and the rest of the vinegar. Bring to a bubble then add the oven-"dried" vegetables; simmer, season with sugar and salt to taste, and take off the heat. Mix well, allow to cool, then chill for at least an hour (preferably overnight).

Serve garnished with the sesame seeds, chilies, and cilantro. This stuff keeps for 3–4 days in the fridge, and actually improves after a day or two.

A PAIR OF OLIVE SALADS

Olives, yeah. They inspire such strong feelings. Truly people either love them or hate them—although I think the balance is mainly in favor. As a shopkeeper it is my privilege to be able to offer out samples of strange stuff, and just occasionally I get to give a visiting child its first ever olive. I wish I could record their facial expressions (of wonder, and horror) to share, but people get so hissy over taking pictures of kids that I have given up asking—sad, really.

THREE OLIVE SALAD

Working on the principle that if you like olives, you really like olive…

A STARTER FOR 2

2 beef tomatoes

1 small red onion, elegantly sliced

scant ½ cup/2¾oz/75g plump black olives, pitted and sliced

scant ½ cup/2¾oz/75g green olives stuffed with anchovies (or pimento for a vegan alternative)

2¾oz/75g Emmental, cubed (optional, use avocado for a vegan alternative)

big handful of fresh cilantro, chopped

4 tbsp nice extra-virgin olive oil

1½ tbsp balsamic vinegar

½ tsp green olive paste

freshly ground black pepper

Cut the top off the tomatoes and scoop out the flesh. Chop the flesh and mix around half of it with the onion, olives, cheese, and cilantro (keep the rest of the chopped tomato for general cooking purposes: I'm nothing if not thrifty!). Spoon the mixed olive salad back into the tomato shells.

Whisk the oil, vinegar, olive paste, and pepper together and pour over the salads. Serve with fancy crackers like table water crackers.

ZEITUN PARVARDEH:
PERSIAN OLIVE SALAD

✳ On pennyroyal

Pouneh, or pennyroyal, is used a
fair bit in Persian cooking and the
enterprising Romans used it in lots
of recipes; Apicius features
it in several of his potted salads,
thus: In a mortar, combine celery
seed, dried pennyroyal, dried
mint, ginger, cilantro, raisins,
honey, vinegar, olive oil, and wine.
Strew pieces of Picentian bread in
your salad bowl, arranging them in
alternate layers with pieces of
chicken, kid goat sweetbreads,
Vestinian cheese, pine nuts,
cucumbers, and dried onions,
finely chopped. Pour the dressing,
made above, over the potted salad.
Strew snow around it until the
dinner hour…

It was also used in ancient
times to repel fleas (its Latin name
Mentha pulegium is derived from
pulex, or flea): this probably has
much to do with its pungent smell.

Now the thing is, pennyroyal is
a pretty dangerous substance when
used fresh: rub the leaves and they
secrete an oil that can procure
abortion or even kill a man if
ingested in sufficient quantities.
The dried variety is, however,
quite safe to use. If you can't find it,
do substitute lesser calamint or
even regular dried mint in
recipes—they all belong
to the same happy herb family.

Parvardeh is a funny old word: it literally means "captive," so technically this
is "captive olive salad," which is just silly. But it is also used to apply to "things
on farms" in general. Which is still silly, since these are really rather sophisticated
olives. The flavor combo looks very odd on paper. Just trust and go for it.

FOR A BIG BOWLFUL

½ cup/2¾oz/75g walnut kernels

1 tsp lemon juice

scant 3 cups/1lb 2oz/500g pitted green olives

2 garlic cloves, minced

2 tbsp pomegranate molasses

1 tbsp extra-virgin olive oil mixed with a little
sunflower oil

2 tsp dried pennyroyal*

1 tbsp fresh pomegranate arils (seeds;
optional)

Put the walnuts in a bowl and cover them with cold water and the lemon juice. Leave to
soak for 2–3 hours before draining thoroughly, allowing to dry, and grinding. You are
probably curious about the soaking thing: the process removes the innate bitterness of the
nuts (would that people could be thus treated) and renders them super-creamy. Iranians
are walnut perfectionists you see.

Mix the olives with the ground nuts and garlic, then stir the pomegranate molasses,
oil, and pennyroyal through them. Leave to marinate in the fridge for at least an hour,
preferably overnight. Serve at room temperature (olives should never be served chilled),
sprinkled with the pomegranate arils, if using. In the unlikely event that they do not all get
consumed at one sitting, your *zeitun parvardeh* will keep for around a week in the fridge.

WELCOME TO COLESLAVIA: A ROUND-UP OF CABBAGE SALADS, OLD AND NEW

Mankind has been chomping cabbage salads for at least 2,000 years (those gourmandizing Romans mention a salad of raw cabbage and eggs), but coleslaw as we know it has only been around for about 200 years, or since the invention of mayonnaise. Dutch settlers in the Americas brought with them cabbage seeds together with knowledge of a simple creation of cabbage and carrot, which they called *kool sla* (cabbage salad). This was swiftly corrupted to become cold slaw, thence coleslaw, and a Western fridge staple was born. The dish in itself is salad simplicity: finely sliced cabbage, with or without other ingredients, dressed with mayo. It is less simple to understand how the supermarkets have changed a fresh and crunchy accompaniment into a soggy, mass-produced abomination. Yup, I am not a fan of store-bought slaw: even late-night, post-night out munchies cannot tempt me to cross to the dark side on this front. Coleslaw should be made freshly. End of story.

BILL BILL'S NOTHING FANCY CLASSIC COLESLAW

BIG HELPINGS FOR 4–6

½ small white cabbage, finely sliced

2 medium carrots, grated

2 sticks of celery, finely diced

1 small onion, finely chopped

salt

5 tbsp good mayonnaise (see p.256)

juice of ½ lemon

2 tsp Meaux mustard (i.e. wholegrain)

2 tbsp finely chopped fresh curly parsley

OPTIONAL EXTRA:

scant 1 cup /3½oz/100g grated red Leicester cheese (or cheddar)

You know how men of a generation like to have a signature dish in the kitchen? Oh-the-hou-ha when they are "creating," and oh-the-mess they leave behind... Anyway, my grandfather's signature dish was coleslaw, and this is his "recipe." He was a bank manager, but should have been on the stage: he loved dressing up, but his closet theatricality really flowed when he was allowed in the kitchen.

Couldn't be simpler, much as Grandpa Bill would have you think otherwise. Place the cabbage, carrots, celery, and onion in a bowl of very cold water for 20 minutes (to crisp the veggies/soften the flavor of the onion) before draining and drying them and rubbing them with 1–2 teaspoons salt. This too should be left for 20 minutes.

Mix the mayo, lemon juice, and mustard together and stir it through the coleslaw, followed by the parsley and cheese, if using. Serve within hours.

CAROLINA-STYLE RED SLAW

This is one for ketchup heads, as it skips mayo and uses the red stuff all the way. Its sharpness makes it a perfect barbecue accompaniment, and it's even quite nice piled on top of pizza...

TO SERVE 4–6
¼ red cabbage
¼ green cabbage
¼ white cabbage
¾ cup/175ml ketchup
5 tbsp/75ml cider vinegar
2 tsp chili sauce
   (or less for a mellower flavor)

½ tbsp maple syrup (or sugar)
1 tsp celery seeds
½ tsp smoked paprika
salt
⅔ cup/3½oz/100g pecans,
   toasted (optional)

Shred the cabbage finely and soak in cold water (see handy hints below). Whisk the ketchup, vinegar, chili sauce, maple syrup, spices, and salt to taste together. Once the cabbage is quite dry, mix it with the pecans, if using, and stir the dressing through it. This slaw benefits from an hour in the fridge before serving.

SOME FUN KETCHUP FACTOIDS

#1 Ketchup (or catsup) as we know and love it was almost certainly created/derived from kecap (see p.44), a Chinese/Malay sauce of fermented fish and soy sauce.

#2 Before it was available in bottles, housewives had to make their own tomato ketchup. So we might forgive Heinz' advertizing slogan: "Blessed relief for Mother and the other women in the household!" There again, we might not.

Coleslaw handy hint #1
Use the slicer thingy on your blender, or a mandolin, to cut your cabbage—it will always perform better than the swankiest of knife-armed chefs.

#3 For those who dismiss tomato ketchup as a junk food abomination—well, I've got news for you. It actually contains more lypocene and vitamin C than fresh tomatoes.

#4 You can make ketchup out of anything. One's current favorite is the Philippine idea of banana ketchup.

Coleslaw handy hint #2
Soaking the cabbage and other veggies in ice cold water for a little while beforehand will give you an even crisper finish.

DATE AND BEET SLAW

This is a bit rad: coleslaw without the cabbage. But it is pretty addictive, and healthy, and a practically perfect pal for ham.

A MOUTHWATERING SIDE
FOR 4
½ bulb fennel, very finely sliced
½ head of radicchio, shredded
1 carrot, grated
2 sticks of celery, chopped
1 bunch of scallions, chopped
scant ¾ cup/¼lb/120g pitted dates, halved
½ cup/125ml plain yogurt

2 tsp date syrup
2 tsp creamed horseradish
juice of ½ lime
¾ in/2cm knob fresh ginger, peeled
    and minced
½ tsp caraway seeds
salt and freshly ground black pepper
2 small (raw) beets, peeled and grated
handful of fresh mint, shredded

Toss the first 6 ingredients together in a bowl. Whisk the yogurt with the date syrup, horseradish, lime, spices, and seasoning. Finally, stir the beet into the slaw, mix in the dressing, and sprinkle with mint. This will survive until the next day, and is a good lunchbox filler.

HARISSA-SLAW

This has proved very popular with our shop customers, so we thought you might like it too. Coleslaw is often used to "cool" things down, so spiking this with hot-hot-hot harissa is an act of delightful culinary mischief.

TO FEED 4
½ white cabbage, finely shredded
1 fat carrot, grated
1 fat apple, grated
1 onion, finely chopped
½ cup/⅔oz/75g raw cashew halves
1 tbsp lemon juice
½ bunch of fresh flat-leaf parsley,
    finely chopped

FOR THE DRESSING:
3 good tbsp mayonnaise
1 tbsp harissa paste (or less if you're not a
    habitual fire breather)
1 tbsp peanut butter
2 tsp orange blossom water
1 tsp ground cumin
salt

Mix all the salad ingredients except for the parsley together in a bowl. Beat all the stuff for the dressing together. Apply the latter to the former, stirring well, then add the parsley.

ONION, LEEK, AND GARLIC SALAD

I have a theory about breath-stinky ingredients, which is that if you eat enough of them they cancel each other out. Anyway, this salad is so healthy you should just eat it and face the socially unacceptable consequences. The allium family are notably good for building up immunity to coughs and colds. What a lot of people don't know is that they also contain natural prebiotics. What are they? Well prebiotics are non-digestible substances that pass through the body and end up in the gut, where they work wonders at stimulating the walls of the intestine, strengthening it and improving all around digestive function. And this, in an age of increasing junk consumption, food sensitivity, and gastric intolerance, is a really helpful thing.

A SIDE DISH FOR 4,
OR MEZZE FOR 8

4 small leeks

1 bunch of scallions

1 bunch of spring garlic (out of season just use extra leeks/garlic chives)

2 tbsp olive oil

2 tbsp sesame oil

1 tbsp soy sauce

1 heaped tsp mustard

1 tbsp balsamic vinegar

¾in/2cm knob fresh ginger, peeled and minced

4 garlic cloves, minced

¼ tsp chili powder

1 level tbsp marmalade

Trim the vegetables, chop off the rooty bits, and get rid of any tired looking shoots. Cut the leeks in half lengthways, then across the middle (if they are woody/mature, cut these further into quarters). Cut the scallions in half, and make an incision through any thick bulbs to enable the marinade to penetrate. Cut the spring garlic in half across the middle, then plunge all of the veggies into a bowl of cold water to wash it. After 10 minutes scoop the roots and shoots out, change the water, and repeat—this is always the best way to wash vegetables. Leave it all to drain thoroughly.

Mix the oils with the soy sauce, mustard, vinegar, ginger, garlic, and chili, and bathe the vegetables in it, ensuring that each is thoroughly coated. Tip the whole bunch into a plastic bag and set aside: the vegetables need a couple of hours to marinate, and marinating stuff at room temperature in plastic gets the best results.

When you are ready to cook, heat your barbecue or griddle, shake the excess oil from each of the veggies (retaining the marinade), and sizzle them for a few minutes, turning regularly, until they are pleasingly charred without actually being burned.

Pour the remaining marinade into a bowl and whisk in the marmalade. Arrange the still warm allium on a platter and drizzle with the sauce.

ZUCCHINI SALAD WITH MINTY TOMATO, RAISINS, AND PINE NUTS

Some useless culinary information for you, just in case you didn't read the intro properly. Iranians (together with quite a lot of Central Asia) believe that all food has hot or cold properties. That's not as in "ouch—hot" or "woah—cold," but rather pertains to its effects on the metabolism (think Avicenna and the four humors). Some stuff—so-called hot food—races through the system while other less digestible food ("cold") moves very slowly. An imbalance of either can leave you feeling either febrile (in the first instance) or leaden, light-headed, and bilious (if you have too many cold substances). As a hopelessly generalized illustration, spices, most meat, cheese, nuts—these are all regarded as having hot properties, while coffee, alcohol, many vegetables, most fish, and some fruit are cold.

The relevance here is that this is a practically perfectly balanced salad: zucchini and tomatoes are "cold," while mint, pine nuts, and raisins are all "hot." This is the sort of dish to which medieval chefs would have aspired to create, and is in fact how much of the cooking of antiquity was evolved.

FOR 6 AS A GENEROUS
SIDE DISH

1lb 10oz/750g zucchini,
    very finely sliced
6 garlic cloves, minced
1 level tsp dried mint
½ tsp salt
1 level tsp coarse ground black pepper
½ cup/120ml olive oil

juice of 2 lemons
½ cup/2¾oz/75g raisins, soaked in water
    for 20 minutes or so
½ cup/2¾oz/75g pine nuts
4 nice large firm tomatoes,
    very finely sliced
big handful of fresh mint, shredded
big handful of fresh cilantro, shredded

Place the zucchini in a bowl, add the garlic, mint, and seasoning, and cover with the oil and lemon juice, mixing well. Cover and refrigerate overnight, perhaps turning the ingredients over in the marinade just before you go to bed (although I do admit that the list of things one has to do just before one goes to bed is usually onerous enough already).

Ready to serve? Drain the raisins thoroughly. Toast the pine nuts gently in a pan, and add them to the zucchini along with the raisins, tomatoes, and fresh herbs. Check the seasoning and dish up; some warm bread would be handy so you can soak some of that garlicky oil goodness.

ROASTED VEGETABLE SALAD WITH TOASTED SEEDS AND ÇEMEN

You could use this as a sidekick to a roast or a barbecue, but it is quite deserving of its own time in the spotlight and makes a filling meal or lunchbox standby.

LUNCH FOR 4

2 medium sweet potatoes, peeled
6 Chantenay (i.e. small, sweet) carrots
6 shallots, peeled
olive oil, for cooking
1 fat red bell pepper, cut into strips
6 plum tomatoes, cut into quarters lengthways
5½oz/150g halloumi, cubed
⅓ cup/1¾oz/50g pine nuts

1 tbsp hulled sesame seeds
⅓ cup/1¾oz/50g sunflower seeds
small bunch of fresh parsley, finely chopped

FOR THE DRESSING:

2½ tbsp çemen (see below)
about scant ½ cup/100ml water
2 tbsp olive oil

Preheat the oven 400°F/200°C.

Cut the sweet potatoes into wedges; if they are very long, you could halve the wedges across. Cut the carrots into quarters lengthways. Cut the shallots too into quarters. Place the veggies in an oven tray and toss with some olive oil before sliding it into the oven. Cook for 15 minutes then add the pepper and tomatoes. Bake for a further 10–15 minutes, or until the potatoes and carrots are cooked. Remove from the oven and set aside.

Now make the dressing. Mix the çemen with enough water to make it of a salad dressing consistency. Whisk in the olive oil. Job done.

When you are ready to serve, arrange the roasted vegetables in a bowl. Now fry the halloumi in a splash of olive oil before scattering it over the veggies. Mix the salad, cheese, and çemen together, stirring carefully so as not to break up the vegetables. Finally, toast the seeds and nuts (dry-frying is quickest). Once they start to turn golden, sprinkle them over the salad along with the chopped parsley. Serve with warm bread and raw onion wedges.

BONUS RECIPE: ÇEMEN—FENUGREEK PEPPER SAUCE

Çemen is the Turkish word for fenugreek, and it is this that provides the overriding flavor for the paste of the same name.

9oz/250g biber salçasi (Turkish pepper paste, available in most Mediterranean stores)
1 tbsp tomato paste
1 tsp red pepper flakes
½ tsp ground cumin

1 tsp ground fenugreek seeds
½ tsp ground cinnamon
¼ tsp garlic powder
juice and grated zest of 1 lemon
2 tbsp olive oil

Mix all the ingredients together to a smooth paste. Use as a marinade, a sauce, or in salad dressings. Makes a wicked burger relish. Çemen will keep for a week or so in the fridge.

WARM EGGPLANT SALAD WITH GARLIC YOGURT AND CARAMELIZED WALNUTS

This is absolutely one of the favorite appetizers we offer at out supper clubs. It has little to do with any vestige of culinary talent that we may possess, and everything to do with the fact that garlic sauce tends to make everything a little bit wonderful and a lot better. Shame we can't just pour garlic sauce on the troubles of the world and make all the bitterness go away...

A STARTER FOR 6
FOR THE WALNUTS:
scant 1 cup/4oz/120g walnut quarters
   (or halves)
1½ tbsp brown sugar
½ tsp chili powder
pinch of salt
1 tbsp groundnut oil

FOR THE SALAD:
3 small-ish eggplants,
   cut into ½in/1cm thick rounds
salt
canola oil, for frying

1 level tsp ground turmeric
1 tsp ground cinnamon
1 large red onion, sliced into rings
4 large tomatoes, thinly sliced
1¾oz/50g arugula
big handful of fresh basil, roughly shredded

FOR THE GARLIC DRESSING:
tiny splosh of oil
8 garlic cloves, finely chopped
generous 1 cup/250ml plain yogurt
1 whisked egg white
½ tsp cornstarch
pinch of salt

First get the walnuts ready. Toss the nuts in a little frying pan along with the sugar, chili, salt, and oil. After around 5 minutes tip them on to some wax paper and allow to cool.

Next, sprinkle the eggplant slices with salt and set aside for 30 minutes.

Meanwhile, make the dressing. Heat the oil in a heavy-based saucepan and sauté the garlic. Set it aside, turn the heat way down, and tip the yogurt in. Add in the egg white, cornstarch, and salt, stirring constantly in the same direction. This is one of those strange instructions that the good witch issues in fairy tales, which the hapless heroine always disobeys, thus giving herself a lot more hardship than she had bargained for: stirring the yogurt randomly will cause it to curdle. Bring the pan's contents slowly to a boil, then turn the heat down and simmer for a few minutes. Take it off the heat and stir the garlic in.

Wipe the eggplants with paper towel. Heat a glug of oil in a frying pan and cook the slices until golden brown on both sides (you will probably have to do this in batches). Just before you remove each batch from the pan, add a little turmeric and cinnamon. Drain on paper towel. Fry the onion in the same pan until cooked but not colored, adding more oil if necessary and then the tomato slices, taking care not to overcook.

Spread the arugula around the outside of a platter, and layer some eggplant on top, followed by a layer of onion, and then tomato. Dress with a little of the warm dressing, and then repeat. Top with the caramelized walnuts and the basil and serve immediately. Warm bread would make a fitting accompaniment.

THINGS IN JARS SALAD, AKA CORNER SHOP SALAD

You've got supper to cook for X number of people, you've got zippety-zilch in your fridge, and you're really struggling to stay with it. This is how Things in Jars Salad came to be devised. We literally emptied our pantry into a bowl one night and presented it as a salad. Serve with cold chicken, or canned tuna, or just as it is with some crusty bread. You could have knocked us down with a parsley sprig when we realized how good it was. Yes OK, it does help that we live over the shop—a shop full of things in jars. But the recipe below uses things that most people have in jars. If you don't have those things in jars, use other things in jars, or fresh things lurking in the bottom of your fridge. Use your desperation as a coefficient alongside your imagination. And make a mental note to stock up with random things in jars next time you're at your local corner store.

A SALMAGUNDI OF
CONVENIENCE FOR 4 OR SO

2–3 slices stale bread, crusts off and cubed

splash of oil

½ tsp rosemary (or thyme)

12oz/350g jar/can artichoke hearts (in brine, oil, what you will), drained and quartered

12oz/350g can/jar asparagus, drained and halved across

generous 1 cup/7oz/200g olives (any you like—we use pimento stuffed ones)

1¾oz/50g sun-dried tomatoes, chopped

10½oz/300g button mushrooms (can, jar, or fresh)

1 tbsp (drained) capers

7oz/200g peppers (any: pickled, hot, sweet, sliced, or even fresh)

1 large red onion, chopped

3 garlic cloves, chopped

5 tbsp/75ml extra-virgin olive oil

2 tbsp balsamic vinegar

salt and freshly ground black pepper

fresh herbs as available, chopped

Fry the bread in hot oil, turning it over so it doesn't catch. After around 3 minutes, add the rosemary, stir a little more, and tip the croutons on to some paper towel to drain.

Mix the drained vegetables, onion, and garlic in a bowl. Whisk the oil, vinegar, salt, and pepper together, adjusting the seasoning according to preference—a lot of things in jars are already quite sour or salty, so this is in your hands. Pour the dressing over the salad and sprinkle the croutons and fresh herbs on top.

Don't forget to recycle all those newly emptied jars: if you're not going to use them for making foraged pickles and preserves (see p.19), donate them to your local corner store's jar bank. And if your local corner store doesn't have a jar bank… get them to start one. All corner stores are microcosms, you see, and your little corner-shaped deeds will ripple out into the space-time continuum at large and make everything better. It's amazing what rubbish we corner shopkeepers tell ourselves to break the monotony of a day behind the counter…

A TWIST ON THE SAME THEME:
PICKLE JAR (AKA MASON JAR) SALAD

Stumbled across this idea on Pinterest, which to be honest is one website I rarely visit: it seems to be full of impossibly talented and beautiful people showing off. Ho-hum. Anyway, the idea is that you make a portable salad in a jar. Not only will it look real pretty (thus creating lunchbox envy), but if you make it right, it'll stay fresh and pert until you want to shake it up and eat it.

Layer 2–3 tablespoons of your chosen dressing at the bottom of the jar, followed by any heavy, non-absorbent ingredients such as tomatoes, potatoes, and beans, followed by any absorbent stuff like grains and pasta, and plonk any salad leaves on top. To add extra thrill to the matter, put a thin layer of nuts or sprinkles (see Chapter 14) between each layer. When you are ready to eat, just up-end the jar into a bowl, toss briefly, and enjoy.

CHAPTER THREE
Roots and squash

Ah. Potato salad. Anyone else recall the stuff that came out of a can in the 1970s? It is actually impossible to write that sentence without inducing a brief involuntary shudder. Remember salad cream? Deary me. Anyway, expunge all thoughts of childhood salad torture. Roots are some of the best ingredients with which to play in the salad bowl. They hold their shape, do what they're told, and still look nice the next day: sounds like the perfect kitchen date, no?

SALAD OLIVIEYEH

This is a twist on a dish popular in many countries. A sort of fancy potato salad, it undoubtedly originated in Russia (it was devised by Chef Olivier around 150 years ago)—the Spanish call their version *ensaladilla a la Russe*; you might know it as Russian salad. Anyway the Persian version is popular right across the land, and is eaten as a snack, at parties, and as a sandwich filling. As with all dishes, some of the ingredients are debatable—one home cook using peas and carrots and the next throwing up her hands in horror at the very thought of it. We obviously think that our version is the best, and it's pretty simple.

FOR A VERY BIG BOWLFUL
3¼lb/1.5kg peeled potatoes (use a smooth textured potato such as Desiree)
butter
English mustard
2 cooked skinless chicken breasts (bit of a waste to use breasts, so the meat from a couple of legs and thighs would be adequate. This is obviously a good way of using leftover roast chicken)
1¾ cups/400g mayonnaise

either 1 large can garden peas or 1 small bag frozen peas, blanched and drained
1 jar (28oz/750g) Persian pickled cucumbers
1–2 bunches of scallions
1 large bunch of fresh cilantro or parsley (according to taste)
1 bunch of fresh tarragon (or 4 tsp dried tarragon), optional
6–8 hard-boiled eggs
lemon juice
salt and freshly ground black pepper

Boil the potatoes then mash them roughly with just a little butter and 2 teaspoons mustard. Flake the chicken meat into the mixture, and add the mayonnaise and the peas. Reserve 4 pickles, and drain and dice the rest. Chop the scallions and chop the fresh herbs (put a bit of each to one side for the garnish). Set 1 of the eggs aside and roughly chop the rest. Stir the pickles, herbs, eggs, and scallions into the potato mixture with a dash of lemon juice, and season to taste. Pack into a deep dish, or if you are serving it immediately, on to a suitably grand platter, smooth the top, and make pretty with sliced cucumbers (remember those 4 you kept back), and sliced egg (likewise). A sprinkling of green stuff is good as well. This is a good filler for buffet spreads, but we usually wrap it in *lavash* bread for extemporized sandwiches off the cuff.

PATATAS BRAVAS SALAD

Patatas bravas is, as I am sure you all know, the *tapas* dish of choice for inebriated *chicos* and *chicas* the length and breadth of Spain. I first tried them in Alicante after a night of clubbing (yes, shopkeepers do dancing): it was 6am and I was presented with a plate of very fiery, smoky potatoes and a glass of Cantueso, the region's (sweet, herby, alcoholic) favorite hangover remedy. The somewhat weird taste combo has stuck very firmly in my mind. Roll forward a few years, and I am looking for something red to contrast with my range of otherwise beige and green deli dishes. Yes, sometimes I cook by color: don't you? Well food doesn't get much redder than *patatas bravas*, although there is an amazing amount of debate as to the best/most authentic recipe. We ignored the debate and just did our own thing (they are normally served hot, for one thing)—but the sauce tastes pretty authentic, we'll have you know. If you add in some chorizo it becomes a whole meal.

A SIDE DISH FOR 6

1lb 2oz/500g waxy potatoes, peeled

salt

1 large red onion, sliced

1 large carrot, grated

1 bunch of fresh chives, chopped

½ bunch of fresh parsley, chopped

1 can (14oz/400g) chickpeas, drained

3 tbsp *ajvar** (or use red pepper paste mixed with vinegar and a pinch of sugar)

1 tbsp apple cider vinegar

2 large tomatoes, peeled and finely chopped

2–3 garlic cloves, peeled and mashed

½ tsp red pepper flakes (optional, depends how hot you want it)

½ tsp ground turmeric

1 tsp smoked paprika

2–3 tbsp olive oil

Cut the potatoes into ¾in/2cm cubes and boil them with a little salt until they are cooked but still fairly firm. Drain and refresh them with cold water to prevent them from cooking any further. Put them in a bowl and add the onion, carrot, herbs, and chickpeas.

Whisk the *ajvar*, vinegar, tomatoes, garlic, spices, and olive oil together, then add salt to taste (*ajvar* can be salty in its own right). Drizzle the dressing over the potatoes. Serve at room temperature as a perfect side dish or *mezze/tapas* dish to go with early evening drinks. It has to be said that it really isn't that nice for breakfast.

* *Ajvar?*

A really useful red pepper dip from Macedonia. If you can't find it to buy, it is easy to make. Roast or chargrill 3–4 red bell peppers until the skin blackens, then put them in a plastic bag to sweat for 5–10 minutes. Flake the skin off (and deseed), and chop or blend them roughly with 2 garlic cloves, 2 red chilies, olive oil, vinegar, and salt to taste.

BAVARIAN-STYLE *KARTOFFELSALAT*

Kartoffel is just a very grand (albeit slightly cartoonish) word for potato. This is potato salad with a twist, though: piquant and with lashings of hidden bacon. And I am sure you agree that everything tastes better with hidden bacon (unless you happen not to eat pork, of course). This makes a great lunchbox filler or side dish—but throw in apple and cheese as optional extras, and it becomes a (slightly naughty autumn) meal.

FOR 6 HUNGRY BAVARIANS
2lb/900g firm potatoes (authenticity demands red skinned potatoes here, but I find waxy salad potatoes will also do)
splash of oil and a pat of butter, for frying
6 rashers (slices) thick streaky (lean) bacon, cubed
1 medium onion, sliced
½ cup/125ml beef stock
scant ¼ cup/50ml canola oil (or sunflower)
scant ¼ cup/50ml red wine vinegar

handful of fresh flat-leaf parsley, chopped
salt and freshly ground black pepper

OPTIONAL EXTRAS:
5½oz/150g smoked cheese, cut into tiny cubes
2 small red apples, cored and cubed
6 dill pickles

OK, so put the potatoes into a pan of water and boil them until they are cooked but still firm (15–20 minutes depending on the variety). Drain and allow them to cool a little.

Next, heat the oil and butter in a frying pan and fry the bacon cubes for a few minutes before removing them to a plate with a slotted spoon. If you are using cheese, add it to the bacon now: it becomes delightfully soft and, well, bacony. Fry the onion in the bacony oil; when they are brown scoop them on top of the meat, reserving just a little bit of the cooking fat.

Once the potatoes are cool enough to handle, peel and cut them into half moon slices. Whisk the beef stock together with the oil and vinegar, adding around a tablespoon of the reserved bacon fat; then pour this "dressing" over the salad. Stir in the bacon 'n' onion combo together with the parsley and any extras you may be using: the potato will inevitably crumble, but do not mix it too vigorously as you are not aiming for "mash." Season the *kartoffelsalat* to taste. This is particularly good served with *sauerkraut* or *kimchi* (see p.57), and beer, of course—a stein of beer.

YAM, HAM, AND THANK YOU MA'AM

This takes that yucky canned potato salad to which I alluded in the opening of this chapter—you know, little cubes of mayo-smeared potato and peas and ham—and stands it on its head. This salad has bite, not slime.

A BUFFET SALAD FOR 5–6

¾lb/350g yam (or use sweet potato)

extra-virgin olive oil and canola oil

1 tsp dried thyme

1 tsp sea salt

½ tsp coarse ground black pepper

1 large red onion, thickly sliced

1 large red bell pepper,
    cut into ¾in/2cm squares

2 tbsp balsamic vinegar

2 tsp maple syrup

1 tsp mild mustard

¼ tsp ground mace

salt and freshly ground black pepper

5½oz/150g mixed salad leaves

10½oz/300g top-notch cooked ham, cut into
    ⅝in/1.5cm cubes

3½oz/100g goat cheese, crumbled

2 heaped tbsp/1¼oz/35g flaxseeds,
    dry-toasted in a frying pan

Preheat the oven to 425°F/220°C.

Peel the yam and cut it into ⅝in/1.5cm cubes, plunging them straight away into cold water (yam is one of those tubers that discolors in a nanosecond). Whisk around 2½ tbsp/40ml extra-virgin olive oil and 2½ tbsp/40ml canola oil with the thyme and seasoning. Drain the yam and pat it dry before tossing it in the herby oil. Do the same with the onion and pepper, and spread the veg out in an oven dish. Bake for around 20 minutes, or until the potato starts to color and the onion/peppers soften. Remove and allow to cool a little.

Beat a scant ¼ cup/50ml extra-virgin olive oil with the vinegar, maple syrup, mustard, and mace, and season to taste.

Arrange the salad leaves on a platter and dot the roasted veggies on top. Add the ham and dribble with the sweet dressing. Sprinkle with goat cheese and toasted flaxseeds, and serve with warm homemade rolls.*

* *Just kidding*

I'm a terrible baker and would hardly prescribe the act thereof for anyone else. Max respect if you are a home baker, though.

JERKED SWEET POTATO SALAD

I am a lucky bunny, for I live and work in one of the most diverse and colorful hoods in the universe. Peckham is a riot of noise and clashing themes and chatter, abuzz with residents from every conceivable nook and cranny of the globe. A walk along Rye Lane is a true feast for the senses: beat boxes and bangra rhythms compete with frenetic salsa and the unmistakable sound of the muezzin, and the aromas from the myriad food stalls are just as complex. But the area is perhaps most famous for its Afro-Caribbean population, and this salad is a celebration of that fact, specifically of the great number of Jamaicans among my customer base.

A SIDE SALAD FOR 6

1lb 2oz/500g sweet potatoes, peeled and
    cut into ⅝in/1.5cm cubes
⅔ cup/150ml olive oil
2 tsp jerk paste*
sea salt
1¼ cups/300ml water
¾ cup/5½oz/150g roasted buckwheat
1 can (14oz/400g) callaloo (or spinach),
    drained
1 small red or orange bell pepper,
    finely chopped**
2 sticks of celery, diced**
1 onion, diced**
½ bunch of fresh flat-leaf parsley, chopped
juice of ½ lemon
juice of ½ orange
salt

Preheat the oven to 375°F/190°C.

Place the potatoes in an oven dish. Mix about a third of the oil with 1 teaspoon of the jerk paste and spoon over the potatoes, turning them over so that they all get coated. Sprinkle a little sea salt on top, and roast for about 30 minutes, or until the sweet potatoes are golden and cooked through. Allow to cool.

Bring the water to a boil in a pan and add the buckwheat. Cover and simmer for 5–6 minutes, or until just cooked through (buckwheat varies, so keep an eye on it otherwise you will end up with an inedible slurry). Drain off any unabsorbed water, fluff with a fork, and tip into a basin to cool.

Place the cooled sweet potatoes and buckwheat in a bowl and add the callaloo, pepper, celery, onion, and parsley, mixing well.

Whisk the remaining olive oil and jerk paste together, add the fruit juices, and season to taste. Pour over the salad, stir, and refrigerate until needed—the dish benefits from being left for 30 minutes or so to allow the flavors to mingle.

* Tip

Or improvise your own by mixing 1 minced garlic clove with ½ teaspoon ground allspice, ½ teaspoon crushed thyme, a pinch of nutmeg, ½ small minced Scotch bonnet or habanero chili, and some peanut oil.

**

These three ingredients are known as the "holy trinity" in Creole and Caribbean cuisine— they form the base of the majority of dishes from the region.

TUBER LORE

No—not a discussion of London underground etiquette, but rather a quick look at some of the funkier root vegetables to be found in the world's salads. In the not-so-wild West few of us play around with cassava, or taro, or jicama, or salsify. And they are rewarding to play with, not least because a lot of them have, through history, been dismissed as peasant fare, fit only for serfs and cattle.

It is true that many tubers have to be cooked, but many that we traditionally cook (overcook) in the West can be enjoyed raw, especially when they are young: turnip, beet, parsnip, parsley root, celeriac—these are all delectable when sliced or grated and served just so as a salad.

Root veggies fall into several (botanical) subsections, which you don't strictly need to know in order to prepare a top salad, but I shall tell you anyway. There are "true roots," tuberous roots, tubers, corms, bulbs, and rhizomes. The difference lies in how much starch they store (the starchier ones such as cassava and yam are super-useful in nutrient poor areas), and whether or not they contain new shoots growing within the root.

Here's a li'l list of some of my favorite saladable roots that aren't carrots or potatoes:

BEET: My fondness for beets knows no bounds (actually, it stops at the door of my laundry room…). Raw, cooked, chunked, grated—there is surely room for it in every salad if not in every color scheme. Beet tops are also highly flavorsome. Make sure you always have it in the house—your kidneys will love you for it.

CASSAVA (aka manioc): this is one that you can't eat raw. Bitter cassava contains all sorts of toxins (causing goiters), so don't even go there. Buy the sweet ones, then peel, core them, and use as potato. They work better as a dip than chunked in a salad. Do try some for no other reason than the fact that it is the third largest source of human calorie consumption (after rice and corn) on the planet: call it culinary education.

CELERIAC (aka celery root): Like celery, this root is an effective anti-inflammatory. When cooked it adds a creamy aniseed flavor to salads, but it is perhaps at its best raw. There are not one but two raw celeriac recipes in this chapter.

GINGER: One of the healthiest foodstuffs known to mankind. It is anti-inflammatory, antibacterial, antiviral, anti-nausea (as many a pregnant lady will testify), anti-all-sorts-of-things. It makes a most excellent poultice (whatever happened to poultices?): pound fresh ginger with turmeric, warm the mixture slightly, and apply it to aching muscles. More relevantly for us, grate it into any salad dressing that calls for a bit of heat or sweetness and you will transform the dish.

HORSERADISH: Almost as healthy as its pals ginger and turmeric. It too is anti-inflammatory, and a powerful weapon against bacteria such as E. coli. Use raw grated in salad dressings.

JERUSALEM ARTICHOKES (aka sunchokes): Highly versatile, although not the most attractive of vegetables. Use raw (see p.92), or boiled, or sautéed in salads. They make an absolutely amazing pickle (use coriander and nigella seeds as seasoning).

KOLOKASSI (aka taro/dasheen): Needs to be cooked carefully as it contains high concentrations of calcium oxalate, which is not something we should be eating. You should peel and wipe it without washing it, then aim to break pieces off the core of the vegetable. It can be roasted, fried, or boiled, but is generally best made into a dip rather than chopped into salad.

LOTUS ROOTS: Need to be boiled before use, but you can find them pre-cooked in cans in most Asian supermarkets. Their *umami* taste requires quite a strong salad dressing (soy, mirin, wasabi...), but they are worth incorporating in salads because of their alien, spongiform appearance.

MANGELWURZEL: The butt of many a rustic joke, these also star in an annual hurling competition in the south of England. The young ones can be boiled and used like potatoes in salads, and the leaves and stalks are tasty too.

PARSNIPS: Glorious in salads, they happen to be the one vegetable that I dislike, hence their relative absence on these pages (sorry). They can be roasted or used raw to great effect. They are particularly good grated and marinated with spices, and work well in *Maghrebi* salads. Fun parsnip fact: best not to forage for wild parsnips, since they look uncannily like a member of the rather less edible hemlock family.

RADISHES: Full of trace minerals and low calorie, they provide a splendid crunch and pepperiness to salads. They've been popular since Roman times, and are often just eaten with salt. As Evelyn says: "these are eaten alone with salt only, as carrying their pepper within them..." Wacky radish fact: the Mexicans celebrate a radish festival (*La noche de los Rabanos*) just before Christmas each year. And why not?

SALSIFY: We really need to cultivate and eat more of this jolly little root. It's very tasty in an "asparagussy" kind of way, and can be eaten from flower to root. The sprouted seeds are particularly tasty. The root itself can be eaten raw when young—thicker, gnarlier ones should be lightly boiled.

RUTABAGA (aka swede): Fun fact—these are known as "swedes" because they (were perceived to have) come from Sweden. Cooked, cubed rutabaga works well in salads, but it is at its best raw, grated, and mixed with fruit and nuts. It is high in fiber and low in calories.

TURMERIC: The West has recently cottoned on to what the East has understood for millennia: turmeric is a seriously powerful healing tool, benefiting the liver and working as an anti-inflammatory. Among agencies researching its health properties currently are those involved with Alzheimer's, coronary disease, cancer of the colon, cystic fibrosis, rheumatoid arthritis, irritable bowel syndrome (IBS), and cholesterol. To incorporate it into salads, buy the fresh root (now readily available in many supermarkets), peel, then grate or dice it. Or you can cook other salad ingredients (potatoes, rice) using ground turmeric.

TURNIPS: I am a confessed turnip fan. They are super good for you, notably as a kitchen remedy for chest infections. You can use them cooked in salads, but the flavor of young, raw neeps is far more delectable.

YAM: Hard to overstate the importance of yams to some societies in the world: it is a staple crop in Nigeria and other parts of West Africa, and is celebrated accordingly with festivals. For salads either chunk and roast, or use puréed (see p.245). Note—they are not the same as sweet potatoes, although most of the US seems to think that they are.

ACORN SQUASH SALAD BOATS

This is yet another example of Nature handily dispensing produce replete with its own serving dish. Got to love baby squash: they are such fun with which to play, and you can fill them with anything from sausages to soup. This recipe sees them stuffed with a hearty mix of toasted pasta and vegetables, with a sliver of Parmesan for a hint of naughtiness.

A WINTER SUPPER FOR 4

2 little acorn squash (or any other mini gourd-like thing)—if they are large, just get one
1 tbsp vegetable ghee
salt and freshly ground black pepper
non-extra-virgin olive oil
1 tsp rosemary
3½oz/100g *moghrabbieh* (or giant couscous)
pinch of ground saffron steeped in a splash of boiling water
juice and grated zest of 1 lemon

1½ cups/350ml low sodium vegetable stock (or water)
1¾oz/50g podded peas
1¾oz/50g artistically shaved Parmesan and a bit for the table
8 cherry tomatoes, halved
big handful of arugula
4 tbsp extra-virgin olive oil
2 tbsp cider vinegar
2 garlic cloves, minced
1 generous tsp Dijon mustard

Preheat the oven to 375°F/190°C.

Cut the squash in half to form 4 coracles (if you are using a larger squash, cut it into quarters to form 4 "regular" shaped boats) and scrape out the seeds, setting them aside. Rub the inside of the squash with the ghee, prick the flesh in several places, then season with salt and pepper before putting the halves cut side up on a baking tray. Cook for about 35 minutes, or until the squash is cooked and just starting to brown. Remove from the oven (leaving the latter on) and allow to cool slightly. Use a small sharp knife to cut the flesh away from the skin in rough cubes (cut to within ¹⁄₁₆ in/2mm of the skin—if you go any closer, your boats will no longer be seaworthy, if you see what I mean). While the oven is still warm, season the retained seeds, put them on an oven tray, and roast for about 10 minutes, or until they start to look quite golden in color.

Heat a splash of oil in a pan and toss in the rosemary, followed by the *moghrabbieh*, rolling it around so that it toasts gently. Once it starts to color all over, add the saffron and lemon, then add the vegetable stock in batches, much as you would for a risotto, stirring well. Turn the heat down, put the pan on a heat diffuser if you have one, and wrap the lid of the pan in a clean dish towel. Leave the couscous to steam gently for about 20 minutes, stirring occasionally, or until it is cooked. Take it off the heat, stir in the peas and squash cubes, top with the Parmesan, and allow to cool a little.

When you are ready to serve, divide the *moghrabbieh* mixture between the squash boats and top it with the tomatoes, arugula, and toasted seeds. Whisk the olive oil together with the vinegar, garlic, and mustard and season to taste. Dribble the dressing over and set your boats out to sail across your supper table. Serve with extra black pepper and Parmesan.

BUTTERNUT SQUASH SALAD
WITH SOUR GRAPES

A very Persian salad. Well, it would be if not for the fact that for most Persians salad is just tomato, cucumber, and onion. What I mean is that the flavor is quintessentially Iranian, comprising fragrant spices, split peas, and verjuice. Verjuice (*verjus*, or *ab ghooreh* in Farsi) has been prepared for centuries as a way of using fruit deemed too sour for other purposes. It can be made from crab apples, but in the Middle East it is usually made from tiny sour grapes. It is somewhere between wine and vinegar in sourness, but less winey than the wine and less vinegary than the vinegar. It is one of the chief "souring" agents in Persian food, and it is not only the verjuice that is used: the whole grapes, both fresh and pickled, and a powder made from dried sour grapes are all employed to great effect. You should be able to find them on the shelves of good delis and all Middle Eastern stores.

LUNCH FOR 4

½ cup/3½oz/100g *chana dal/lapeh*
   (split chickpeas)
1 small–medium butternut squash
½ tsp ground cinnamon
1 tsp ground cumin
1 level tsp ground turmeric
sea salt and coarsely ground black pepper
3 tbsp non-extra-virgin olive oil
chili powder, to taste
3oz/80g mesclun (mixed leaves)
12 cherry tomatoes, halved

1 onion, sliced
1½ tbsp pickled sour grapes (or unsweetened
   cranberries, or the diced flesh of 1 lemon)
3½oz/100g feta, crumbled (optional)

FOR THE DRESSING:

¼ cup/60ml extra-virgin olive oil
3 tbsp verjuice (or a mixture of dry white wine
   and wine vinegar)
1 tsp tomato paste
½ tsp Tabasco (just for fun)
salt

Pick through the *chana dal* and set them to soak in cold water for 30 minutes or so.

Next, place them in a pan of cold unsalted water, bring to a boil, then turn down the heat and simmer for a further 30 minutes, or until just cooked. Refresh under cold water.

Preheat the oven to 375°F/190°C.

Halve the butternut squash carefully, reserve the seeds, then cut the flesh into 1¼in/3cm cubes. Mix the spices and seasoning with most of the olive oil, then toss the squash cubes in the mixture before spreading them out on a non-stick baking tray. Roast for around 20–25 minutes, or until golden and cooked through. While it is roasting, pick through and clean the reserved seeds and spread them out on a separate oven tray. Sprinkle with the rest of the olive oil, salt, and a little chili powder, and roast in the oven for about 10 minutes, or until crunchy and golden.

Mix the cooked *chana dal* with the mesclun, tomato, onion, and sour grapes and arrange the still-warm squash on top. Whisk the dressing ingredients together and drizzle over the salad. Top with the roasted seeds and feta, if using.

BEET AND RED ONION SALAD WITH PATÉ CROUTONS

Paté appetizers are all very well but they are mostly, let's face it, pretty boring: a slab of puréed liver with token greenery and some sort of bread. For a part-time vegetarian like me, who enjoys a morsel of paté but really doesn't want to wade through a whole chunk of the stuff, this mostly veggie salad is perfect.

AN APPETIZER FOR 4
FOR THE DRESSING:
scant ¼ cup/50ml walnut oil
    (or use extra-virgin olive oil)
2 garlic cloves, minced
½in/1cm knob fresh ginger, peeled
    and minced
1½ tbsp balsamic vinegar
salt and freshly ground black pepper

FOR THE SALAD PROPER:
3 small–medium cooked beets, cut into
    ¾in/2cm (ish) cubes

1 large red onion, roughly chopped into ⅝
    in/1.5cm pieces
1 large red apple, roughly chopped into ⅝in/
    1.5cm cubes
1 bunch of watercress
9oz/250g coarse, firm paté, cut into
    ⅝in/1.5cm cubes
1 egg beaten with 1 tsp water
1 tbsp flour
1 level tsp aniseed, lightly crushed
oil, for cooking
2 slices (stale will do) bread, cut into
    ¾in/2cm cubes

First, whisk the dressing ingredients together and set aside: garlic dressings are always best when given a little time to infuse.

Mix the beets, onion, apple, and watercress in a bowl (if you do this much ahead of time, keep the apple in some cold water with a drop of lemon juice to stop it discoloring). Next, roll the paté in the eggwash; mix the flour with the aniseed, then roll the egged pate cubes in this too. Heat a good glug of oil in a frying pan and fry the paté cubes, turning regularly (and gently, so as not to mash them up), giving them enough time to heat through thoroughly and turn golden brown. Scoop them out and drain them on paper towel before frying the bread cubes.

Pour the salad dressing over the beet compilation, and toss the croutons on top. Serve immediately.

BEET, GINGER, AND MANGO SALAD *SUPER-HEALTHY*

Beets and ginger go together nearly as well as Fred and Ginger, dancing round the taste buds in seamless fusion. This salad packs a detoxing, anti-inflammatory, pro-digestive, phytochemical punch. It will probably put hairs on your chest and help you see in the dark as well. Its sweet-sour overtones means that it works very well with rich meats such as duck or lamb, but you know, I could possibly live on it, just as it is.

A SIDE FOR 2
OR LUNCH FOR 1

3 medium beets (yes: you can cheat and buy
    pre-cooked)
½ in/1cm knob fresh ginger,
    peeled and minced
1½ tbsp extra-virgin olive oil
1 tbsp pomegranate molasses

juice and grated zest of ½ small orange
juice and grated zest of ½ lime
½ tsp ground fennel seeds
salt and freshly ground black pepper
1 fat mango: sharper, greener varieties would
    work well here*
2–3 scallions, finely chopped
big handful of fresh mint, shredded

Peel the beets and cut them into roughly ⅝in/1.5cm cubes. Put them in a pan of unsalted cold water and bring to a gentle boil (25 minutes or so should do the trick—you need them tender but firm). Drain and refresh under cold water to stop them from cooking further.

Whisk the ginger, oil, molasses, juice, and zest, fennel seeds, and seasoning together and pour it over the beets. Peel and cut the mango into chunks, then stir it into the salad along with the scallions and mint. Mix gently and refrigerate for 30 minutes or so to let the flavors meld. Serve with napkins and a deservedly virtuous smile.

* Tip
If you live in one of the strange mango black holes that exist in some areas, substitute papaya, apple, kiwi, pineapple, or pear.

SPICED CARROT, ORANGE, AND RADISH SALAD *SUPER-HEALTHY*

This is a real head-turner of a salad. It is kind of Moroccan: both Paula Wolfert and Claudia Roden (the joint doyennes of North African food writing) offer a range of orange based salads, and this is an amalgamation of their recipes (with a pinch of Peckham). To be honest, the main ingredients make a perfect threesome in more or less any combo.

A ZINGING SIDE DISH FOR 4

2 tbsp top-notch olive oil, preferably Moroccan (it is decidedly more olive-y than other oils)

juice of 1 lemon

1 tsp orange blossom water

¾ in/2cm knob fresh ginger, peeled and chopped

1 tsp *ras el hanout*

sea salt and freshly ground black pepper

2 large carrots, peeled

1 bunch radishes, topped and tailed (but retain the green tops)

2 oranges

⅓ cup/1¾oz/50g slivered pistachios OR sliced black olives (either work well)

few sprigs of fresh mint

Mix the olive oil together with the lemon juice, blossom water, spices, and seasoning, and leave for the flavors to mingle for 30 minutes or so.

Grate the carrots and finely slice the radishes (with a mandolin if you have one). Use a thin bladed knife to cut the peel and pith from around the oranges, working from "top" to "bottom" so to speak. Remove any seeds then cut the orange into thin half moon slices. Arrange the orange, carrot, and radish in layers on your finest Fez plate. Top with the pistachios, and dribble the dressing over the whole bunch. Finish with the mint. Admire. Don't forget to take a quick photo for your delightfully well-organized social media pinboards.

RAW TURNIP, CELERIAC, AND PARSNIP SALAD *SUPER-HEALTHY*

This pretty little side dish should prove to be a talking point, since the main ingredients are more usually served cooked. Although—since it is crafted with a vegetable peeler—the first time that I served it, the family actually thought that it was avant-garde for all the wrong reasons and that I had dished up a plate of vegetable peelings. The crunchiness provides a good counterpoint to any main dish of what my granny would have called "slosh": casseroled food, or things with mashed potatoes—meals that in themselves lack texture.

A CRUNCHY SIDE DISH FOR 4

1 tsp fenugreek seeds
1 tsp coriander seeds
½ tsp cumin seeds
½ tsp fennel seeds
½ tsp sea salt
½ tsp red pepper flakes
¼ cup/60ml extra-virgin olive oil

juice and grated zest of 1 lime
1 tsp rose water
2 pert-looking parsnips
2 baby turnips
9oz/250g celeriac (celery root)
½ bunch of fresh cilantro,
    finely chopped

Toast the first 4 spices in a frying pan. When they start to pop and smoke, take them off the heat and allow them to cool before blending them with the salt and red pepper flakes. Whisk the olive oil with the lime and rose water, then stir the spice mix in. Set aside for the flavors to mingle.

Peel the vegetables (and dispose of the peel pronto—it is easy to mix the prepared veggies with the unwanted peel). Using a vegetable peeler, "shave" the roots by cutting off long strips. Mix the strips together in a tub or bowl and stir the dressing through it, mixing well (I use my hands). Leave the salad to marinate for 2–6 hours. Just before serving, check the seasoning (you may want to add a little more salt), then stir in the cilantro.

MIXED ROOT *REMOULADE*

I once worked in a very lah-di-dah restaurant that used to blanket all manner of food with mayonnaise and then call it *remoulade*. I used to think they made it up, but as it turns out, it's a thing: *remoulade* is basically just mayonnaise with stuff in it. In France, celeriac *remoulade* is practically a national institution. This version adds a few Peckham spices, and mixes up the tubers so that if you can't find one you can use something else.

A LITTLE FRENCH NUMBER
FOR 4–6

4 tbsp nice mayonnaise
    (make your own see p.256)
2 tbsp crème fraîche
¼ tsp ground saffron steeped in a splash of
    boiling water
1 tbsp poppyseeds
½ tsp nigella seeds

1 tbsp Dijon mustard
salt (if necessary) and ground white pepper
5½oz/150g carrots
5½oz/150g celeriac
5½oz/150g daikon (white radish; or use
    regular ones)
juice of ½ lemon
5½oz/150g beets
big handful of fresh curly parsley, chopped

Mix the mayo with the crème fraîche, saffron, seeds, and mustard, then add salt and pepper to taste.

Peel and grate the first 3 tubers and add the lemon juice, turning well. Add the *remoulade* sauce, then finally peel and grate the beet and stir this in. Sprinkle liberally with parsley. *Que c'est bon.*

JERUSALEM ARTICHOKES WITH AVOCADO HOLLANDAISE

Dunno if it's just me, but Jerusalem artichokes (sunchokes) always make me sit up straight and mind my manners. This is silly, since in many countries they are regarded as being fit only for cattle; I must have eaten them somewhere very fancy in my formative years. I am also slightly in awe of Brussels sprouts: my father was apparently force fed so many at school during WWII (rationing, remember?) that they were taboo in our house when I was a nipper. Anyway, teaming these vegetables with avocado hollandaise makes this one impressive little *umami*-packed side dish, even if I say so myself.

Useless artichoke fact: the Jerusalem of the title is, like the best peculiar names in the world, a corruption, in this case of *girasol/e* (sunflower in Spanish and Italian), for this tuber is a member of the sunflower family.

A POSH WINTER SIDE SALAD FOR 4

2–3 large Jerusalem artichokes (sunchokes) or 5–6 smaller ones
2–3 pre-squeezed lemons/limes or dash of juice
12 Brussels sprouts
⅓ cup/1¾oz/50g almonds, toasted

FOR THE HOLLANDAISE:

1 large ripe avocado
juice of 1 lime
big handful of fresh chervil (or parsley)
½ tsp ground black pepper
1 egg yolk
11 tbsp/5½oz/150g butter

Peel and finely slice the chokes then plunge them immediately into cold acidulated water (just add a dash of lemon juice, or float 2–3 pre-squeezed limes or lemons in the water). Shred the sprouts roughly.*

Put the avocado, lime juice, herbs, pepper, and egg into your blender and give them a quick whiz. Melt the butter carefully, skimming off any white solids that come to the top, then trickle it very slowly into the avocado mixture while the motor is running. If you do not have a blender, mix the first 5 ingredients in a little bowl over a pan of boiling water, then slowly whisk the butter in and take off the heat. You want the sauce to thicken, but to be thinner than normal hollandaise, so if it looks too thick add a splash of cold water.

Drain the chokes and arrange them on a platter along with the Brussels sprouts. Drizzle with the hollandaise, top with the almonds, and stand back to marvel at what a pretty shade of green it is.

* Tip
I like this salad raw, but if you are cooking for Great Uncle Albert (dentures and all) you may want to blanch the chokes and sprouts—the former for about 2 minutes, and the latter for 30 seconds—before refreshing them under cold water and proceeding as above.

CHAPTER FOUR
Peas and beans

If it's *bean* salad, what is it now? Badum-tish! Ah—the oldies are the best.
Beans and peas are great ingredients for salads: tasty in their own right, über-
healthy, filling, and they get along with the other children. You have but to cook
your favorite legume and add a little oil and lemon and you already have a
great snack: add some other stuff and you have a dream salad team. I never
ever tire of them.

FOULS MEDAMMES SALAD

Fouls Medammes (or *fuls medammas*) are basically mature fava beans. Whereas in the Middle West we tend to eat our fava beans green, tender, and young, in the Middle East the preferred way to consume them is when they are browned and dried. More or less every country in Arab-shire prepares a version of the dish, which is quite often served for breakfast: the beans are soaked overnight, cooked until soft, then served hot with chili, *tahini*, or lemon along with diced vegetables, boiled eggs, and relish. This recipe sees it served cold with the trimmings on the side—a mini *mezze* of a salad. Perfect for your *Arabian Nights*-themed party.

A SELF-ASSEMBLY SIDE SALAD
FOR 4–6

1¾ cups/10½oz/300g whole dried fava beans, soaked overnight
pinch of baking soda (to accelerate the cooking process)
3 tbsp sesame oil
1 level tbsp *tahina*
juice of 1 lemon
around ½ cup/120ml cold water
½ tsp ground cumin
salt and freshly ground black pepper

TO SERVE:

3 perfectly hard-boiled eggs, peeled and quartered
3 firm tomatoes, finely diced
2 baby cucumbers, finely diced
1 onion, finely diced
3 green chilies, finely chopped
4 garlic cloves, finely chopped
1 bunch of fresh cilantro, chopped
chili sauce
extra lemon wedges
plain yogurt
sea salt
warm bread

Cover the beans with water, add the baking soda, then bring to a boil and cook for 1½ hours, or until tender. Drain and allow to cool before mixing with the sesame oil.

Whisk the *tahina* together with the lemon juice, water, cumin, and seasoning. If you are preparing ahead, you may need to dilute this "dressing" with a little water, since it thickens in the fridge.

Serve the beans in a bowl in the middle of the table with the dressing alongside. Arrange all the other "condiments" in little bowls for people to help themselves.

INSALATA DI FAGIOLINI:
ITALIAN GREEN BEAN SALAD

I've always felt that green beans need quite a lot of help to taste good—like so many prom queens, they look pretty and pert enough, but lack substance when push comes to shove. And when over-boiled they can taste wretchedly watery. This very simple Italian treatment takes them from plain (tasting) Jane garden staple and raises them to a tongue-titillating Tuscan (or thereabouts) temptress of a salad.

LUNCH FOR 2 OR
A SIDE DISH FOR 4

18–20 cherry tomatoes (or around 5 super
    regular ones)
4 garlic cloves, peeled
½ cup/125ml extra-virgin olive oil
2 sprigs of fresh thyme
    (or 1 generous tsp dried)
sea salt and freshly ground black pepper

14oz/400g green beans—Italian flat beans are
    ideal, but runner, French, or string beans
    will all do well, topped and tailed and
    de-stringed as necessary
1 tbsp balsamic vinegar
handful of fresh chives, duly snipped
scant ¼ cup/1oz/25g (or so) piece of good
    Parmesan, grated (optional)

Preheat the oven to 375°F/190°C.

Place the tomatoes in a little roasting dish: if you are using big tomatoes you will need to quarter them. Slice 3 of the garlic cloves, and add them to the dish along with a good glug of the olive oil and the thyme. Sprinkle with salt and pepper, cover with foil, and bake for around 15 minutes, whereupon the tomatoes should be soft and the garlic cooked. Remove from the oven and allow to cool.

Bring a pan of salted water to a boil and cook the beans for 2–3 minutes before draining and refreshing under the cold tap. Allow them to drain until quite dry (pat with paper towel if necessary) before adding them to the tomato/garlic combo. Whisk the remaining olive oil together with the vinegar and pour over the vegetables, mixing gently. Cover and allow to marinate for an hour or so in the fridge before serving garnished with the chopped chives and Parmesan as required. Then just shut your eyes and let the somnolent sound of the breeze in the cypress trees and the gentle aroma of herb-strewn olive groves carry you away… well, something like that anyway.

WARM FLAGEOLET BEAN SALAD WITH CAMEMBERT DRESSING

For those of you unfamiliar with cross-channel day trips (that's over the English Channel to France), they can be rather more of an undertaking than they may sound. You go on them full of optimism, spend the whole day under the channel, buy a load of stuff in French superstores that you didn't know you wanted at slightly higher prices than home, together with a load of wine that's so dire you end up giving it away, barely squeeze in a cup of *café au lait* and an order of *pommes frites*, and before you can say "*Zut Alors!*" it's time to go home. You vow you'll never do it again, and then a few months down the line...

Anyway, there was a time when channel-hopping made sense. Our palates were less refined, so cheap wine was acceptable and there were lots of mysterious products that were unavailable in the UK: mustards in little reusable glasses, CDs of jazzy left bank numbers that you think will make you look more intellectual, all manner of unfathomable gadgets for dealing with garlic, cheese (but oh-my, what cheese), *sauçisson* just-a-bit-too-*sec* to use, bread that will be hard by the time you get home... and flageolet beans.

I can't figure the hold that these mild flavored and somewhat slimy beans have on me: perhaps it's the delicate green color. But I love them and often have them for lunch with just a little lemon, onion, and garlic. They are truly at their best in salads—and they are readily available pretty much everywhere now so there is no excuse. This is my very French day trip salad.

A SUPPER FOR 2 OR
A HEARTY SIDE DISH FOR 4
generous ½ cup/3½oz/100g dried flageolet
    beans, soaked overnight (or use 2 cans,
    14oz/400g each)
9oz /250g baby or fingerling potatoes,
    scrubbed and halved (or quartered if big)
salt
7oz/200g *sauçisson sec*, skinned (good quality
    veggie sausages could be substituted)
3–4 garlic cloves, minced

olive oil, for frying
1 head of chicory, pulled apart
1 red onion, sliced
1oz/30g watercress (a handful in other words)

FOR THE DRESSING:
3½oz/100g Camembert, rind removed
2 tbsp crème fraîche
½ tbsp Calvados (or use extra apple vinegar)
1 tbsp apple or cider vinegar
freshly ground black pepper

Put the beans in a pan of unsalted* water, bring to a boil; then turn the heat down and simmer for around 1 hour, or until tender. Drain and leave somewhere cool while you make the rest of the salad.

Boil the potatoes in salted water for around 6 minutes, then drain and set aside.

Chop the *sauçisson* into chunks and fry along with the garlic in a splosh of olive oil before scooping them out and draining them on paper towel. Now tip the still-hard drained potatoes into the pan and sauté them gently until they are cooked through.

Next, make the dressing: throw all the ingredients in a little saucepan and warm very gradually until the cheese melts: you are not aiming to boil it, merely to render it mixable and pourable. Gently whisk the cheesy gloop, then take it off the heat.

Toss the chicory, onion, and watercress in a large bowl, then carefully mix in the beans, potato, and sausage. Drizzle the Camembert sauce over the top and serve straight away with warm French bread and a bottle of *bière*.

* A note on beans

Always use unsalted water for legumes. Salt slows and in some cases prevents the beans from cooking. This is to do with something alarmingly technical called osmotic pressure and I am no physicist. Suffice it to say that the old maxim of "water following sodium" is true, and that cooking stuff in salted water actually desiccates it.

A TRIO OF LENTIL SALADS...

In that child-like game that we all play wherein we imagine having to forsake all foods except one, I have to say the one thing I would choose to retain is lentils. I am far too young to have been a hippy the first time around, naturally, but I'll stand up and be counted if there is a second flower-fueled coming. I love the things, hence not one but three lentilly salads. If you don't have the right lentils, just use different ones, but not red as they turn to mush as soon as you so much as look at them.

A note about cooking lentils: THEY DON'T NEED SOAKING, and they only take 30–40 minutes to cook. You don't need to buy cans—in fact I was pretty surprised to find such a thing existed.

In the meantime, some lentil-related useless information:

1. The word "lentil" is derived from the Latin *Lens culinaris*, and it is that our word "lens" stems: it's all to do with the shape.

2. I would have liked my favorite lentil quote to have come from Confucius, or Pliny, or Larousse. Actually it's by the late comedian Les Dawson: "A square egg in a dish of lentils won't make a marrow bend with the wind, nor will it make rhubarb grow up the milkmaid's leg."

3. They're a top source of protein for non-meat eaters, and are full of trace minerals and folate. They won't actually turn you into Iron Man but you'll feel a lot better for chomping down a few portions each week.

PIQUANT PUY LENTIL SALAD

A SIMPLE SIDE FOR 6–8

1¼ cups/9oz/250g Puy (French) lentils

1 large onion, sliced

1 large red bell pepper, cut into very thin strips

2 limes

3–4 tbsp extra-virgin olive oil

2 tsp ketchup

3 red bird's eye chilies (or less if you're cooking for Aunt Mavis)

3 garlic cloves, minced

salt

big handful of fresh cilantro, chopped

1 bunch of scallions, diced

½ cucumber, diced real fine

4 large firm tomatoes, cored and diced

This dish is as attractive as it is tasty, which is some feat as lentils have been called many things, but pretty isn't usually one of them.

Put the lentils into a pan of unsalted water, bring to a boil, and cook for around 30 minutes, or until just cooked. Refresh and drain.

Put the drained legumes in a pretty serving bowl and add the onion and pepper. Use a thin knife to peel one of the limes, removing the pith, and chop the flesh, discarding any seeds. Add this to the lentils.

Grate the zest of the other lime, then halve and juice it. Mix the zest and juice with the olive oil, ketchup, chili, and garlic, then season to taste (this dish needs salt, so don't be shy). Dress the lentils, mixing well, then stir the cilantro carefully through the salad. Just before you are ready to serve, mix the onion, cucumber, and tomato together. Make a well in the top of the lentil salad and pile the tomato mixture on top.

MINTED AND GARLICKED GREEN LENTILS

This is a version of my mother-in-law's default lentil dish: simple, nourishing stuff. The addition of bready croutons and plentiful herbs turn it into fairly funky fare.

A HEALTHY LUNCH FOR 4 OR
AN X-FACTOR SIDE DISH FOR 8
1½ cups/10½oz/300g green lentils,
    picked through
8–10 fat garlic cloves, minced
good glug of oil, for frying
1 baguette (stale will do)
½ tsp green cumin seeds

1 tsp coriander seeds
juice and grated zest of 1 fat (or 2 small) lemon
3–4 tbsp extra-virgin olive oil (less if you're on
    a low-fat diet, you poor soul)
sea salt and coarsely ground black pepper
big handful of fresh parsley, chopped
big handful of fresh mint, shredded

Put the lentils in a pan of unsalted cold water, bring to a boil, then turn down the heat and simmer until cooked (around 30 minutes). Drain and set aside.

Fry the garlic in the oil, stirring well so it doesn't burn, then scoop it out with a slotted spoon. Cut the bread into 1¼–1½in/3–4cm rounds. Carefully pull out the middle bits and cut these into small cubes. These you should then fry in the garlicky oil until they start to brown, then drain on paper towel. Next, fry the crusty outer rings of the bread, taking care not to break them: they will need turning in the oil so as to crisp all surfaces. These too should be drained on paper towel. Finally, fry the spice seeds until they just start to pop.

Assembly time. Mash the garlic and toasted seeds together in a mortar and pestle, then whisk in the lemon and olive oil, seasoning to taste. Place the lentils in a bowl and mix with the dressing and herbs. When you are ready to serve, arrange the baguette discs on a plate, fill each with lentil salad, and top with the bread croutons. Amazing however you choose to serve it, especially awesome with lamb.

BACONED BROWN LENTILS

This salad is like breakfast, but with added lentils. It's kind of drool-inducing but that's probably my lentil addiction talking.

A WINTER BRUNCH FOR 2

FOR THE LENTILS:
1 onion, finely chopped
pat of butter and splosh of oil
scant ⅔ cup/4½oz/125g brown lentils,
    picked through
1 sprig of fresh thyme (or ½ tsp dried)

FOR THE SALAD:
¼lb/120g bacon lardons
olive oil, for cooking
2¾oz/75g nice mushrooms (fancy or basic
    or a mixture, your choice), thickly sliced
3½oz/100g cherry tomatoes (about 10),
    halved

2½oz/70g baby spinach leaves
1 small red onion, finely sliced

FOR THE DRESSING:
2–3 tbsp extra-virgin olive oil
1 tbsp balsamic vinegar
1 tsp Dijon mustard
1 tsp brown sauce (like HP, or use steak sauce)
salt and freshly ground black pepper

TO SERVE:
1 large egg
⅓ tsp ground turmeric
pinch of salt
2 slices bread
oil, for frying

Fry the onion in a little butter and oil (adding oil to butter stops it burning as oil has a higher smoke point), and as they start to brown add the lentils and thyme. Top up with water to about ¾in/2cm above the surface of the lentils, then bring to a boil. Turn down the heat and simmer until cooked (about 30 minutes—add more water if necessary). Set aside.

Fry the lardons in a splash of oil. I have allowed enough for you to sneak 2 or 3 pieces, so don't feel too bad when this, inevitably, happens. Remove the bacon with a slotted spoon then fry the mushrooms. Once they start to shrink, add the tomatoes and cook until they just begin to soften. Tip the lentils into a bowl and carefully stir in the mushrooms and tomatoes. Whisk the ingredients for the dressing together.

Now, for some French toast... Whisk the egg with the turmeric and salt, then dunk the bread into the mixture, allowing it to soak up the liquid. Heat a generous splash of oil in a frying pan and fry the eggy bread, turning it so that becomes golden on both sides. Remove and cut each slice diagonally.

Arrange the bread around the outside of a platter (or on individual plates). Mix the spinach and onion through the still warm lentil mixture, and toss carefully with the dressing. Spoon the lentil mixture into the middle of the platter and serve immediately.

CHICKPEA, LAMB, AND RED CURRANT SALAD

Lamb on its own can be a bit weird in salads: the slight sweetness, the texture, the greasiness… It needs strong flavors to contrast and carry it—and this recipe does just that.

The lamb marinade is based on a throwaway comment by the deeply and importantly talented Tom Norrington Davies: you can tell a good chef when even their asides ooze culinary knowhow. You can, of course, use leftover lamb, in which case just disregard the first part of the recipe. Red currants are obviously a summer fruit; cranberries would make a good winter substitute.

A FINE SUPPER FOR 6–8

FOR THE MEAT:
1 heaped tbsp black olive paste (or tapenade)
1 tsp thyme
1 tsp rosemary
6–8 garlic cloves, minced
1 tsp ground black pepper
1–2 tbsp olive oil
1 small (around 2¼lb/1 kg) leg lamb, boned

FOR THE SALAD:
1¼lb/600g small white potatoes, cut into
    ¾in/2cm cubes
salt

2 cans (14oz/400g) chickpeas
1 head of Chinese (Napa) cabbage, shredded
2¾oz/75g watercress
2 big handfuls of a mixture of fresh mint,
    parsley, and cilantro, chopped
1 fat red onion, sliced
10½oz/300g basket red currants, destalked

FOR THE DRESSING:
4–5 tbsp extra-virgin olive oil
1 tbsp red currant jelly
2 tbsp balsamic vinegar
big handful of shredded mint
salt and freshly ground black pepper

Mix the olive paste, herbs, garlic, pepper, and olive oil together, and rub the mixture all over the lamb. Place the meat in a clean plastic bag and put it in the fridge to marinate for a couple of hours or so.

When you are ready to start cooking, preheat the oven to 425°F/220°C.

Place the lamb in an oven dish and bake for 20 minutes uncovered, then cover it with foil and cook for a further 25–30 minutes, or until the lamb is cooked to your preference. Shred the lamb and allow it to cool a little.

In the meantime, cook the potatoes in salted water for 8–10 minutes, or until they are just cooked, then drain and refresh them.

Toss the potatoes, chickpeas, salad greens, herbs, onion, and red currants in a bowl and arrange the lamb across the top. Whisk the dressing ingredients together and drizzle over the salad.

Serve with warm flatbread and a nice yogurt dip on the side (see p.241).

THE TALE OF HOW THE PEA GOT ITS BLACK EYE

Once upon a beansprout, many moons ago, and long before he voyaged to America and became infamous, Anansi* was a poor spider farmer in West Africa. That's as in "a spider who happened to be a farmer," not "a farmer who grew spiders," for spider cultivation would just be silly.

On each of the animals under the sky, Nyame, the great sky god, had bestowed one type of crop for them to tend: Brer Rabbit was given a market garden as he was good at digging and burying stuff, and Brer Fox was given a maize plantation, as he was the wiliest of the lot and only he was able to patrol it to keep the other critters out. Brer Lizard was given the cress family, as they shared a love of wet-and-dry living, and Brer Bear got a fruit orchard, as bears are known to be rather partial to fruit and thus more inclined to look after it carefully.

And so it went on, until all that was left was Anansi, the cheeky spider: the only crop that was left was a lowly, plain, pale bean. It was, admittedly, a suitable task for our eight-legged friend, as he could spin a web around the young plants to keep them safe from pests, but he was not impressed.

The seasons passed, and while all the other animals apparently reaped a fine harvest, indolent Anansi fell into a trough of depression. Mrs. Anansi tried to encourage him, but in the end it was mostly she and their brood of spider-lets who did the work around the farm, while he spent his days sighing and spying on his neighbors, and his evenings drinking himself into an arachnoholic stupor. He was convinced that he was a victim in the grand scheme of things, and that whole of the animal kingdom had conspired to put him down, and he gazed with envy at the thriving farms of his neighbors. Nyame was not pleased about this, no sirree, but he'd give the insect a little more time.

One evening Anansi went to the village bar. The other animals were there, chatting (mooing, cooing, roaring, mewing) in the corner, and Anansi (who had already had a few glasses of rum) became convinced that they were bad-mouthing (beaking, snouting) him. He swung over with that confident but ridiculous swagger that only a moderately intoxicated man-spider can manage, and confronted them.

"I know what you're all trying to do," he cried, "But it won't work!" And he shook all of his fists at them, which was probably quite terrifying as he had eight of them. Well, dear reader, soon punches were flying all over the place, and Anansi, being rather small, was scurrying for home.

The next morning he felt very sorry for himself. He had a sore head, and his missus was positively scowling at him. To make matters worse, when he looked in the mirror he discovered that he had two real shiners. And he had alienated all the other farmers. He put his head in his impressive collection of hands and wept.

Mrs. Anansi felt very sorry for him. So she baked up a batch of banana cake, and dragged him over to the neighbors' houses to apologize. First they went to see Brer Rabbit, who gladly accepted Anansi's apology, and over carrot tea confessed that business wasn't all that good. Caterpillars had eaten half of his greens, and his potatoes had been afflicted with some strange blight: he had had to work extra hard and had only just broken even. The story was the same at Brer Fox's house, and in fact all across the county: farming was a hard job, it seemed. Anansi felt very remorseful, but vowed from then on to be a better neighbor, a model farmer, and a deserving husband.

Nyame was not entirely convinced by this resolve, and so, while the spider family was sleeping, he visited their bean plantation and adorned each of the legumes with a black eye, to remind Anansi firstly of his disgraceful brawl, and secondly, that viewing the world through jealous eyes can only lead to trouble.

Anansi was distraught to find his crop thus tarnished in the morning, and grabbed a handful of the pods to show his wife. "Look—we are ruined!"

he uttered. But his wife found the new "design" enchanting, and cooked up a batch for breakfast. The whole family agreed that while the taste was unaffected, the dish looked a lot more alluring. Nervously Anansi took a wagon of the whacky-looking beans to market, craftily hawking them as a new "miracle product"—and was overjoyed when he sold out within half an hour.

He was like a new spider, working happily in the fields by day (wherein he found that many hands— well, eight arms—do indeed make light work), reading tales of horrific two-legged humans to his children by night—and in his spare time he helped his neighbors by spinning webs to keep out pests. Business boomed, and friendships were rekindled, but Anansi was ever mindful of his humble start in life, for that black eye was always there, staring at him…

*Anansi the spider is the popular folk hero of stories from West Africa (Ghana, specifically) across to the West Indies. His guises range from a minor deity to clown/trickster: he is generally regarded as the god of storytelling. He is often associated with that other rascal, Brer Rabbit. There is actually an authentic tale of how his gluttony drives him to steal a pot of hot beans and hide it under his hat, therein scalding away all his hair. He appears in this tale with considerable license.

FASOLIA: BLACK-EYED PEAS WITH LEMON AND DILL

Black-eyed peas are generally believed to have originated in West Africa, and thence to have traveled East to China, and West (carried by trafficked slaves) to the United States—where they are now very much embedded in the cuisine of the nation. They are so beloved in the US that they are eaten for luck on New Year's Day in a dish known as Hopping John—which is rice and peas by any other name. This recipe, however, derives from the Eastern end of the Mediterrnean—Greece, the Levant—where the beans are popular prepared simply with lemon. In Turkey they are often cooked whole in the pod, but here we will use the ubiquitous dried version.

TO MAKE A BIG BOWLFUL
(FOR 4 AS A SIDE DISH)
generous 1 cup/7oz/200g black-eyed peas
1 onion, chopped
2 sticks of celery, diced
1 fat carrot, grated
½ bunch of fresh cilantro, chopped
2 tbsp dill (or 1 ½ tbsp if using dried)
5 tbsp/75ml extra-virgin olive oil
2 lemons
salt and freshly ground black pepper

Put the beans in pan of unsalted water and bring to a boil. They do not need soaking and will take but 35–40 minutes to cook. Refresh under cold running water and tip into a colander. When they have drained, tip them into a bowl and add the other vegetables along with the herbs. Whisk the olive oil together with the juice of 1 of the lemons and season to taste before pouring over the beans. Cut the other lemon into wedges and serve alongside the salad. I could probably eat this for lunch every day forever, even though I know that they might just have been produced by a spider… (see p.106).

THINGS IN CANS SALAD

I know quite a lot of serious food-types who completely eschew the convenience and occasional delight of using canned food on the grounds that it's beyond the culinary pale. I also know quite a few serious oddballs who refuse to eat canned stuff as they firmly believe that it is toxic/radiated/spawn of the devil. Me? I am an averred fan, and it's not just the five-minutes-for-lunch shopkeeper in me talking either. Canned food is perfect for emergencies, whether it be a camping trip to Patagonia or simply the arrival of a few unexpected dinner guests. And the nutrients in canned stuff are often better preserved than those of fresh stuff, which has often been traveling for a few days.

You can make Things in Cans Salad from any things in cans (and for that reason this piece is more of a template than a cut-out-and-keep recipe), but the handiest things to keep in your pantry for this are obviously beans.

EMERGENCY SALAD FOR 8

3 cans assorted beans: chickpeas, red kidney beans, lentils, black-eyed peas, lima beans, fava beans, gungo peas, pinto beans, black beans—these all hold their shape well in salads. Canned cannellini beans, white kidney beans, and green peas tend to get a bit mushy, as do borlotti beans for some reason*

big handful of fresh herbs, chopped (you should ALWAYS have fresh herbs in your fridge—see p.11)
1 large onion, chopped (and any other crunchy veggies you might have in your fridge)
4–5 tbsp olive oil
juice of 1 large lemon/lime (you should ALWAYS have lemons in your fridge)
few garlic cloves, minced
salt and freshly ground black pepper

Rinse the beans (unless you are actually using beans already in some sort of sauce) and drain well. Mix with the herbs and onion. Whisk the oil, lemon, garlic, and seasoning together and allow to sit for as long as possible before stirring through the salad. Smile quietly to yourself as you serve it with "here's a little something I made earlier" panache...

* Tip
Other things in cans you can use include corn, frankfurters (serve them sliced and sizzled on top), artichokes, asparagus, olives, clams, truffles—hey, just use your imagination. I personally draw the line at canned potatoes, and canned 'shrooms are always pretty vile too—but someone must like 'em since they keep making them.

SALADITOS: LUPINI BEAN SALAD

I first came across *saladitos* when I was pretending I could cook for a living out in Spain: it took me quite a few years to work out that these addictive little beer chasers are actually lupini beans. Over there they are normally eaten as a *tapas*, but they are stunning in this simple side salad.

A word about using raw, dried lupini beans: I don't want to put you off or anything, but they take around five days to prepare. They contain certain bitter toxins, you see, and in order to draw these out you need to soak them in brine for a good few days, changing the water twice daily. This process is what you might call a pain in the rear, so I thoroughly advocate cheating and buying pre-cooked/brined ones.

AN ADDICTIVE LITTLE
SALAD FOR 4

14oz/400g can/jar lupini beans in brine,
    drained and rinsed (you could use whole
    baby fava beans if you can't find lupinis)
14oz/400g can processed
    (aka marrowfat) peas, drained
12 cherry tomatoes, halved
1 small onion, diced
big handful of watercress

FOR THE DRESSING:

2 tsp mint sauce (see p.257)
2 tbsp extra-virgin olive oil
1 tbsp red or white wine vinegar
3 garlic cloves, minced
pinch of sea salt
⅓ tsp red pepper flakes

This is a snap. Mix the beans, peas, tomatoes, onion, and watercress together in a bowl. Whisk the dressing ingredients together and stir through the salad. End of story. Excellent with just about any meat dish really.

SPROUTED BEAN BONANZA
SUPER-HEALTHY

Sprouted beans, so good for you—and yet in serious need of a PR makeover. It's their perennial association with hippydom that does them in, which is a shame as you don't strictly need to wear sandals and patchouli to enjoy the powerful combination of flavor and phytonutrients they offer. We've been cultivating and using sprouts for millennia: one of the oldest recipes in the world is that for *sameno*u, an Iranian confection prepared ceremonially from sprouted wheat grass, and the Chinese have been using beansprouts in their cuisine for at least 3,000 years.

* Your in-the-margin guide to sprouting

Good (safe) things to sprout include mung beans, black-eyed peas, soy beans, lentils, aduki beans, and chickpeas (not forgetting wheat and alfalfa—but they're not beans of course). Other beans can have lots of something called lectins, and these are not good if ingested in high quantities (for the same reason you shouldn't eat too many beansprouts). Wash your chosen legume several times then leave it to soak in plenty of water overnight. After about 24 hours, drain the water away and wrap them in a super-clean damp dish towel (better still, muslin). Put the beans somewhere warm and dark overnight. The next morning spread the beans out in a shallow layer and cover with moistened paper towel or cloth: keep watering the cloth until you can see sprouts (beans sprout at very different rates—mung are the easiest and the quickest). As soon as sprouts appear, remove the covering cloth and put the beans somewhere sunny. Water them several times daily until the sprouts are the desired length. Keep in the fridge until needed. Always rinse well before using.

A VIRTUOUS LUNCH FOR 2
splash of sesame oil
3oz/80g shiitake mushrooms, sliced
1⅔ cups/7oz/200g sprouted peas/beans*
⅓ cucumber, peeled and cubed
1 red onion, sliced
½ bunch of fresh cilantro, chopped
2 tsp *tahina*

2 tbsp water
juice and grated zest of 1 fat lime
   (or 2 little ones)
1½ tbsp extra-virgin olive oil
sea salt and Turkish-style red pepper flakes
   (or use black pepper)

Heat the sesame oil in a pan and stir-fry the shiitake mushrooms for just a few minutes before taking off the heat and allowing to cool. Why cook them? Because it makes them more nutritious, tastier, and easier to digest.

Mix the sprouted beans with the cooled 'shrooms, cucumber, onion, and cilantro. Blend the *tahina* with the water, lime, olive oil, and seasoning and mix the dressing through the salad. Enjoy with wheat bread and that feeling of superiority that you get when you treat your body as a temple.

EDAMAME SUPERFOOD SALAD

**✱ Notes

*Edamame beans are just immature soy beans. They shot to fame when the press started touting soy as a good nutrient for post-menopausal women (the beans are full of phyto-oestrogen, you see), but they are also a good source of plant-based protein and work to lower cholesterol. Dried soy beans take about a week to cook, so these softer pods are much more user-friendly.

**Ah. Nigella. The source of black seed oil, which is the original super-food (the Koran states that it "cures all ills except death"). The seeds are full of omega 3 and omega 6, which are good for the brain and joints.

***Hemp seeds are the proud bearers of more omega-3 and omega-6 than you can shake a stick at, along with trace minerals and vitamin E.

****Moroccan argan oil is produced from the fruit of the rare argan tree: it is harvested (eaten) by goats and the oil-rich stones are then extracted from the animals', um, waste material. It is high in vitamin E and all sorts. The argan trade is one of the first fairtrade arrangements, as all the proceeds thereof go back to the Berber women who produce it.

Some of my favorite things in life are beans, but when you can't eat wheat or dairy, and don't much like meat, your choice of food on the hoof is limited (although I'm very fond of fries, don't get me wrong). You start to realize how many unnecessary ingredients food manufacturers sneak into our diet. Inevitably I end up chomping on some virtuous but tasteless super-food salad (which these days ALWAYS has edamame beans in it), pretending not to be a tad envious of my burger chowing husband. This, then, is based on all of those salads—but with a bit of added flavor, for "healthy" does not have to be synonymous with tasteless. Actually, edamame beans are pretty cool.

A POWER LUNCH FOR 1 HUNGRY EXECUTIVE (OR SHOPKEEPER)

2³⁄₄oz/75g frozen edamame beans, defrosted (or 4½oz/125g fresh bean pods)*
¼ fresh pomegranate, pith removed, broken into arils (posh word for seeds)
1 tbsp corn kernels
1 scallion, chopped
½ carrot, grated (juice the other half for the dressing, see below)
big handful of arugula
1 level tsp nigella seeds, lightly toasted**
2 tsp raw hemp seeds, toasted***

FOR THE DRESSING:

1 tbsp olive oil
1 tsp argan (or pumpkin seed) oil****
1 tbsp carrot juice (see above)
1–2 tsp lime juice
½ tsp mustard
pinch of red pepper flakes
½ in/1cm knob fresh ginger, peeled and minced
sea salt

If you are using fresh beans, boil them in unsalted water for about 10 minutes before draining and cooling them, then removing them from their pods. Mix all the salad ingredients in a bowl, then whisk all the dressing ingredients together, seasoning to taste. Apply the latter to the former and stir. Enjoy on its own, or with rye bread/crackers if you feel you need a carb injection. Or you could actually have it with fries, just for fun (fries make you happy, which releases serotonin, which improves your health, which makes them a super-food too, no?).

ADUKI BEAN SALAD WITH CELERY, WALNUTS, PEAR, AND CREAM CHEESE *HEALTHY STUFF*

Aduki beans are neglected little guys—although they are big in Japan* and used in lots of sweet dishes over there. We should all be eating a lot more of them as they are full of folic acid, trace minerals, and soluble fiber. Chinese herbal medicine rates them for their healing properties. I'm guessing that this bland list of nutritional attributes isn't really selling them to you on the taste front but I can assure you that they also have a darn good, sweet-nutty flavor.

Pears are super-healthy, containing many valuable phytonutrients. Celery and walnuts are both practically super-foods, so this salad has everything going for it. Cream cheese always represents a little bit of wonderful in your day, so no apologies for its inclusion—but if you are on the Monte-Peruvian 6:1 Upside-down Tofu and Fries Diet you could always use low-fat stuff instead.

A CRUNCHY HEALTHY SIDE DISH FOR 4–6

1 cup/6oz/175g dried aduki beans, soaked overnight
3 sticks of celery, chopped
2/3 cup/3½oz/100g shelled walnuts, roughly chopped
2 small–medium ripe pears, cut into ½in/1cm cubes
1 bunch of scallions, chopped
2/3 cup/5½oz/150g cream cheese
1½ tbsp apple (or cider) vinegar
2 tbsp water
1½ tsp chopped fresh (or dried) dill
freshly ground black pepper and celery sea salt (or regular sea salt) to taste

Drain the aduki beans then bring them to a boil in a pan of unsalted water. Turn down the heat and simmer for about 45 minutes, or until just cooked. Drain once again (health buffs would have you keep the cooking water and drink it—the stuff is meant to be very good for the kidneys) and allow to cool. Mix the beans with the celery, walnuts, pear, and onions.

Make the dressing by beating the cream cheese with the vinegar, water, dill, and seasoning. If you are making this as a solitary pleasure just stir the dressing through the salad. If you are entertaining, for aesthetic purposes it might be better to serve the dressing in a bowl on the side. If there is any left, this one lasts well in the fridge so use it for your lunchbox the next day.

*Tip
The sad writerly fact is that I have waited years to be able to use this phrase in a sentence. The rock songs of one's youth are responsible for an awful lot of gibberish in later life, no?

CHAPTER FIVE
Grains and pasta

Part of the image problem that salad has can be ascribed to the fact that it is not
regarded as "filling." Simple: we'll add a truckload of (mostly healthy) carbs to
bulk it out. Crunchy wholewheat, soft pasta, toasted couscous, sticky sautéed
grains… in your face, salad critics: now tell us you're still hungry… The salads in
this chapter are robust affairs which you can for the most part make ahead.
This means that they will work well in your lunchboxes and on picnics.

GREEN PASTA SALAD WITH PISTACHIO PESTO

This is a simple salad, but it is very tasty—and such a pretty shade of green. I usually use *kritheraki* or *orzo* pasta for this (the one that looks just like rice), but you can use any pasta that takes your fancy. One's carnivorous husband likes this with added chopped mortadella, but frankly I think the meat is quite unnecessary.

A CREAMY SIDE SALAD FOR 4

10½oz/300g *orzo*

⅔ cup/3½oz/100g shelled pistachios

3–4 garlic cloves, peeled

handful of fresh basil

big handful of fresh parsley and cilantro

2½ tbsp balsamic vinegar

scant ½ cup/100ml extra-virgin olive oil

salt and freshly ground black pepper

1 bunch of scallions, chopped

1 fat zucchini, cut into matchsticks

scant 1 cup/5½oz/150g pitted green olives, sliced

1 tsp sumac (optional)

Bring a pan of salted water to the boil, add a dash of olive oil, and tip in the pasta. Cook for 8–9 minutes (or as per the instructions on the package if you are using another type of pasta) then drain and run under cold running water a little to cool it down.

Put the pistachios in your blender (or use a mortar and pestle) and crush them with the garlic and most of the herbs (retain a little parsley/cilantro for the garnish). Add the vinegar then trickle the olive oil in real slow so that an emulsion is formed. Season the pesto to taste.

Put the pasta in a bowl with the onions, zucchini, and olives and coat liberally with the pesto. Chop the retained herbs and sprinkle on top along with the sumac, if using.

SEASIDE SALAD

We should all be eating more seaweed. It is one of the best sources of iodine and other trace minerals, and once you get used to the occasionally funky smell its *umami* flavor grows on you. We should probably all be eating more clams as well. They are plentiful enough and yet they are not as easily found in stores as their media savvy seafood friends the mussel and the scallop. Razor clams are two a penny on our shores, but you'll want Palourdes clam in this recipe since it remains firm when steamed or boiled, and is a better shape for a salad.

This dish should leave you feeling that you must go down to the sea again, to the lonely sea and the sky...

AN APPETIZER OR LIGHT
LUNCH FOR 4
1¾lb/800g fresh Palourdes clams, de-fuzzed
    and scrubbed
handful of rolled oats
2 tbsp/1oz/30g butter
1 onion, chopped
2 garlic cloves, minced
1 glass of white wine (leftovers will do)
½ bunch of fresh parsley
7oz/200g pasta shells (conchiglie by any
    other name)

8 plum tomatoes, thinly sliced
1 bunch of scallions, chopped

FOR THE SEAWEED PESTO:
½ sheet nori, soaked for 10 minutes,
    then drained
big handful of fresh parsley
½ soft avocado
1 tsp (drained) capers
5 tbsp/75ml olive oil
juice of ½ lemon
sea salt and cracked black pepper

Put the clams into a bowl of salted water along with a handful of oats (this helps to clean the fish—see note on p.183) and leave for an hour. Drain, then tap any clams that are open: if they do not close, discard them.

Heat the butter in a pan and throw in the onion, followed by the garlic. Once they start to brown, add the wine and the stalks from the parsley (waste not want not and all that). Lower in the drained clams and steam them for around 6 minutes, or until they have all opened (throw any unopened ones away). Scoop the clams out and set aside.

In the meantime, bring a pan of water to a boil and cook the pasta according to the instructions on the package (around 7 minutes should do the trick). Drain and refresh.

Next for the pesto. Simply blend all the ingredients together, seasoning to taste.

When you are ready to serve, tip the pasta into a bowl with the tomatoes and scallions. Add the clams (being a bit of a peasant I add them shell and all, but you can remove the shells if you like), then chop the parsley and stir this through the salad. Dress with the seaweed sauce. Smell that ozone already.

GNOCCHI AND *PAPRIKASH* SALAD

Paprikash in its normal incarnation is a Hungarian chicken or beef casserole, usually served with *nokedli*, which are soft dumplingy things. I have subbed *gnocchi* for *nokedli* because they are more robust for a salad, and, more importantly, readily available, should you choose not to make your own. I've had a special thing going on with *gnocchi* since I discovered that my relationship with wheat had gone bad. When they are properly made, you see, it is with potato and buckwheat flour (or semolina). Trips to Italian restaurants (all that pizza… all that pasta… all that garlic bread) for those on other than conventional diets are only rendered bearable by the existence of risotto and gnocchi.

BONUS RECIPE:
QUICK(ISH)
HOMEMADE
GNOCCHI

Bake 2 large floury potatoes (King Edward are good), then skin them and mash (while still hot) with around ⅔ cup/3oz/80g buckwheat flour (or regular all-purpose flour), 1 beaten egg, some salt and pepper, and a sprinkling of dried herbs (oregano or basil) if you like. On a floured board, form the "dough" into a long flat oblong, then cut it into ¾ x ½in/2 x 1cm pieces, scraping each one with a fork (this makes the gnocchi more receptive to a coating of sauce). Either boil in salted water for around 2 minutes, stirring well to prevent clumping, or fry in hot oil, as in the recipe above. *Ben fatto* (well done)—just like Mamma used to make (well probably someone's mother, somewhere—mine is actually from Kent).

SUPPER FOR 4

scant ½ cup/100ml sour cream
3 garlic cloves, minced
2 tbsp (noble sweet) paprika
juice of 1 lime
2 tsp Worcestershire sauce
½ tsp smoked paprika
½ tsp cayenne pepper
½ tsp sea salt
2 fat skinless chicken breasts, cut into narrow strips OR (for a veggie version) 1lb/450g Portobello mushrooms (roughly 6), sliced
olive oil, for frying

1 pack (14oz/400g) gnocchi (or make your own, see bonus recipe)
2 red onions, chopped
2 fat red bell peppers, chopped
2 tbsp olive oil
1 heaped tsp English mustard
1 tbsp apple cider vinegar
salt and freshly ground black pepper
1 small oakleaf lettuce
1 bunch of scallions, chopped
handful of fresh chives, cut into 2in/5cm strips
2 tsp dried dill
big handful of fresh parsley, chopped
toasted slivered almonds

Beat half of the sour cream with half of the garlic, half of the paprika, and all of the lime juice, Worcestershire sauce, smoked paprika, cayenne, and salt. Add the chicken strips (or mushrooms), stirring them until thoroughly coated. Cover and refrigerate for 2 hours.

When you are ready to cook, heat a good glug of oil in a frying pan and throw in the gnocchi. Sear them for around 3 minutes per side until they are golden brown, then leave to drain on paper towel. Next, fry half the red onion and half the pepper in the same pan (adding more oil if necessary). As the vegetables start to soften, add the marinated chicken (or 'shroom) strips and fry for a few minutes per side or until thoroughly cooked.

Whisk the olive oil together with the rest of the cream, paprika, and garlic, and add the mustard and vinegar. Season the dressing to taste.

Time for assembly. Shred the oakleaf into a bowl with your hands. Add the rest of the onion and pepper together with the scallions, herbs, and almonds. Toss in the still warm gnocchi and chicken, and drizzle with the sour cream dressing. Serve immediately with warm bread.

SPAGHETTI SALAD

Because we all cook too much spaghetti sometimes ... This is a great way to use up that ton of spaghetti that we somehow always get stuck with after a spaghetti with meatballs blow-out. You could also use leftover oven roasted veggies. Nothing if not thrifty, me. That is not to say that it's not worth cooking spaghetti just to make this salad: it's a firm favorite with our customers, since it looks, well, silly—and food that makes people smile is the best kind of food.

SERVES 4

4½oz/125g spaghetti (whole grain is nicer, and healthier), broken into 2½in/6cm strips

1 fat zucchini, halved lengthways and cut into ¾in/2cm chunks

1 fat orange bell pepper, cut into ¾in/2cm squares

1 red onion, cut into chunks

4–5 garlic cloves, bashed

2 tbsp extra-virgin olive oil

salt and freshly ground black pepper

1 tsp dried thyme (or good sprig of fresh)

3 spicy smoked sausages (Italian style, or chorizo, or andouille)

12 cherry tomatoes, halved

generous ½ cup/3½oz/100g pitted black olives

FOR THE DRESSING:

handful of fresh basil

big handful of fresh parsley

1½ tbsp balsamic vinegar

2 garlic cloves

1 tbsp grated Parmesan cheese

½ tsp coarse ground black pepper

⅓ tsp salt

5 tbsp/75ml (ish) extra-virgin olive oil

Preheat the oven to 375°F/190°C.

Bring a pan of water to the boil, add salt and a dash of olive oil, and tip the spaghetti in. Cook for around 7 minutes, or until it passes that super-silly test whereby you throw it at the wall to see if it sticks, then drain and refresh. Leave to drip dry in a colander. If you're using leftover "sketti," just cut through it so it is in more manageable pieces.

Place the zucchini, pepper, onion, and garlic in a small oven dish, drizzle with the olive oil, seasoning, and thyme and bake for 10 minutes. After this time, slice the sausages thickly on a bias and add to the baking veggies. Cover the dish and cook for a further 15–20 minutes, or until the sausage is just cooked. Allow to cool a little.

Make the dressing by putting the herbs, vinegar, garlic, cheese, and seasoning in your blender (or whisk it by hand) and trickling in the olive oil to form a pleasingly green emulsion.

When you are ready to serve, tip the spaghetti into a bowl and mix in the (still warm) oven roasted veg/sausage mix. Add the tomatoes, olives, and dressing and serve immediately with warm bread: pizza-style garlic bread would be especially nice here. The salad can be thrown in the fridge and enjoyed the next day, but it will taste better at room temperature rather than chilled.

NEW ORLEANS COUSCOUS SALAD

Couscous, according to my significant other, tastes like ground cardboard…
unless it is heavily disguised. This salad he can handle—it has a ton of stuff in
it to disguise the basic granular blandness of the grain.

It is based on a sandwich—the muffaletta sandwich, which is a bit of a
New Orleans institution, quite apart from being one of the best-named dishes
ever. Created by Sicilian settlers, it is a kind of Deep South Dagwood, with
layers of all sorts to titillate the taste buds—and this is why it makes for such
a good lunch/brunch dish. Want a veggie version? Just add more cheese and
scrap the meat.

LUNCH FOR 4–6
1 cup/7oz/200g whole-wheat couscous
   (because it is better for you)
around ¾ cup/180ml boiling water
3½oz/100g mixed pickled vegetables
   (drained weight), roughly chopped
generous ½ cup/3½oz/100g stuffed olives,
   sliced
1 tbsp (drained) capers
2¾oz/75g prosciutto, roughly chopped
3½oz/100g salami (you choose which),
   roughly chopped
3½oz/100g provolone cheese (or use
   Cheddar)
big handful of fresh basil, roughly shredded

FOR THE DRESSING:
4 tbsp olive oil
1½ tbsp balsamic vinegar
4–5 sun-dried tomatoes in oil, drained
   and chopped
1 tsp dried basil
4 garlic cloves, minced
salt (only a little, the other ingredients are salty
   enough) and freshly ground black pepper

TO GARNISH
4 tomatoes, quartered
1 onion, quartered

Place the couscous in a bowl and pour the boiling water on top. Cover and allow to steam
for around 15 minutes, stirring occasionally. Fluff with a fork and allow to cool.

Next, make the dressing, as the flavors need time to marry. Whisk all the ingredients
together and set aside for 30 minutes or so.

Finally, mix all the salad ingredients together, garnish with the quartered tomatoes
and onion, and stir the dressing through it. This keeps well so you may want to make extra
for your next day lunchbox.

WHOLE RYE SALAD WITH BOURBONED CURRANTS AND CARAWAY

Rye is the mysterious dark horseman of the grain world. Like wheat berries, rye berries are a bit of a pain to cook: you need to soak them overnight, but they are worth it: rich and nutty and so healthy. Rye is super-high in fiber and low in gluten, so it is a good friend to the perennial dieter.

Useless grain facts: Rye was not always valued as a foodstuff: in fact Pliny reckoned that it was a "very poor food and only serves to avert starvation." And one's normally carb-loving beau has actually spat it out on the few occasions I have tried to feed him rye bread. However, it became highly prized in Scandinavia and North Eastern Europe as it is extremely hardy and thrives in poor soil.

A HEALTHY SUPPER FOR 2–3
(WITH A DASH OF HIDDEN
NAUGHTINESS)
5½oz/150g rye berries (i.e. whole rye grains),
    soaked overnight in about 2 cups/500ml
    acidulated cold water*
½ cup/2¾oz/75g currants
3 tbsp Southern Comfort
    (or other sweet bourbon)**
7oz/200g sweet potato, peeled and cubed
    (⅝in/1.5cm cubes are good)

2 medium carrots, cut into chunks
1 red onion, coarsely chopped
drizzle of olive oil
1½ tsp caraway seeds
sea salt and freshly ground black pepper
3 tbsp extra-virgin olive oil
juice of 1 lemon
juice of ½ orange
salt and freshly ground black pepper
⅔ cup/2⅔oz/75g pumpkin seeds
1¾oz/50g arugula

Cook the rye in its soaking water: keep an eye on the liquid levels and top up with cold water if necessary. The berries should take around an hour to cook: you want them done but still with some bite to them. Refresh under cold water and leave to drain.

While the rye is cooking, set the currants to soak in the Southern Comfort. Next, preheat the oven to 350°F/180°C.

Spread the sweet potato, carrots, and onion out on an oven tray, drizzle with oil, sprinkle with the caraway seeds and seasoning, and bake for about 20 minutes, or until the veggies are just tender. Remove from the oven and set aside.

When you are ready to serve, drain the currants, retaining the liquor. Whisk the olive oil with the fruit juices and the remaining Southern Comfort, and season to taste. Place the grains and oven-roasted veggies in a bowl, then stir in the currants, pumpkin seeds, and arugula. Drizzle with the boozy dressing and enjoy.

✳ Notes

*In this case just add 3 tablespoons plain yogurt or lemon juice to the water and stir. You could substitute the more readily available wheat berries – these also respond well to soaking in acidulated water.

**Don't want to use alcohol? Just use water to soak the raisins, and add 1½ tablespoons cider vinegar to the dressing instead.

KISIR: TURKISH BULGAR AND TOMATO SALAD

ON THE FIRST WHEAT EATERS...

Huge chunks of life as we know it evolved in the Middle East. None is more significant than the development of agriculture in the area we've come to know as the Fertile Crescent. At early settlements such as Jarmo and Tell Abu Hureyra, in Iraq and Syria respectively, evidence of grain cultivation dating back to 7,000BC and 9,000BC has been uncovered. It is believed that a mini ice age interrupted the nomadic hunter-gatherer lifestyle of the inhabitants of the region, causing them actively to plant stuff for the first time in order to safeguard food supplies. Communities grew into villages, and civilization was born.

The earliest grains used would have been emmer and einkorn, which are both varieties of wheat, along with goat grass, rye, and barley. Our modern wheat varieties are descended from a hybrid of emmer and goat grass.

Wheat remains an important part of the diet in the belt extending from Eastern Turkey down through Iraq and Syria.

This is basically Turkish *tabouleh* (see p.17). The most noticeable difference is that it is red instead of green, as it contains far less in the way of herbs, and is tinged by a piquant blend of tomato, pepper, and pomegranate paste. It is very much regarded as an everyday salad: all of my Turkish customers seem to make it regularly. This kind of figures as all Turkish households have bulgar and pepper paste, in the same way that all American households stock potatoes and ketchup I guess. This is Meryem's recipe, with a bit of interference from her friend Deniz, and a couple of interjections from Deniz' mother Aiseh—because conversations held in corner stores are never straightforward.

SERVES 6 AS A SIDE SALAD

olive oil, for frying
1 large onion, chopped
1 small red bell pepper, chopped
1 tsp ground cumin
6 large tomatoes, chopped
1 tbsp *biber salçasi* (hot Turkish pepper paste or just use 1 tbsp tomato paste and add chili powder to taste)

⅔ cup/150ml tomato juice
1 cup/7oz/200g medium bulgar
3 tbsp olive oil
1 tbsp pomegranate molasses
salt
1 bunch of scallions, chopped
big handful of fresh parsley, chopped
big handful of fresh mint, shredded

Heat the olive oil in a frying pan and toss in the onion and pepper, stirring until the veggies soften without catching. Add the cumin and half the tomatoes, and cook for a couple of minutes before spooning in the pepper paste and tomato juice.

Tip the bulgar into a bowl and pour the contents of the frying pan onto it, mixing well. Cover, set aside for 10 minutes, then check to see if the wheat is cooked to your liking (the chances are good that you will need to add a further ¼–½ cup/50–100ml of boiling water, but wheat and preferences vary greatly). Allow the *kisir* to cool to room temperature.

Whisk the olive oil and pomegranate paste together and season to taste before using it to dress the bulgar. At the last minute stir the rest of the tomatoes through the salad along with the onions and herbs. *Kisir* goes with just about everything.

FREEKEH SALAD WITH ORANGE AND APRICOT *SUPER-HEALTHY*

Freekeh is smoked wheat. It has been a part of the diet in the Levant and Egypt for millennia, and even gets a mention in medieval Baghdad texts. Young green wheat is sun-dried and then torched. Because there is so much sap inside the wheat, only the chaff burns off, leaving the inner kernel roasted but intact. The wheat is then rubbed and thrashed, and left in the sun a little more: it is either packed whole or cracked so that it resembles coarse bulgar. It is now being touted as a super-food (among other things it may help you "see in the dark" owing to its high lutein levels): this is much to the amusement of my ethnic customers, who find it funny when us Westerners "discover" a "new" ingredient.

A VEGAN SIDE SALAD FOR 6

non-extra-virgin olive oil, for frying

1 onion, chopped

2 sticks of celery, chopped

5½oz/150g freekeh (if you can't find any, buckwheat or barley will do fine)

¾ cup/175ml vegetable stock

5 tbsp/75ml orange juice

1oz/30g sour orange peel (available dried in Middle Eastern stores: grated Seville or ordinary orange zest will do in a pinch)

1 tsp cracked coriander seeds

1 tbsp pomegranate seeds (optional)

½ tsp cumin seeds

1 tsp fennel seeds

1 tsp rose petals

½ tsp red pepper flakes

5 tbsp extra-virgin olive oil

generous ½ cup/3½oz/100g dried apricots (preferably organic), soaked for 30 minutes in cold water

⅔ cup/3½oz/100g macadamia halves, toasted (do use other nuts if you like)

1 bunch of fresh chives, chopped

½ bunch of fresh mint, shredded

1 bunch of fresh cilantro, chopped

2½ tbsp cider vinegar

sea salt and freshly ground black pepper

Heat a splash of oil in a saucepan and sweat the onion and celery. Once they are soft, turn up the heat, add the freekeh, and stir well so that it toasts a little. Now add the vegetable stock and orange juice, bring the liquid to a boil, cover the pan, and turn down to a simmer. Cook for around 40 minutes (unless you are using the cracked grain, in which case it will take half this time), stirring occasionally and adding a little water if necessary. Once it is cooked (it should still be quite firm) remove and allow to cool.

Bring a pan of water to a boil and blanch the orange peel for around 3 minutes, then drain. Next, heat a dribble more oil in a frying pan and toast the peel with the coriander, pomegranate, cumin, and fennel seeds for a couple of minutes. Tip them into a grinder or mortar and pestle and grind them together with the rose petals and red pepper flakes. Add this mixture to the olive oil, and leave for 30 minutes or so for the flavors to mingle.

Drain and chop the apricots and add these to the freekeh along with the nuts and herbs. Whisk the vinegar into the spiced oil and season to taste before stirring it through the freekeh. This keeps well for a day or so and leftovers make a good lunchbox filler.

MAGHREBI BARLEY AND CHICKPEA SALAD

I've long been on a mission to rehabilitate barley into our diet. It is often seen as a pauper's grain, when in fact it is rich in all the good stuff, and tasty to boot. The Romans recognized this as they called gladiators "hordearii," or "men of barley"—it was rumored that they feasted on barley prior to a fight because the grain boosted their strength. And Avicenna noted it as suitable food for convalescents. Furthermore, the Scots pretty much venerate the stuff...*

Its sweet, nutty chewiness makes for hearty salads with an unusual texture.

A HEARTY SIDE DISH
FOR 4 GLADIATORS
(OR 6–8 MERE MORTALS)
dash of oil, for frying
1 tsp coriander seeds, lightly crushed
½ tsp cumin seeds
1 cup/8oz/225g pearl barley
2 tsp paprika
1 tsp ground ginger
1 can (14oz/400g) chickpeas, drained
1 red onion, sliced

3oz/80g baby spinach leaves, roughly shredded
1 fat carrot, julienned
1 small bunch of fresh mint, roughly chopped

FOR THE DRESSING:
4 tbsp extra-virgin olive oil
1½ tbsp wine vinegar
1 tsp orange blossom water
½ tsp harissa paste
3–4 garlic cloves, minced
salt

* Note
You can blame Rabbie Burns and the legend of John Barleycorn for that. John Barleycorn is the human embodiment of barley, a Wicker man-type character who lives and dies so man can eat (and more importantly drink—for whisky and beer are of course barley derivatives).

John Barleycorn was a hero bold, of noble enterprise; for if you do but taste his blood, 'twill make your courage rise...'

Heat a pan and add a splash of oil. When it is sizzling, add the coriander and cumin, stirring constantly, followed by the barley. Stir for a couple of minutes, then slowly add cold water (you will need around 1¾ cups/400ml), a little at a time, much as you would for a risotto. Once the barley is just cooked, turn the heat off, wrap the lid of the pan in a dish towel, and allow the grains to steam gently for around 20 minutes. At the end of this time stir the paprika and ginger through the barley and allow to cool.

While it is cooling, whisk the dressing ingredients together.

When you are ready to serve, tip the barley into a bowl and use your hands to separate the grains. Add the chickpeas and other salad ingredients, and then stir the dressing through it.

MILLET, CRANBERRY, AND SAFFRON SALAD

Millet is an overlooked little grain, often dismissed as bird food, although it has a lot going for it. Canny farmers from the ancient Chinese through to modern Africans have long known that millet is a top crop when it comes to arid, less-than-perfect conditions. It also keeps for years, so it is a good grain to lay down against harsh winters. The Romans used it for all kinds of things, most notably *pulmentum*, which was an early version of polenta. If you add too much water or cook it for too long it quickly turns to a porridge-type slurry, which is, in fact usually its designated culinary function in colder climes: millet porridge is popular across Russia and northern China. Millet is gluten-free and provides handy variety for those on a wheat-free or coeliac diet. To get the best out of it for a salad, toast the grains and use a little less water.

A SIDE DISH FOR 4

1½ cups/9oz/250g millet

1¼ tbsp/½ oz/18g butter

¼ tsp ground saffron steeped in a splash of boiling water

a little oil, for cooking

1 small bulb fennel, sliced into 1¼–1½in/ 3–4cm strips (keep the fronds)

¾ cup/4½oz/125g unsweetened dried cranberries (barberries also work well)

1 bunch of scallions, chopped

½ bunch of fresh cilantro, finely chopped

FOR THE DRESSING:

4 tbsp nice olive oil

1 tbsp (Arabic or Turkish, i.e. sweeter) pomegranate paste

juice and grated zest of 1 small sour (Seville) orange (or use a lime instead)

¾in/2cm knob fresh ginger, peeled and minced

1 level tsp ground fennel seeds

salt and freshly ground black pepper

Toast the millet in a saucepan, stirring constantly, until it just starts to brown. Next, add water, a little at a time, as in the recipe above. As a rough guide, you will need around scant 2 cups/450ml of liquid, and the cooking process should take around 15 minutes. Once the millet is just cooked, stir half of the butter through it together with the saffron, then turn the heat off and wrap the lid of the pan in a clean dish towel, thus allowing the millet to continue to steam and separate.

In the meantime, heat the rest of the butter and a little oil in a frying pan and fry the fennel. Just as it starts to soften and brown, add the cranberries, stirring well, then take off the heat.

Tip the millet into a bowl and fluff it with a fork before allowing it to cool a little. Once it is warm rather than hot, add the fennel and cranberries, followed by the scallions and cilantro. Chop the reserved fennel greenery into the salad for good measure.

Finally, whisk the dressing ingredients together and stir through the millet. Serve warm—although this is almost as nice as a lunchbox filler the next day.

QUINOA AND GARLICKY
EGGPLANTS *SUPER-HEALTHY*

Quinoa. Kwinoa. Keenwah. Call it what you will darlings, it's still all the rage (2013 was actually the "Year of Quinoa," as declared by the UN), and as "grains"* go it is one of the healthier ones: it is high in protein and amino acids, and this is a good thing. It was first cultivated in ancient Peru and Bolivia, and remains a treasured part of the diet in that part of the world. I can't get my other half to eat it for all the gold in El Dorado though, as he reckons it looks like spiders' eggs when it's cooked…

A VEGAN LUNCH FOR 4–5

1 cup/6oz/175g quinoa
scant 2 cups/450ml good vegetable stock
    (or good water)
1 medium eggplant, cut into ¾in/2cm chunks
½ small cauliflower, broken into florets
1 large onion, cut into ⅝in/1.5cm chunks
6 garlic cloves, finely sliced
non-extra-virgin olive oil, for cooking
1 tsp brown sugar
1 heaped tsp garam masala
1 tsp turmeric

½ tsp chili powder
sea salt
⅔ cup/3½oz/100g roasted peanuts
1 can (14oz/400g) chickpeas
1 small bunch of fresh cilantro, finely chopped
plain yogurt (optional)

FOR THE DRESSING:
3 tbsp olive oil
1 tbsp pomegranate molasses
1 tbsp balsamic vinegar

Rinse the quinoa thoroughly in a fine gauge sieve (this rids it of any innate bitterness). Pour the stock into a pan and add the quinoa. Bring to a boil then turn down the heat and simmer for about 10 minutes, or until the stock is absorbed and the grain cooked "al dente." Fluff with a fork and allow to cool.

Preheat the oven to 375°F/190°C.

Place the eggplant, cauliflower, onion, and garlic in an oven dish. Dribble with a little oil and sprinkle with the sugar, spices, and salt before covering with foil and baking for about 30 minutes, or until the vegetables are soft. Allow to cool a little.

Tip the quinoa into a bowl and mix with the peanuts, chickpeas, and cilantro. Whisk the dressing ingredients together, seasoning to taste (it is stating the obvious, but if you have used roasted and salted peanuts, you may wish to use less salt in the dressing). Finally, pile the roasted garlicky veggies on to the quinoa and pour the pomegranate sauce over the salad. Serve with lashings of plain yogurt.

* Tip
Your botanist geek friend will tell you that quinoa is a "pseudo-cereal" (like buckwheat—see below) as it is not actually a grain, but rather a distant cousin of tumbleweed and spinach.

KASHA (ROASTED BUCKWHEAT) SALAD WITH *KIELBASA*

Kasha is roasted (or toasted) buckwheat.* So far so good. What is odd about buckwheat is that it is not actually a type of wheat at all, but rather a cousin of the rhubarb family. It gets treated as a grain, however, hence its inclusion in this chapter. It is healthy stuff, and so it is much beloved by the gluten intolerant, not to mention swathes of Eastern Europe and Russia, where is it more or less a national carbohydrate institution.

You can use whole (unroasted) buckwheat (which is paler: kasha itself should be a rich golden brown color), but toast the grains before playing with them—this serves both to improve the flavor and expedite the cooking process.

Kielbasa is a generic name for Polish sausages, and as I don't want to send you off on a wild goose/sausage chase, I will leave it to you to choose which you use. I tend to work with the thick U-shaped ones as Mr. Shopkeeper has a bit of thing for them and I can guarantee that there is always some hidden in the fridge.

LIGHT LUNCH FOR 4
1½ cups/9oz/250g kasha
scant 2 cups/450ml vegetable stock
2 garlic cloves, chopped
1 bunch of scallions, chopped
2 sticks of celery, chopped
1 nice eating apple
big bunch of fresh dill, chopped
    (or use 1–2 tbsp dried dill)

handful of fresh flat-leaf parsley, chopped
1 U-shaped Polish-style smoked sausage,
    sliced into ¼in/5mm rounds
scant ½ cup/100ml sour cream
juice and grated zest of ½ lime
½ tsp mild curry powder
1 level tsp strong-ish mustard
salt and a pinch of sugar

Place the kasha in a pan, add the stock and garlic, and bring to a boil. Turn down the heat and simmer for about 8 minutes, then check the buckwheat—it should be cooked but still have some crunch to it (kasha is very easy to overcook). Once it is cooked to your liking, drain it in a sieve (there shouldn't be much cooking stock left in the pan) and run some cold water over it to arrest the cooking process. Allow to drain thoroughly.

Mix the drained kasha with the scallions and celery. Core and cube the apple, and add this in too, along with the dill and the parsley. Grill (or fry) the sausage slices until just starting to brown, and set aside.

Whisk the sour cream with the lime, the curry powder, mustard, and seasoning, and spoon it into a little bowl.

Tip the kasha on to a plate, arrange the still warm sausage on top, and serve with the dressing alongside.

* Note
Yes: it is also the general Russian word for "porridge," before all you cunning linguists call in.

WHOLE GRAIN BULGAR WITH APPLE, HAZELNUTS, AND *PEKMEZ* *SUPER-HEALTHY*

Whole grain bulgar was a revelation to me: it does taste super nutty, and holds its texture without being too "crunchy" (euphemism for "resolutely refuses to cook"). If you are fond of a post-prandial snooze at your desk, best leave this one alone: the added fruit, nuts, and seeds make this a nutritious salad that will give you enough energy to sail through the afternoon.

A LUNCH FOR 2 (OR FOR
1 PERSON 2 DAYS RUNNING)

¾ cup/5½oz/150g whole grain bulgar
scant ¼ cup/50ml apple juice
2 tbsp cider vinegar
scant ½ cup/100ml boiling water
3½oz/100g celeriac (celery root)
1 large crunchy apple, cored
1 tbsp lemon juice
1 carrot, grated
1 red onion, finely sliced

⅔ cup/3½oz/100g shelled hazelnuts
    (or walnuts), halved
scant ½ cup/1¾oz/50g pumpkin seed kernels
big handful of fresh parsley, chopped
3 tbsp extra-virgin olive oil
1½ tbsp *pekmez* (grape syrup)
½ tsp Turkish pepper flakes (or use a little chili
    powder)
salt (you will need quite a bit as bulgar
    soaks it up)

Spread the bulgar out in a shallow bowl and pour the juice, vinegar, and boiling water over. Cover the dish and leave for 15–20 minutes, or until the wheat is "cooked" to your satisfaction (you may need to add a little more boiling water).

Peel the celeriac and cut it into matchsticks. Do the same with the apple and immediately coat them with the lemon juice to prevent discoloration. Once the wheat has cooled to room temperature, add the vegetables, hazelnuts, and seeds, then mix in the herbs. Whisk the oil and *pekmez* together, season to taste, and stir through the salad. If you want to push the boat out, serve with a big dollop of thick yogurt on top. You may now fix your colleagues with a nutritionally superior gaze…

CHAPTER SIX
Rice

Personally I've been to just one too many buffet parties that offered, among other dire things, a bowl of Uncle Ben's Rice studded with erstwhile frozen mixed veggies. Rice salad, in the wrong context, makes me decidedly twitchy. Which is why I have dedicated a whole chapter to the stuff. This is also in part due to my Iranian connection (aka husband). For many Iranians a meal is not actually a meal without rice, and anything devoid is but a snack, so if you are going to try and fob them off with salad as a main course, you'll need to include rice. As with grains, rice is filling, and so the contents of this chapter make for great workday lunches. And they can for the most part be prepared the night before.

MULLAH NASRUDDIN
AND THE FEAST OF RICE

Mullah Nasruddin (aka Hodja or Juha) is the clown/
philosopher/wiseman/fool of the Middle East:
a larger-than-life, donkey-riding judge/mullah whose
exploits are used to highlight and solve practically
any foible or dilemma. Here he kindly illustrates
the importance of rice in the region: bread was
(and remains) the staple carbohydrate, and rice
was regarded as the food of the rich.

*Nasruddin was on a long journey, traveling back
to his homeland after a pilgrimage. Tired, dusty, and
very hungry, he espied a caravan of wealthy looking
merchants dining on a lush* pulao *(rice dish): it was
so fragrant that the aromas of cardamom and saffron
wafted across the desert night to where he stood. It had
been a long time since he had enjoyed a meal of rice:
dry bread and dates were the normal fare of travelers.
Drooling, he approached where they sat and
prostrated himself on the ground.*

*"Allah have mercy! How can I escape from the
clutches of these highwaymen? This road is infested
with looters and pillagers and doers of no good: pity me
and let your poor, hungry servant escape in one piece!"
cried our devious friend.*

*"Why we are no thieves!" said the merchants,
appalled to be mistaken for such. "We are honest
tradesmen, and good Muslims to boot. Our* sofreh
*(dinner spread) is filled by honesty and hard
work alone."*

*"Well that does make a difference," said the
Mullah, smiling and squatting to join them at their
repast. "But I'm still a little anxious. Now how can we
prove for all concerned that you are good, alms-giving
characters?" And with that he reached out and began
to partake of the rice…*

I wonder what he'd have made of the *pulao* salad
that follows…

BOGOLI PULAO SALAD: PERSIAN FAVA BEAN RICE SALAD WITH SESAME AND DILL

Bogoli pulao is possibly my favorite among the classic rice (or *pulao*) dishes of Iran. In this version it becomes a ridiculously addictive salad. Out of season, using frozen fava beans is just dandy: if you shop carefully you may even find them already shucked.

AS A GENEROUS SIDE DISH FOR 4

2 cups/10½oz/300g brown basmati rice (using cooked leftover rice is an option of course)
big pat of butter
salt
1 generous tbsp dried dill (or use fresh dill)
¼ tsp ground saffron, steeped in a splash of boiling water
9oz/250g baby fava beans, shucked*
dash of (preferably untoasted) sesame oil or use regular cooking oil

½ cup/3oz/80g hulled sesame seeds
1½ tbsp *tahina*
1½ tbsp olive oil
juice and grated zest of 1 large lemon
a smidge of salt and freshly ground black pepper
½ bunch of scallions, chopped
⅔ cup/3½oz/100g raw pistachios (or pumpkin seeds)
½ bunch of fresh cilantro, chopped

Easy peasy. Rinse then soak the rice for around 30 minutes (brown basmati is just that little bit more resistant to cooking than white). Drain then add butter and salt and cook according to your preferred method. Stir the dill through it, then drizzle with the saffron and allow to cool.

Next, blanch the fava beans in boiling salted water (3–4 minutes should do). Drain and again allow to cool.

Now toast the seasame seeds. Rub a frying pan with sesame oil, then toss the seeds over a fairly strong flame until they start to turn golden brown. Turn them out onto paper towel and set aside.

Time for the dressing. Whisk the *tahina*, olive oil, lemon, and seasoning together until they form an emulsion. Add a little cold water if it looks too thick.

When the rice is cool, stir in the fava beans, sesame seeds, scallions, pistachios, and cilantro. Pour the dressing over and mix well. Check the seasoning and chill until required.

✳ Tip

Great word, shucked. It's one of my favorite culinary verbs. Everyone loves obscure verbiage, no? Here's a few more that you could use to dazzle your dinner party guests:

✳ To bard: to wrap a lump of meat in strips of fat or fatty meat.
✳ To French: to score through food (in an artistic fashion rather than in desperation) to enable it to cook more swiftly.
✳ To quadrille: to sear meat or fish so that it bears a criss-cross pattern (as in the marks from a grill).
✳ To strig: to pluck the stem from produce/herbs.
✳ To vandyke: to fashion fruit into fancy crinkly flower shapes.

That's OK: you don't have to thank me. Geekery is its own reward.

BIRYANI SALAD WITH RAITHA DRESSING *USES LEFTOVERS*

Us corner shopkeepers—we might have to eat pretty fast, but we do eat well you know. After all, we do have the best of everything at our fingertips.

This salad is a combo of my greengrocer's wife's *biryani* recipe and circumstance (i.e. a hot dish gone cold). It is a super-filling and very addictive number: I have to ration myself or allow for an unscheduled siesta when I make it. Come to think of it, the greengrocer is often to be found having a post-prandial snooze in his back room. You know, a "back in ten minutes sign" would be so much more civilized than our current "back in five minutes" one.

TO FEED 4 HUNGRY
GREENGROCERS
1¼ cups/9oz/250g basmati rice
salt
pat of ghee (or butter mixed with oil)
1 large onion, chopped
3 garlic cloves, minced
¾in/2cm knob fresh ginger, peeled
    and minced
2–3 green chilies, chopped (optional)
2 tsp garam masala
½ tsp ground turmeric
1 cup/3½oz/100g slivered almonds
scant ⅔ cup/3½oz/100g raisins soaked in
    cold water

1 bunch of scallions, chopped
9–10½ oz/250–300g leftover cooked diced
    chicken (or cooked shrimp, or shredded
    lamb, or cubed fried eggplant)
1 bunch of fresh cilantro, chopped
poppadoms (or crackers), to serve
your favorite chutney, to serve

FOR THE DRESSING:
3 tbsp grapeseed oil (or canola)
scant ½ cup/3½oz/100g plain yogurt
1 heaped tsp mint sauce (see p.257)
1 tbsp balsamic vinegar
sea salt and freshly ground black pepper

Rinse the rice. Bring a pan of salted water to a rolling boil, tip the rice in, and cook for around 7 minutes; the rice should be soft outside, but still hard inside (pinching a grain between your thumb and forefinger should determine this). Drain thoroughly in a sieve.

Melt the ghee in a saucepan and fry the onion, garlic, ginger, and chilies. Once the onion starts to brown, add the spices then spoon the rice into the pan, mixing well. Using the handle of a wooden spoon, poke 3–4 "fumeroles" down to the bottom of the pan (this allows the rice to steam evenly). Turn the heat right down (time to use a heat diffuser if you have one), wrap the lid of the pan in a clean dish towel, and allow to steam gently for about 30 minutes. At the end of this time, transfer the rice to a cold bowl and allow to cool.

Toast the almonds by dry-frying them until they are golden brown, then set these aside to cool also. Now is also the time to drain the raisins.

Once the *biryani* is quite cool, stir the nuts, raisins, scallions, chopped chicken (or whatever), and nearly all of the cilantro through the rice. Whisk the dressing ingredients together and pour over the salad. Mix once more, garnish with the reserved cilantro, and serve with poppadoms and chutney.

SOUR CHERRY AND RICE SALAD

This is a twist on a Persian classic, *albaloo pulao*, which is a hot dish of meat and sour cherries layered with rice. Rice salad is not something you would find in the Middle East: rice is eaten hot and there are rarely leftovers. But I think it is all kinds of excellent.

Fresh sour cherries are fruit gold dust, rare indeed. We jump through logistical hoops and battle with legions of the devil's own bureaucrats to get them to you. But this recipe uses the dried version twinned with sour cherry jam, both of which are much easier to source. If you really can't find dried sour cherries, substitute unsweetened dried cranberries.

AN ACCOMPANIMENT
FOR 4
5½oz/150g red (Camargue) rice
    (use basmati or long grain if you can't
    find the red stuff)
3½oz/100g dried sour cherries, pitted
1 bunch of scallions, chopped
½ cup/1¾oz/50g slivered almonds, toasted
½ bunch of fresh flat-leaf parsley, chopped

FOR THE DRESSING:
2 juniper berries, crushed
½ tsp dried thyme
1 tsp sour cherry jam
2 tsp balsamic vinegar
grated zest and 1 tbsp of the juice of 1 orange
    (go ahead and drink the rest)
5 tbsp extra-virgin olive oil (nice mixed with
    hazelnut oil as well, half and half—but
    don't go to all the expense of buying a
    bottle just for this salad)
salt and coarsely ground black pepper

Cook the rice in boiling water for about 30 minutes (it does take longer than regular rice), then drain it well and tip it into a bowl. Mix in the cherries, scallions, and almonds and stir well.

Whisk the ingredients for the dressing together, seasoning to taste, and pour over the salad. At the last minute stir the parsley through it (this way its greenness is preserved). This is otherwise a red salad, and the colors merrily all leach into each other.

CHILIED PEANUT
BLACK RICE SALAD

This is another salad evolved during my "back in 5 minutes" shop lunchbreaks. Peanut butter is full of protein and has a healthy oil content, so although it feels like naughty food, it is good for you. Which is just as well considering my intake.

You can use leftover cooked rice for this (especially if you are on a five minute lunch break), but it is all the better for using a chewy, nutty rice. Black rice (also known as forbidden rice—which is an apt name as my Iranian family-in-law disliked it so much that they have banned it from their dinner table) is ace here (and it is a bit of superfood in its own right), but brown basmati also works well.

A HEARTY SIDE DISH FOR 4

1 cup/7oz/200g black rice, soaked for at least 2 hours
1 tbsp toasted sesame oil
1⅓ cups/7oz/200g raw shelled peanuts
3 tsp brown sugar
1 bird's eye chili (or more if you dare), minced
1½ tsp soy sauce
2 peaches, pitted and cubed
1 bunch of scallions, chopped
big handful of fresh cilantro, chopped

FOR THE DRESSING:

3 tbsp extra-virgin olive oil
1 heaped tbsp peanut butter
1½ tbsp balsamic vinegar
¾in/2cm knob fresh ginger, peeled and minced
salt

Drain the rice and bubble it in boiling salted water for about 35 minutes. Check that it is cooked, then drain once again and leave to cool.

Make the dressing by beating all the ingredients together then set aside for the flavors to marry.

Heat the sesame oil in a wee pan, add the peanuts, sugar, and chili (make sure the room is well ventilated as sizzling chilies are quite choky) and once the nuts start to brown, add the soy sauce, then take off the heat.

Toss the cooled drained rice with the peaches, chili nuts, and scallions then stir the dressing and the cilantro through it. This is just grand as a side for plain grilled chicken—but it is even better scoffed in the back room of the shop with a line gently building behind the door.

STICKY RICE SALAD WITH TOFU SAUCE

This is a really filling salad but it is kind of wholesome, and kiddy friendly. Few children about town can be fobbed off with a cheese sammie in their lunch boxes these days, and this ticks a lot of playground-cred boxes.

Sticky (aka glutinous) rice is pretty easy to cook—the trick is in the soaking beforehand. Useless sticky rice fact: parts of the Great Wall of China are held together with the stuff—so if you get bored with it as a foodstuff, you could use it to repair your masonry.

SERVES 3–4

1⅓ cups/10½oz/300g sticky rice (often known as glutinous rice or "sweet rice")

1 level tsp salt

3 tbsp rice vinegar

2 tbsp sesame seeds

2 tbsp shelled peanuts

3oz/80g fresh edamame beans (or use young fava beans)

1 fat carrot, finely diced

3oz/80g green peas

3oz/80g corn kernels

FOR THE DRESSING:

2 tbsp toasted sesame oil

3½oz/100g silken tofu, cut into chunks

1 tbsp miso paste

1 tbsp Chinese plum sauce

½in/1cm knob fresh ginger, peeled and minced

2 garlic cloves, minced

salt and freshly ground black pepper

Put the rice into a bowl of water (enough to cover and then some) along with a little salt and leave to soak for an hour. Drain and tip it into a sieve (or a sticky rice steamer, if you are blessed with such a utensil), and sit it over a pan of boiling water. Steam for around 10 minutes, then fluff it with a fork and leave to steam for 3–4 minutes more. Check that the rice is cooked to your satisfaction, then take off the heat and tip into a bowl. Pour the rice vinegar over, stirring well, and allow to cool.

Whisk the dressing ingredients together, season to taste, and stir through the salad.

Toast the sesame seeds and peanuts gently in a dry frying pan and tip on to a plate to cool.

Finally, bring a pan of water to a boil and blanch the edamame, carrot, peas, and corn for about 2 minutes before draining and refreshing them under cold running water.

When you are ready to serve, mix the rice with the nuts and blanched veg. Best served at room temperature and eaten with the fingers. If serving in a kiddie lunch box, don't forget to include a fortune cookie.

MUSHROOM BONANZA SALAD

Mr. Shopkeeper loves mushrooms. On the rare occasions he is allowed to do the grocery shopping, he always comes back with packages of funky 'shrooms and an expression of childlike glee on his face. Unfortunately his love of exercise is not commensurate with his love of cooking, or he could forage for them. It has, however, never been easier to buy exotic fungi in supermarkets and markets.

A FUNGAL INDULGENCE FOR 4
scant 1 cup/6½oz/180g long-grain brown rice
salt
7 tbsp/3½oz/100g butter
    (or vegetable ghee)
1 level tsp ground turmeric
1 tsp ground coriander
oil, for frying
4 garlic cloves, minced
1lb/450g assorted mushrooms
    (eg 5½oz/150g each of oyster, shiitake,
    chestnut/cremini),* wiped and roughly
    chopped (if large)

1 cup/3½oz/100g slivered almonds, toasted
2¾oz/75g arugula
big handful of fresh tarragon, chopped
    (or use 2 tsp dried)
big handful of fresh parsley, chopped

FOR THE DRESSING:
5 tbsp olive oil
juice of 1 lemon
2 tsp French mustard

Cook the rice in boiling salted water until just done (15–20 minutes), then drain, tip back into the pan, and stir around half of the butter through it, together with the spices. Cover the lid of the pan with a clean dish towel and leave the rice to steam for a further 10 minutes before tipping it into a bowl and allowing it cool.

Melt the rest of the butter in a frying pan and add splash of oil to stop it burning. Add the garlic and the mushrooms, stirring well and cook until softened, then drain off any excess moisture and allow to cool.

When you are ready to assemble the salad, mix the rice with the 'shrooms, almonds, arugula, and herbs. Whisk the dressing ingredients together and stir through the salad. Mr. Shopkeeper found this most agreeable with some sautéed strips of rare steak as a garnish.

* A note on mushrooms
If you're asking me round for dinner, please don't include those creepy, finger-like enoki 'shrooms—they are surely the spawn of the devil...

RED RICE SALAD WITH RAW FISH AND WASABI DRESSING (OR SALLY'S SUSHI SALAD)

Sushi. It's all pretty mainstream now. Even gas station kiosks seem to sell emergency sushi snack packs along with soda and chips. But I still get a little bit excited by the concept every time I indulge. It's raw fish, so it feels dangerous. But then, so does buying "fresh" food from a gas station…

Red rice. Also known as Camargue rice. Love the stuff. It's so squidgy between the teeth and nutty. Perfect stuff for salad since it holds its shape and adds real texture to the occasion. Incidentally, red rice is also the name of a weencey village in the south of England: I did toy with the idea of creating a British version of sushi, but I'm not sure it'll catch on.

LUNCH OR SUPPER FOR 4
1¼lb/600g skinless tuna fillet
juice and grated zest of 3 limes
2–3 garlic cloves, minced
¼ tsp salt
dash of toasted sesame oil

FOR THE SALAD:
1 cup/7oz/200g Camargue rice
1 sheet dried seaweed (nori)
1 red onion, diced
2 small carrots, julienned
½ cucumber, julienned
12 radishes, finely sliced

⅓ cup/1¾oz/50g sesame seeds, toasted
big handful of fresh cilantro, chopped

FOR SILLY SALLY'S SECRET
SPICY SUSHI SALAD SAUCE:
1 tbsp peanut oil (or just use canola)
1 tbsp toasted sesame oil
1 tsp wasabi paste
¾in/2cm knob fresh ginger, peeled
    and minced
scant ¼ cup/50ml mango juice
scant ¼ cup/50ml coconut milk
tamari (or soy) sauce, to taste

Aprons on? Cut the fish into bite-sized chunks, place it in a tub or bowl, and add the lime, garlic, salt, and oil. Swoosh the fish around so it gets coated in the marinade, and refrigerate for 2 hours.

Cook the rice in boiling salted water for around 15 minutes (Camargue rice is quite resistant to the cooking process but it is because of this crunchiness that we love it so). Drain and refresh under cold water.

Next, soak the seaweed (around 5 minutes) before draining and squeezing as much of the water out of it as possible. Dab with paper towel just to take up any surplus moisture.

Mix the cooled rice, chopped vegetables, and seaweed together. Remove the fish from the marinade and gently fork this through the rice.

Whisk the dressing ingredients together and spoon over the salad. Top with the sesame seeds and the cilantro.

HAWAIIAN RICE SALAD

I've often wondered if the people of Polynesia really live on ham and pineapple, but the rest of the world seems to assume that they do. I spent rather more time than I would have liked making pizzas for a living, and so Hawaii for me is ever synonymous with a Number 5: I guess I'll just have to go there one day to dispel this rather daft association.

This salad is a bit cheesy and retro, but it is equally full of zing and fun. Hawaiians are great party animals, and celebrate anything joyous by throwing a *luau* or feast, so hopefully you'll get into the spirit of things, wear your best floral shirt, and have the neighbors over.

A PARTY SALAD FOR 4–6
generous ¾ cup/200ml water
pat of butter and a pinch of salt
¾ cup/5½oz/150g long-grain rice (or basmati)
2 tbsp/1¼oz/35g hulled sesame seeds
¼ cup/1oz/25g fresh shredded coconut (or use dry unsweetened)
1 large pineapple
1 tbsp butter
1 onion, sliced
2–3 garlic cloves
1in/3cm knob fresh ginger, peeled and minced

1 tbsp brown sugar
1 bunch of scallions, chopped
1 small can (8oz/225g) water chestnuts, sliced
5½oz/150g ham, shredded (optional, replace with tofu or omit altogether if you like)

FOR THE DRESSING:
3 tbsp coconut oil*
1 tbsp balsamic vinegar
juice and grated zest of 1 lime
½ tsp Tabasco
sea salt

Put the water, butter, and salt into a pan and bring to a boil. Add the rice, bubble away for a few minutes; then turn down the heat really low, wrap the lid of the pan in a clean dish towel, and simmer for another 20 minutes. The rice should be perfectly cooked and the grains separated. Set it aside to cool completely.

Toast the sesame and coconut by dry-frying in a frying pan, then allow to cool.

Remove the top from the pineapple, and use a sharp knife to dig out the inside of the fruit, keeping the excavated bits as intact as possible. (Do not throw the pineapple shell away.) Remove the chewy core of the fruit (although this is meant to be the most nutritious part), and cut the rest into ⅝in/1.5cm cubes (try to retain any surplus pineapple juice released by all this chopping to go into the dressing later).

Melt the butter in a pan and fry the pineapple and onion. As they start to brown, add the garlic, ginger, and sugar and cook for a few minutes more, then take off the heat.

Heat the coconut oil in a little saucepan (it is solid at room temperature) then whisk in the other dressing ingredients (including any reserved pineapple juice).

Now mix the rice with the toasted coconut/sesame mixture, scallions, chestnuts, and ham, if using. Stir the still warm pineapple mixture into the rice and pile the salad into the empty pineapple shell. Pour the dressing over it, put the top of the pineapple back on, garnish with tacky paper umbrellas, and serve.**

PAELLA SALAD

On *Paella*...

Many moons ago, when I still thought the lack of security and income that was associated with catering was quite fun, I ran away to Spain for a season. After months of working for dubious sorts in sweatbox kitchens on the Costa del Whatever, I went off to tour the interior of Spain in a totally unreliable little Cinquecento (which, in a flash of brilliant unoriginality, I called Rocinante). Which is how I found myself camping in the middle of La Mancha, clutching an unskinned but undeniably dead rabbit.

The fellow occupants of my campsite, in the true spirit of *paella* making, had suggested that we each chip in an ingredient to make a communal *paella* on a wood fire under the shady shoreside trees. I had confessed to having some cooking experience; thus it was determined that I should cook the thing. Having never cooked a *paella* in my life before, skinning the rabbit was the least of my worries. Desperation is a good teacher.

Paella is a kind of salmagundi of a dish: even its origins are mixed, combining a Roman vessel (the *patella*, which morphed into the modern flat *paella* pan) with the Arabic import of rice to the region. There are plenty of *paella* purists out there who will argue the finer points of the dish, but to do so is to miss the point: with the exception of *paella Valenciana* (which is just chicken and rabbit), the very concept of *paella* is all about using what you have on hand.

Much as I'd like to think of you lighting a fire in the nearest olive grove and cooking lunch with your neighbors, this salad may be more practical—it has all the flavor of the original dish, but is more portable. I have made it with seafood, as the best *paellas* I have ever had have been made on the beach in the glorious windswept region of Albufera, just south of Valencia.

A PICNIC SALAD FOR 8–10

15 raw jumbo shrimp

generous 2 cups/500ml fish stock

¼ tsp ground saffron steeped in less than
    1 tbsp boiling water (or use ½ tsp
    ground turmeric)

1 twig of fresh rosemary

salt

1 tsp lightly crushed peppercorns

15 live fat mussels

scant 2 cups/14oz/400g short-grain rice
    (preferably Calasparra, or *paella* rice)

glug of non-extra-virgin olive oil, for frying

8 garlic cloves, minced

9oz/250g fresh squid rings

1 onion, chopped

1 fat red bell pepper, roughly chopped

6 tomatoes, peeled and chopped

7oz/200g sugar snap peas, chopped

1 bunch of fresh parsley, chopped

FOR THE DRESSING:

5 tbsp extra-virgin olive oil

juice of 1 fat lemon

½ tsp smoked paprika

1 tsp paprika

salt

¿Vamos? Peel the shrimp, reserve the flesh, and place the shells and heads in a saucepan with the fish stock, saffron, rosemary, salt, and pepper. Simmer for about 30 minutes, adding the mussels for the last 5 minutes. Fish out the mussels, setting them aside to cool, then strain the fish stock into a clean pan.

Bring the stock to a boil, add the rice, turn down the heat, and simmer for about 10 minutes, or until cooked. Drain and cool.

Next, heat a good shot of pure olive oil in a frying pan, add around half of the garlic together with the raw shrimp and the squid and cook until the shrimp pinken (if there is such a word, and even if there isn't, there should be) and the squiddly diddly starts to brown. Again, allow to cool.

Whisk the salad dressing ingredients together with the remaining garlic.

When you are ready to assemble the salad, toss the rice together with the onion, pepper, tomato, peas, and parsley and stir the dressing through it. Arrange the mussels (still in their shells), shrimp, and squid on top. Serve in your very best picnicware under an olive tree, accompanied by bread and some nice *vino de la casa*.

JAMBALAYA: PAELLA'S CREOLE COUSIN

Jambalaya and a crawfish pie and filé gumbo,
'Cause tonight I'm gonna see my ma cher amio
Pick guitar, fill fruit jar, and be gayo,
Son of a gun, we'll have big fun on the bayou.

Yup. I make no secret of my Carpenters vinyl collection. The word *jambalaya* will of course forever be associated with this song, at least in the ears of many Westerners of a certain age.

This is another dish with as many recipes as there are kitchens in America's Deep South, and, like *paella*, it is a real "gallimaufry" of cultural and culinary influence. Even the name is a hodgepodge of sorts, although most etymologists claim that the word is derived from the French word *jambon* (ham—but you knew that, yes?).

The recipe is pretty much the same concept as above—and indeed is probably based on some kind of *paella* as prepared by Spanish immigrants in New Orleans.

ANOTHER PICNIC FOR 8–10
1 small joint cured ham (at least 10oz/300g)
2 bay leaves
1 sprig of fresh thyme
1 can (14oz/400g-ish) chopped tomatoes
2 cups/14oz/400g long-grain rice
10½oz/300g smoky cooked sausage (chorizo or salami will do), sliced
3 sticks of celery, finely chopped
1 fat onion, finely chopped

1 bunch of scallions, chopped
1 red bell pepper, diced
1 green bell pepper, diced

FOR THE DRESSING:
5 tbsp canola oil
juice of 2 limes
2 green chilies, minced
4 garlic cloves, minced
salt and freshly ground black pepper

Rinse the ham and place it in a pan of water. Bring to a boil, discard the water, and cover with fresh cold water. Bring to a boil again, add the herbs, and set to simmer for around 45 minutes (for an average small joint, or as per the instructions on the package). Once the meat is cooked, remove and set it aside to cool. Strain a generous 2 cups/500ml of the stock into a clean pan, add the tomatoes, bring it to a boil, and tip in the rice. Turn down the heat and simmer for around 20 minutes, or until the rice is cooked. Turn off the heat, wrap the lid of the pan in a clean dish towel, and allow to steam gently for another 10 minutes. Finally, tip the rice into a bowl, fluff with a fork, and allow to cool.

Meanwhile, whisk the dressing ingredients together and set aside. Cut around 10½oz/300g of the cooked ham into cubes and reserve.

To assemble, mix the rice with the cubed ham, salami, celery, onions, and peppers. Stir the dressing through the salad. Great for buffets and even better enjoyed with a few beers overlooking the bayou.

CHAPTER SEVEN
Cheese

Cheese salad has come a long way since my school days. School lunches, eh?
OK—so things are getting better, but back in the day, a cheese salad (which
was rated the "healthy lunch" option) comprised about a cup of cheap
grated Cheddar and some very limp lettuce leaves. It was utterly dire.
There is, I reckon, quite a large percentage of the population who believe that
cheese makes everything all right—truly it's the little things that help us get by.
Just a little bit of cheese in a bowl of leaves can instantly raise your meal game
(of course lots of cheese is invariably better than a little bit of cheese, and I am
no advocate of dietary restraint but you want to titillate your salad rather
than kill it). It is also a sneaky but effective way to get recalcitrant offspring
to eat salad.

A GENERIC ITALIAN: MOZZARELLA, BASIL, AND TOMATO SALAD

You can't go wrong with this combo: the ingredients get on with each other, so well that it is impossible to make a bad "Italian" salad. Don't tell Mr. Shopkeeper though: he thinks this is one my cleverest dishes. Aw. If you want to impress you can give it its proper ethnic name: *insalata caprese*.

A SLINKY APPETIZER FOR 2

1¾oz/50g arugula

big handful of fresh basil, roughly shredded

4½oz/125g buffalo mozzarella, sliced into small wedges

1 fat beef tomato, thinly sliced

1 white (sweet) onion, thinly sliced

¾ cup/4½oz/125g black olives

4½oz/125g pancetta (optional), fried until crisp

generous ⅓ cup/1¾oz/50g pine nuts, toasted (optional)

sea salt and freshly ground black pepper

extra-virgin olive oil, for drizzling

Scatter the leaves on a platter and top with the mozzarella, tomato, onion, and olives together with the pancetta and pine nuts, if using. Season and drizzle with olive oil. Serve with a separate bowl of balsamic vinegar and plenty of bread for dunking and mopping.

"*Molto delizioso!*" as Lucia* might have said.

* Tip

If you are unfamiliar with the delicious cattiness of the E.F. Benson novels *Mapp and Lucia*, I suggest you rush out and secure yourself a copy of at least one of the six tomes forthwith. They won't teach you anything about Italian food, but they will have you crying with laughter.

HORIATIKI: A CLASSIC GREEK

You know: never has such a simple dish been so played with and over-worked. Across the (undoubtedly wonderfully entertaining) pseudo-tavernas* of the world, and in the kitchens of misty-eyed vacationers back from their two weeks of sun, sea, and Retsina, and in the kitchens of every mobile barbecue caterer across the land, all manner of versions of this salad are being pumped out. *Horiatiki* just means "peasant's salad," and is no more capable of being defined by one simple recipe than the Greek people by one simple wine-dark, sea-glancing, mountain-conquering epithet. But the format below is about as authentic (or simple in this case) as it gets (and no I didn't "forget" the vinegar). Feel free to add in whatever it behoves you so to do (including vinegar) or whatever you find skulking in your fridge. The one refinement I do recommend, however, is the "bonus serving idea" at the end.

A SIDE DISH FOR 4

6 large proper tomatoes (i.e. not watery ones from a supermarket)

½ cucumber, peeled

1 green bell pepper, deseeded

1 large red onion

generous ¼ cup/1¾oz/50g fat black olives (preferably *Kalamata*)

sea salt and freshly ground black pepper

5½oz/150g proper feta**

3 tbsp extra-virgin olive oil

1 level tsp dried oregano

TO SERVE:

1 bottle Retsina (Greek wine)

1 Bouzouki CD

Chill the Retsina. Cut the tomatoes into chunks and slice the cucumber into half moon slices. Cut the pepper into thin slices, likewise the onion. Mix it all together in a bowl along with the olives, and season to taste. Cut the feta into decent sized slabs and dot them on top. Drizzle the olive oil over everything, and sprinkle with the oregano. Open the Retsina, put the Bouzouki CD on, and commence embarrassing vacation dance. Smile. Job done: *poli kalo*.

BONUS SERVING IDEA (YOU'RE GONNA LOVE THIS)

We clocked this idea for *horiatiki* at a friend's family home in a village halfway up a Cypriot mountain. You need a (preferably day-old) chunky loaf of bread (the Greek-style sesame braids are great). Trim the top off and scoop out most of the doughy bits inside (but don't throw them away). Spoon the salad into the cavity, dressing and all, and replace the "lid." Allow to sit for around 15 minutes, so that all the olive oily goodness soaks into the bread. And there you go—a salad in an edible receptacle. The bread you hacked out of the middle can be fried as croutons (check out the Prop Cupboard, p.262 for more ideas)—waste not want not and all that.

* Tavernas

I used to work in one, so I know about these things. Dancing on the tables and smashing plates… and that was just the staff.

** Feta

Feta has protected nomenclature, which means that only real Greek feta can use the name.

A MANCHEGAN CHEESE SALAD

Queso Manchego at its best (aged, or *viejo*) is a fine dish in itself, and it would be a culinary crime to try and incorporate it into another recipe. Slices of the cheese, on their own or twinned with *jamon Serrano*, and washed down with a glass of sweet wine or sherry—this constitutes the finest *tapas* of the bunch, a feast fit for Castillian kings.

But the younger cheeses from the region work well in salads, adding a nutty tang. Factor in another Spanish classic, *membrillo* (quince cheese—see bonus recipe below), together with La Mancha's other famous products—saffron, olives, and sunflowers, and you'll be tilting at windmills already.*

LUNCH FOR 4
FOR THE DRESSING:
scant ¼ cup/50ml extra-virgin
    olive oil**
¼ tsp ground saffron steeped in a splash
    of olive oil
juice of ½ orange
juice of ½ lemon
1 sprig of fresh rosemary
sea salt and coarsely ground black pepper

FOR THE SALAD:
1 small head of frisée (curly endive),
    roughly shredded
4oz/120g not too mature Manchego cheese
3½oz/100g *membrillo***
1 medium red onion, sliced
1 tbsp caper berries
generous ½ cup/3½oz/100g pimento-stuffed
    olives
½ cup/2¾oz/75g sunflower seeds, toasted

*

Obscure reference to Don Quixote, with whom I am a teensy bit obsessed, because somehow he makes being goofy work for him.

** Olive oil

Controversially I rate Cretan (*Kolymvari*) and (the more expensive) Moroccan olive oils far more than Spanish or Italian: they are darker, fruitier, and lack either the (on the whole) blandness of the former or the bitterness of the latter. But please don't all write in: there are always exceptions, and this is just my very humble opinion.

Whisk the salad dressing ingredients together: the rosemary needs time to infuse.

Assemble the salad by arranging the leaves on a platter. Shave the cheese as artfully as possible, and cut the *membrillo* into tiny cubes. Pile the cheese, quince, red onion, caper berries, olives, and seeds on top of the frisée, then remove the rosemary from the saffron dressing and drizzle over the salad. Serve with crusty white bread. And perhaps a little sherry…

***BONUS RECIPE! *MEMBRILLO*:

Readily available in fancy delis, but it's so easy to make your own. Peel and chop a bunch of quinces, but leave the cores in. Bring them to a boil in a pan of water, turn down the heat, and simmer for 1 hour, or until soft. Press though a sieve (or pick the seeds out and blend), add the same weight in sugar, and put back on the stovetop over a low heat (preferably on a heat diffuser). After an hour or so transfer the gloop to a shallow, parchment paper-lined oven dish and put it into the oven on its lowest setting. After an hour remove the *membrillo* and leave somewhere to firm up even more. Refrigerate and use as a spread or with cheese. It keeps for up to a month.

A MANCHEGAN TALE

You may well have wondered why Manchego cheese comes with such a pretty zigzag design on its crust. There again, perhaps you haven't. But I shall tell you anyway.

Many many years ago, long before the age of chivalry, the world was darker, harder, and hazardous for those of a frail or gentle disposition. In the middle of the middle of Spain, in a region known as La Mancha (the stain), there lived a young maiden, Conchita. She was a will-o-the-wisp of a girl, unassuming to the extent that even her parents barely registered her existence. Her sweet nature did not go unnoticed in the village where she lived, however, and it was not uncommon for her to spend her day running errands for the elderly, the lazy, and the downright cunning. She simply could not say no to people.

Thus is was that when she grew into a head-turner of a young woman, she found it hard to turn her many suitors away, and before long she found herself with child. This was a matter of great shame for her parents, who compelled the young man responsible to marry Conchita: the wedding was at night, the bride wore black, and the couple were discreetly moved to a cottage at the edge of the village.

It was not long before the pressure of a suddenly acquired family was too much for her young husband, and he fled, leaving Conchita alone and ostracized. She still visited the sick and the elderly, although her bump was beginning to slow her down and the other villagers were very hostile.

At night she was afraid, but she gathered in the goats and sheep and snuggled up to them: it was a cold winter and it was quite common for the animals to sleep indoors. One evening as she was lighting the fires, a viper sidled up to her. She was alarmed and made as if to run, but the viper spoke to her, assuring her that all he wanted was a warm bed for the winter. As ever, she was unable to say no, but advised the creature that he should stay out of the way.

Towards the end of the winter she had nearly run out of food, the baby's birth was imminent, and the whole thing was starting to look less like a fairy tale and more like a pastoral tragedy. In despair she combed the house looking for scraps of food… and came across the snake. The creature had curled itself around an old pot of curds and whey behind the chimney breast—and so good was his camouflage that she had not only forgotten about the whey, but she had simply not noticed her largely unwanted guest all winter long.

"Are you hungry, my child?" asked the snake, uncoiling himself to reveal a solid yellow lump covered in ziggy zaggy markings from his skin. The contents of the pot had solidified, and the pot had rotted away, leaving a perfect, patterned, mature cheese… Conchita fell upon the cheese with glee, and was so grateful she kissed the snake on its nose.

You probably spotted this one a mile away, no? The snake was no other than Ferdinand, Prince of Guadalajara: a scheming warlock had murdered his pregnant wife and turned the prince into a snake for all eternity, or at least until a beautiful, sweet-natured, pregnant girl kissed him. Where would the story world be without coincidence, eh?

Of course they fell in love, and Conchita presently gave birth to a boy whom Ferdinand was proud to raise as his own. The villagers were united in remorse at their treatment of the lass, and even the stoniest hearted among them was happy to see her fortunes change, especially when the minorly royal couple set up a cheese-making factory in the village. *Queso Manchego* was born.

All of this proves that Don Quixote does not have the final word when it comes to Manchegan magic. And that no good deed goes unrewarded.

PUB PLOUGHMAN'S SALAD WITH CHIPS

It doesn't get much more British than a ploughman's lunch. I have long suspected that there is some brewing federation byelaw requiring this rather wonderful creation to appear on every pub menu the length and the breadth of Blighty.

The concept binds chunky cheese with chutney, pickled onions, bread, and some sort of garnish. For the hungry wayfarer, or bar-propping regular, or, one presumes, actual bona fide ploughman, it is a veritable (if fattening) feast. For the uninitiated, I should explain it goes hand-in-hand with a noisy pub garden, buzzing wasps, warm ale, and the knowledge that someone has blocked you in in the undersized parking lot—all essential components of the UK pub tradition.

I've taken all the basics and wrapped them into something just a smidge healthier—because new-age ploughmen surely watch their waistlines.

LUNCH FOR 4

1 bag (4oz/120g) fancy mixed salad greens

¼ iceberg lettuce, roughly shredded

4oz/120g fine Cheddar (you choose the strength), cut into ½in/1cm cubes

1 red apple, cored and sliced (optional)

2 sticks of celery, chopped

4 pickled onions, cut into quarters

4 pickles, cut into ½in/1cm chunks

2 pickled eggs,* quartered

12 cherry tomatoes

2 x 1oz/30g bags sour cream and onion chips

⅔ cup/3oz/75g grated red Leicester (or Cheddar)

½ tsp caraway seeds

1 tsp poppyseeds

FOR THE DRESSING:

1½ fat tbsp fruity chutney

3–4 tbsp extra-virgin olive oil

1 tbsp white wine vinegar

⅓ tsp English mustard powder

salt

Toss the green leaves, iceberg, cubed Cheddar, apple, celery, pickles, and tomatoes in your most rustic looking bowl.

Preheat your broiler before lining the pan with a strip of foil and spreading the chips out. Sprinkle the grated cheese and seeds on top, then grill for around 2 minutes, or until the cheese is bubbling. Allow to cool for a few minutes before adding them to the bowl.

Whisk together the dressing ingredients and drizzle over the salad. Serve atop a hay bale accompanied by warm bread, chilled beer, and some nice toe-tapping folk music.

*BONUS RECIPE! JO-JO'S SPECIAL PICKLED EGGS:

Jo-Jo was my grandmother and one of my best friends. I inherited her recipe notebook, which is full of fiendish ways to upstage the old dears at the bridge club. One of my favorites are these pickled eggs—gosh they're easy to make at home. Hard-boil 8 eggs (10 minutes boiling from cold), then cool and peel. Boil a generous 1 cup/250ml cider vinegar with 1 small chopped onion, 1½ tablespoons sugar, 2 teaspoons curry powder, 1 teaspoon coriander seeds, and 1 teaspoon mustard seeds. Simmer for 5 minutes then take off the heat. Pack the eggs into sterilized jar and pour the still hottish vinegar over them, wiggling the jar to make sure that there are no air pockets. Seal and refrigerate. They'll be ready after 4–5 days, and keep for up to a month. Great for all manner of salads.

SALAD *PAYSANNE* WITH BRIE CROUTONS

Peasant salad. Hmm. The very sad pedant in me always sniggers in supermarkets when it gets to the salad section: there is row upon row of offerings—potato salad, mushroom salad, tomato salad, pasta salad… and then "family" salad. As in chopped up family? One equally assumes peasant salad is composed of diced peasants. No? OK—it's just me. I'll go and stand in the corner.

In the meantime, Salad *Paysanne* can comprise pretty much anything that the peasant in question has in their fridge/pantry/smallholding. It is perhaps as helpful a term as "mixed salad." So what I am trying to convey with this recipe is the essence of that excellent house salad you had in that quaint roadside restaurant that you stopped at "on the way to the Dordogne, you know the one where Lisa fed the cat when you told her not to, but oh the view and what lovely food—what was the name of the place again David?—anyway that was just the best salad ever…" Well, that.

LUNCH FOR 4 HUNGRY
PEASANTS

4 small waxy potatoes, peeled

3 large eggs

3oz/80g green beans, cut into 1in/3cm pieces

1 small frisée lettuce (or any crisp, slightly
    bitter leaf)

handful of lamb's lettuce

12 cherry tomatoes

oil, for frying

2¾oz/75g lardons

1 tbsp flour

1–2 tbsp breadcrumbs (from stale bread)

5½oz/150g soft brie, cut into ¾in/2cm cubes

FOR THE DRESSING:

4–5 tbsp olive oil

1 heaped tsp Dijon mustard

2 tbsp red wine vinegar

salt and freshly ground black pepper

Put the potatoes into a pan of salted water and bring to a boil. Turn down the heat and simmer for 5 minutes, then add 2 of the eggs, together with the green beans. Cook for 7 minutes, then remove and cool the eggs under running water. The potatoes and beans should be just cooked at this stage, so they too should be drained and refreshed—but potatoes vary so do check. Peel and quarter the eggs, slice the potatoes thickly, and set all of the ingredients aside.

When you are ready-ish to serve, arrange the lettuce and tomato in a bowl along with the potato slices, egg, and beans. Heat some oil in a frying pan and cook the lardons before scooping them out of the oil with a slotted spoon and draining them on paper towel.

Beat the remaining egg in a bowl, then place the flour and breadcrumbs on separate plates. Dip the brie in the flour, followed by the eggwash, followed by the breadcrumbs. Add a little more oil to the pan—you want about ½in/1cm depth—and bring it back to sizzle point. Now fry the brie croutons until they are golden before draining these too on paper towel.

Spoon the still warm lardons and hot brie on to the salad. Whisk the dressing ingredients together and pour over the top. Serve straight away with some decent chunky farmhouse bread.

SWISS CHARD AND *LABNEH* SLAW
SUPER HEALTHY

The Middle East may not be famed for its cheeses, but the glorious creamy naughtiness that is *labneh* more than compensates. It's a bit of a confusing substance, as the word can be used to apply from anything to salted yogurt to sun-dried "cream cheese." I am using the latter here—it is easy enough to find in Middle Eastern stores, usually rolled into balls, coated with thyme, and preserved under olive oil. If you can't find any or live in the Outer Hebrides, improvise with some creamy goat cheese.

Swiss chard is an oft neglected little guy, at least here, which is a shame since his robust flavor and wacky color-ways are both desirable assets for an aspiring salad.

SERVES 3–4 AS A SIDE DISH

1 tsp caraway seeds

a big bunch of Swiss chard (preferably rainbow chard as it is so pretty), thoroughly washed

1 fat carrot, peeled and grated

1 large sweet white onion, finely sliced

1 nice apple, cored and grated

⅔ cup/1¾oz/50g sunflower seed kernels

4 balls of *labneh*
   (or around 6oz/175g goat's cheese)

FOR THE DRESSING:

3–4 tbsp grapeseed oil

1 tbsp *pekmez* (grape syrup—if you can't get it just use extra vinegar)

1 tbsp apple or cider vinegar

sea salt and freshly ground black pepper

First, toast the caraway seeds by dry-frying them in a little frying pan. Set aside to cool a little.

Next, check over the chard—any of the stalks (ribs) that are chunky need to be cut out and reserved for cooking/stock/stir-frying. Shred the rest of the leaves/stalk and place in a bowl along with the carrot, onion, apple, caraway, and sunflower seeds. Crumble the *labneh* and scatter it on top.

Finally, whisk the dressing ingredients together and pour over the salad, mixing very gently. Serve with rich meat or fish dishes.

WARM BROCCOLI AND HALLOUMI SALAD

I probably eat this for lunch once or twice a week. It does, after all, contain two of my nation's new best foodstuffs. Well, notwithstanding the fact that the Brits reputedly live on fish and chips and roast beef. In the winter this can be dressed up with hot sauce, but in the warmer months it works well as a salad. Shopkeepers, one way or another, eat a lot of salads, as what starts as a piping hot lunch often cools to a trendy room temperature while they serve customers in between mouthfuls… ho-hum.

A SHOPKEEPER'S LUNCH FOR 1
splash of olive oil
1 small head of broccoli, broken into
    small florets
3 thick slices halloumi (roughly 2¾oz/75g),
    cubed (2 is probably enough for
    most mortals, but I'm an unrepentant
    halloumi glutton)

4–5 cherry tomatoes, halved
½ tsp mint sauce (see p.257)
1 tbsp balsamic vinegar
freshly ground black pepper

Heat the oil in a pan or wok and throw in the broccoli. Cook for 3 minutes, stirring well, before adding the halloumi. Cook for another minute or so, still stirring, until the cheese starts to brown. Add the tomatoes and cook for a minute more. Take off the heat and add the mint sauce and balsamic vinegar. Enjoy while still warm. This is what "back in 5 minutes" signs are made for.

GOAT CHEESE FLORENTINE SALAD WITH POACHED QUAILS' EGGS

Cheese, eggs, spinach—the stuff of dream brunches. Perfect fare—simple yet showy—for when you're trying to impress an, um, overnight guest...

Eggs Florentine began life as a twist on eggs Benedict, the classic American dish of muffin, bacon or ham, eggs, and hollandaise sauce. In modern kitchen parlance, the term Florentine seems randomly to get attached to anything with spinach in it, without so much as a nod to its origins as "food from Florence." I tried telling someone recently that their front teeth were "a la Florentine" but the reference fell a little flat...

BRUNCH FOR 2
FOR THE HOLLANDAISE:

1 egg yolk

2 tbsp lemon juice

1 tbsp cold water

8 tbsp/4½oz/125g (salted) butter, carefully melted

¼ tsp grated nutmeg

freshly ground black pepper

FOR THE OTHER BIT:

few leaves of frisée (curly endive), torn

1 small bunch (1¾oz/50g) of spinach, julienned

10 cherry tomatoes, halved

3 tbsp olive oil

1 tbsp wine vinegar

½ tsp English mustard

salt and freshly ground black pepper

2 crumpets or English muffins

3½oz/100g goat's cheese log, sliced into 4 discs

4 quails' eggs

paprika

Make the hollandaise first. Place the egg yolk, lemon juice, and water in your blender* and switch the motor on. Trickle the melted butter in very slowly, then add the nutmeg and some pepper. Keep at room temperature until needed (if making ahead, chill then bring back to room temperature before using).

Toss the frisée, spinach, and tomatoes in a bowl. Whisk the oil, vinegar, mustard, and seasoning together and stir through the leaves.

Next, heat the broiler. Slice through each crumpet/muffin horizontally to make 3 thin discs from each. Toast these discs on both sides and arrange them on 2 plates. While the oven is still hot, put the cheese on to a piece of foil and grill it gently for about a minute either side so it softens and begins to brown. Keep it warm while you get the rest ready.

Put a wee pan of water on to boil, add salt, swirl the water around, and crack the eggs in. Make ready a small bowl of iced water next to the oven, then after around 1½ minutes, scoop the eggs out and lower them into the cold water (thus arresting the cooking process).

Time for assembly. Divide the salad leaves between the 2 plates of toasted crumpet/muffin, top each with 2 discs of cheese and 2 (well-drained) eggs, and finally, spoon some of the hollandaise on top. Sprinkle with paprika. Don't forget to act nonchalantly, like you cook this sort of stuff for yourself every day.

* Hollandaise
This is traditionally hand whisked over a double boiler, so if you don't have a blender, do it the old-fashioned way.

RACLETTE AND ONION SALAD WITH PICKLED WALNUTS

Raclette, like fondue, is trending all over again. It is a Swiss dish comprising scraped, melted cheese and not much else (though traditional accompaniments include potatoes, pickles, and smoked meat). It is also the name for a type of cheese developed for the purpose. Wandering medieval cow herders reputedly used to leave their cheese by the evening fire, waiting for it to soften so they could scrape it on to their bread. Nowadays you can buy table-top electric grills and host jolly raclette parties in the comfort of your own home: just remember that your weight-watching friends may not be too impressed by the menu…

I can't claim that this salad version is much healthier (although there's some good stuff in there), but it is at least less rich.

BONUS RECIPE:
PICKLED WALNUTS
These would traditionally have been prepared as a way of preserving the very short walnut season. Green (soft) walnuts can be picked in June(ish): you will need to prick them to make sure that they have not started to harden inside. Fresh walnuts make a very good hair/leather dye—and will stain your hands for weeks, so wear gloves when handling. Prick each of the nuts a couple of times with a fork and then plunge them into a pot of brine (1 part salt to 6 parts water should do). Leave for around a week, refreshing the brine after 3 days. Prepare your pickling vinegar by boiling the required amount of vinegar with 2 teaspoons tamarind paste, a few cinnamon sticks, chili flakes, Persian hogweed (or ground angelica), and nigella seeds. Drain the walnuts and leave somewhere warm for a few hours to dry: they will darken considerably in color. Pack them into sterilized jars and cover with the vinegar. Seal and leave for 5–6 weeks. Great with cheese, they will keep practically forever.

A DECADENT TREAT FOR 4
(IF YOU CAN BEAR TO SHARE)
4oz/120g mesclun (mixed green leaves)
1 bunch of fresh chives, chopped
⅓ cucumber, cut into very thin slices
3 tbsp walnut (or olive) oil
1 tbsp tarragon (or red wine) vinegar
1 tsp French mustard
salt and freshly ground black pepper

2 medium onions, thinly sliced
splash of canola oil
9oz/250g raclette cheese (Gruyère, Emmental, or Jarlsberg all make good alternatives), thinly sliced
6–8 pickled walnuts (see bonus recipe, left: sweet pickles or pickled beets would make a fair substitute), quartered
4 very thin slices rye bread

Mix the mesclun with the chives and cucumber. Whisk together the oil, vinegar, mustard, and seasoning to taste.

When you are ready-ish to serve, fry the onions in a little oil until they are brown. Heat the broiler, then arrange the slices of raclette on top of the onions and "grill" until bubbling hot and starting to brown.

Dress the leaves with the vinaigrette and arrange the pickled walnuts therein. Using a spoon, dot dollops of the bubbling onion/cheese on top. Toast the bread and place around the salad. Serve immediately, warning guests that that cheese will be mighty hot.

STILTON, WALNUT, AND BANANA SALAD

This is an unusual combination, and comes to you via my friend Reg,* courtesy in turn of one Professor John Fuller. If the banana element completely fazes you, just go with convention and use pear. If you're cooking for fusspots/carnivores, you can make it meatier by adding crispy bacon or lardons.

Probably best not eat this one just before you go to bed, otherwise (to paraphrase W. Gilbert) your slumbering will so teem with horrible dreams that you'll curse the food writer...**

*

I learned a lot about food from my friend Reg (who played restaurant manager to my second chef), mostly in the form of scribbled notes left attached to my "creations." The best was the one written entirely in capitals and read "ARE YOU TRYING TO DRIVE ME TO DRINK?" I'm living proof that you do learn from your (culinary) mistakes...

* * Cheese

For the armchair scientists among you, it is now widely held that cheese does indeed give you bad dreams as it contains tyramine (as does red wine, soy products, and a lot of other stuff). The body struggles to digest this compound, and is distracted from offering the normal relief provided by REM sleep. Guess the nightmares are the body's way of punishing you for your late night indulgence.

* * * Chickweed

One of the few plants that grows pretty much everywhere, pretty much all the time. Super-easy to grow or forage, and full of good stuff. It is yet another ingredient that used to be in common usage and yet has been largely forgotten.

AN APPETIZER SALAD FOR 4
FOR THE DRESSING:
1 tbsp walnut oil
    (or just use extra-virgin olive oil)
1 tbsp extra-virgin olive oil
1 tbsp port
1 tbsp balsamic vinegar
1 tsp maple syrup (or use honey)
grated zest of 1 orange
1 tsp English mustard
salt and freshly ground black pepper

FOR THE SALAD:
2 bananas
1 small wedge lemon
2¾ oz/75g chickweed***
    (or use lamb's lettuce)
1¾ oz/50g watercress
⅓ cup/1¾ oz/50g shelled walnut halves, lightly
    toasted (dry-fried)
4½oz/125g Stilton cheese, roughly cubed

First, whisk the ingredients for the dressing together and set aside.

Peel and chop the bananas, rubbing the slices gently with the lemon wedge to prevent discoloration.

To assemble, mix the leaves together and arrange on individual plates (both Stilton and banana are quite soft and will not brook too much passing around/dishing out from bowl to plate). Top with the banana, nuts, and cheese, then drizzle with the port dressing. Serve with warm brown bread.

CHAPTER EIGHT
Fish

Mullah Nasruddin chanced upon a wise man who was lost, and kindly gave him directions. Since the wise man was hungry, he offered to buy the mullah a meal if this latter could also show him a good restaurant in the town. The mullah was delighted to oblige, and took him to the best restaurant. When they enquired of the restaurateur what his recommendation would be, they were told to order the fish speciality, which of course they did.

When the two fish dishes arrived, one was much bigger than the other. Without any hesitation the Mullah seized the larger one for himself. Startled, the wise man hesitated before querying the Mullah's action, saying that it contravened all moral and social norms. The Mullah looked surprised, and replied, "Why, sir, what would you have done?" The wise man naturally answered that he would have claimed the smaller fish for himself. "Well there you go then, my friend!" cried the Mullah, and placed the smaller portion on the wise man's plate.

This chapter offers you fish dishes of all sizes and to suit all palates, wallets, and occasions. It is my humble opinion that there is no finer way of serving fish than in salad form. For it is an elegant but delicate foodstuff, and is easily overshadowed by a surfeit of cooked vegetables, rice, or potatoes. A piquantly dressed bowl of salad is the perfect foil for the oily smokiness of seafood. A wedge of crusty bread alongside is usually all you need…

PROPER SALAD *NIÇOISE*

That this is a World Great in the wonderful realm of salads, and that it evolved in Nice (hence *Niçoise*, duh), no one can deny. But debate over what exactly goes into it is passionate, if not heated—and if you've ever seen Frenchmen arguing over culinary stuff, you will know that this is a serious matter.

Fortunately one does actually have contacts in Nice, albeit very lowly ones (no yachts involved), and so I sent out some feelers. Extensive (and unfortunately off-site) research led me to the recipe below.

This *salade* evolved as an institution in the last half of the nineteenth century, but was based on the simple local fare hitherto enjoyed by the town's fisher folk. The original probably just comprised stale bread (known in the region as *pan bagnat*, although this has now come to refer to a sandwich) topped with tomatoes, anchovies, salt, and olive oil. This grew to include black Provençale olives, hard-boiled eggs, tuna, scallions, and garlic, with a little mesclun (green salad leaves) thrown in for color. Romaine lettuce, little boiled potatoes, artichoke hearts, and green beans often get added (unusually it was the great Escoffier who was chiefly responsible for these corruptions), but they are (as far as I can determine, but let's not fall out over this) inauthentic extras. When I make this at home I usually commit salad sacrilege and add lima beans: I will leave it up to you as to how far you wander from the quayside...

Here then is my "proper" *salade Niçoise*.

TO SERVE 4 AS AN APPETIZER
OR SIDE

2 garlic cloves, peeled

6 very lovely tomatoes

4 perfectly hard-boiled eggs

2 cans (1¾oz/50g) anchovy fillets, drained
   (because 1 is never enough)

1 can (7oz/200g) tuna steak, drained

generous ½ cup/3½oz/100g plump purply
   black olives

1 bunch of scallions, chopped

3oz/80g assorted salad greens (mesclun)

FOR THE DRESSING:

scant ¼ cup/50ml good extra-virgin olive oil

2 tbsp red wine vinegar

sea salt and freshly ground black pepper

Choose your finest salad bowl, and rub one of the garlic cloves around the inside. Mince both garlic cloves and reserve.

The tomatoes would traditionally have been peeled and deseeded, but I can rarely be bothered. Simply quarter them, likewise the eggs. Now mix all of the salad ingredients gently in your seasoned bowl. Whisk the reserved garlic with the oil, vinegar, and seasoning and pour over the *salade Niçoise*. Serve with French bread, *bien sûr*.

XATO: CATALAN SALT COD SALAD WITH SPECIAL SAUCE

Salt cod (or *bacalao*) was a mystery to me until I spent a rogue year pretending I could cook for a living in Spain. I would hazard a guess that it is also a bit of a mystery to you: it is simply not something that enters our heads when we're pondering the universal dilemma of WHAT ON EARTH TO COOK FOR DINNER. Which is a shame as it is now readily available, cheap, and very tasty.

I took great delight in serving this salad to fairly ungrateful, loudmouthed expats who pretended to love ethnic Spanish food (and the "real Spain") but secretly just wanted shrimp cocktails and roast beef; it was a surprisingly popular dish, but that, I suspect, was because I didn't tell them what was in it. Food geeks might want to know that the special sauce is a variation on *salsa Romesco*.

A LIGHT LUNCH FOR 4
7oz/200g dried salt cod
½ onion, roughly chopped

FOR THE SAUCE:
1 red bell pepper
½ cup/2¾oz/75g blanched almonds
½ cup/2¾oz/75g roasted hazelnuts
2 anchovies (you use the rest of the can below)
2 garlic cloves
3 slices stale dry (or toasted) bread

4 tbsp red wine vinegar
scant ½ cup/100ml olive oil

FOR THE SALAD:
1 small head of frisée (curly endive), pulled into pieces
2 firm, proper tomatoes, finely sliced
12 anchovies (use drained, canned, see above)
2¾oz/75g flaked tuna
½ cup/3½oz/100g cured black olives
few sprigs of fresh tarragon (or watercress)

* First World Problems
I did actually hear an imperious lady ask for paint "the color of *salsa Romesco*" in a certain chirpy chain of DIY stores once: the nonplussed expression of the teenage sales assistant was priceless.

** Note on Spanish garlic bread
In Spain garlic bread is served in a wonderfully basic manner—but let us call it "artisan," that way (in London and NYC at least) we can charge you twice the price. Warm bread is brought to the table with a dish of olive oil, a pot of salt, and a garlic clove. The idea is that you dip your bread in the oil, sprinkle it with salt, and rub it with the garlic. ¡*Que bueno*!

Soak the cod in cold water for 24 hours, changing the water a couple of times (this serves both to reconstitute it, and to render it less salty). Hardcore Catalans eat salt fish just as is, and I must admit I prefer it that way, but most people like to blanch it first. I will leave it up to you as to whether you cook it or not. If you do then place it in a pan, cover with water, add the onion, and bring to a boil. Turn down the heat and simmer for 10 minutes, or until the cod becomes easy to flake and skin (if your salt cod is still with skin). Drain and refresh under running water. If you are using it uncooked, just chop it roughly.

Preheat the oven to 375°F/190°C.

Roast the pepper in the oven for about 20 minutes, then cool slightly before throwing it in a plastic bag for a few minutes (this makes it sweat, thus enabling you to skin it with ease). Toast (dry-fry) the almonds for a few minutes and set aside.

Put the pepper, nuts, anchovies, garlic, bread, and vinegar in your blender and give it a quick whizz before trickling in the olive oil (to form an attractive, pale orange sauce*).

Put the lettuce, tomatoes, anchovies, tuna, olives, tarragon, and cooled, drained salt cod into a bowl, mixing gently. Spoon the dressing on top. Serve with garlic bread "the Spanish way."**

GREAT QUEEN STREET'S HOME-CURED BASS, FENNEL, AND CLEMENTINE SALAD

This is a wonderful salad: dreamed up by chef Sam Hutchins at Great Queen Street and brought to life below by the restaurateur/incredibly talented chef/ food writer Tom Norrington Davis. It's a splash of color and lightness in deep mid-winter, when fennel bulbs and clementines are at their best. If bass is hard to come by you could use pollock, gurnard, or cod fillets. The fish is not raw, it is cooked (or, to be more precise, macerated) by the acids in the lemon and orange juices. If you don't like the idea of raw (ish) fish, the salad works just as well with tranches of grilled or smoked fish.

AN EXQUISITE SUPPER
FOR 4–6
1 large-ish (around 2¼lb/1kg) sea bass
    (or another, pale-fleshed fish of your
    choice), ask the fishmonger to scale,
    clean, and pin bone the fish for you
sea salt
1 lemon
4 clementines
1 level tsp fennel seeds

½ tsp whole coriander seeds
pinch of ground black pepper
2 bulbs fennel
1 small red onion or shallot
1 tbsp red wine vinegar
salt and freshly ground black pepper
generous ¾ cup/200ml (or thereabouts) extra-
    virgin olive oil
1 small bunch of fresh flat-leaf parsley

Cure the fish first. Season the fleshy surface of the fillets with a generous pinch of sea salt and allow them to rest while you prepare the other seasonings. Combine the juices of the lemon and 1 of the clementines. Set aside.

Roughly grind the fennel and coriander seeds. Combine and set them aside.

Next comes the tricky part. You need a good, sharp knife. Lay the fish fillets out on a chopping board, one by one, with the tail pointing to the right. Now, starting at the tail end and working backwards, slice the fish as thinly as possible, stopping just shy of the skin, as if it were smoked salmon. Lay the slices on a large plate in a single layer. Don't let any slices sit on top of one another: they all need to be exposed to the dressing. Once you have sliced the fish, you season it: first with the lemon and clementine juice, then the ground fennel and coriander seeds. Leave the fish to cure further in this marinade for about 30 minutes.

Meanwhile, you can prepare the fennel bulbs and the shallot. Peel, halve, and slice both as thinly as possible. Dress the slices with the vinegar, a little salt and pepper, and a good drizzle of olive oil.

Finally, chop the parsley and segment the remaining clementines. Toss the fruit, parsley, and vegetables together, check the seasoning, and arrange in a serving dish. Top the salad with the slices of the delicious, marinated fish and serve it at room temperature.

FISKESALAT MED PEPPERROTSAUS: NORWEGIAN FISH SALAD WITH HORSERADISH

The Norwegians are good with fish. They have to be. It's all the crinkles around the edges—they've got so much coastline it would be a crying shame if they failed to exploit it. This is a classic combo: it's got all the flavors you associate with Scandinavia—sour cream, dill, and horseradish, plus a little extra from me. It's so rich that a little goes a long way, but with some toasted rye croutons as an appetizer it's a real winner.

AN APPETIZER FOR 6–7

10½oz/300g skinless white fish fillet (cod, halibut, hake...)
2 bay leaves
3 shallots (or 1 small onion), finely chopped
generous pinch of ground saffron, steeped in 2–3 tsp boiling water
1 tbsp apple vinegar
generous 1 cup/250ml sour cream
2 tbsp freshly grated horseradish (or use 3 tbsp creamed horseradish)

½ tsp each salt and ground white pepper
2 tbsp dried dill (or fresh)
7oz/200g smoked trout, cut into ¾in/2cm chunks
3 thin slices rye bread
1 head of little gem lettuce, washed
2 large tomatoes, thinly sliced
3 fat pickles, sliced
2 perfectly hard-boiled eggs, peeled and sliced

Poach the white fish with the bay leaves until the former is just cooked (i.e. still nice and firm). Drain, discarding the bay leaves, and allow to cool before cutting into ¾in/2cm chunks.

Place the cooled fish in a bowl with the shallots. Add the saffron water to the vinegar, then beat this into the sour cream along with the horseradish, seasoning, and half of the dill. Pour the sauce over the fish, mixing very gently so as not to break it up. Cover and chill for around an hour.

When you are ready to serve, add the smoked trout to the marinated white fish and check the seasoning (you may want more salt). Toast the rye bread until it is quite crisp, then cut each slice into 4 small squares. Arrange the lettuce on a platter (or individual plates), with the rye squares on top. Top each of these with a slice of tomato, and then pile a little of the *fiskesalat* on to each square, and garnish with sliced pickle and eggs. Sprinkle with the reserved dill. *Vær så godt*, as they say in downtown Oslo. Enjoy!

SCALLOP SHELL SALADS WITH *CHIMICHURRI*

Shellfish is a dream to work with because it offers so many possibilities for flashy presentation. And the scallop is the best of the bunch, for it comes replete with its own dinky serving dish.

Chimichurri is pesto or *pistou* by any other name: an Argentinian parsley number, usually deployed as a sauce for steak.

* Scallops

Your best option when buying scallops is to get them already out of the shell (preferably dry-packed, as these are additive free—if you use wet-packed rinse them well before using). If you buy from a good indie fishmonger, they will normally let you have some shells to play with. If you do buy whole scallops in their shells, use an oyster shucker or other small pointy knife to pry the shell open, then place the shell so that its flat side is face down on your chopping board. Next, slide a filleting knife all the way through the shell towards the flat hinge (this will sever the scallop from the shell). Now you should be able to open it and pry the scallop out. Peel away the frill round the edge and any nasty looking black bits to leave the white and orange edible parts. A useless trivia-night scallop-shaped factoid for you: these dudes are associated with Saint James, and are thus often found on heraldic crests, as they denote that the family in question has made a pilgrimage to Santiago de la Compostela.

SERVES 6 AS A QUAINT BUT ELEGANT APPETIZER

FOR THE *CHIMICHURRI*:
6 garlic cloves, minced
3 scallions, minced
½ bunch of fresh flat-leaf parsley, finely chopped
2–3 sprigs of fresh oregano, chopped (or use 1 tsp dried)
½ tsp cayenne
sea salt
scant ½ cup/100ml extra-virgin olive oil
2 tbsp white wine vinegar

FOR THE SALAD:
⅓ cup/1¾oz/50g pecan quarters/pieces
¼ cucumber, julienned
1 red bell pepper, julienned
2 scallions, julienned
big handful of frisée lettuce, pulled into sprigs
6 scallop shell halves, washed
pat of butter and a little oil
12 scallops (18 to make it a more substantial snack)*
juice of 1 lime
pinch of ground saffron steeped in a splash of boiling water

Pound the garlic and scallions together (you could do this in a blender if you like), then add the herbs, cayenne, and salt to taste. Trickle in the olive oil and vinegar, and whisk into a green emulsion of sorts. Set aside until needed.

Toast (dry-fry) the pecans for a few minutes then take off the heat. Mix the cucumber, pepper, and scallions together with the frisée. Add the pecans and distribute the mixture between each of the seashells.

Heat a little butter and a drop of oil together in a frying pan, and just before it reaches smoking point, lower the scallops in. Allow them to sizzle away for around 1½ minutes (without poking or moving them), before turning them over and cooking for another minute. Take off the heat and spoon 2 of the scallops onto each shell, leaving the butter in the pan. Put the pan back on the heat, tip in the lime juice and saffron water, and bring the liquid back to sizzling point before tipping it over the scallops. Drizzle a little of the *chimichurri* around the outside of the salad greens, and pour the rest into a serving dish. Serve the scallop salads immediately with the *chimichurri* on the side. Some warm moppy-uppy bread would be good too.

SUPER FANCY LOBSTER SALAD

A woman should never be seen eating or drinking, unless it be lobster salad and Champagne, the only true feminine and becoming viands. (Lord Byron)

Trying to impress your lady, guys? Not sure if I agree with Byron, being a cockles and Guinness girl myself, but I'm guessing few women would fail to be impressed by their fella preparing a champagne and lobster supper for them. Like most seafood, lobster has a reputation as an aphrodisiac: any noticeable "effects" are probably psychological (for the act of cooking such luxury food for someone is surely one of love...), but this king of crustaceans is rich in protein, vitamin B12, and zinc, all of which help the old libido.

You can purchase pre-cooked lobster, but for freshness and authenticity, you will need to buy a live lobster and dispatch it yourself. Choose the liveliest looking lobster, since this is likely to be the freshest, but make sure that its claws are tied together—these guys are vicious. You'll find some handy hints on snappy-critter-cooking on p.177: the main difference is in cooking time—lobster needs cooking for around 15 minutes per 1lb/450g. When cooked, your crustacean will turn a rich reddy pink: remove it from the boiling water and cool.

Remove the meat from the shell by cracking the lobster along the backbone and splitting it in half. Crack the pincers and legs to extract the flesh: if the legs are very spindly, you may be better off just sucking them in private—chef's pickings and all that.

OK—to the salad.

DÎNER A DEUX

1 fat live lobster (1¼–1½lb/600–700g is ideal), or equivalent cooked
salt
generous ¾ cup/200ml water
½ tsp cayenne
¼ tsp ground saffron
½ tsp English mustard
5½ tbsp butter/3oz/80g, cubed and chilled
big handful of fresh cilantro, chopped
handful of fresh basil, chopped
juice and grated zest of 2 limes
2¾oz/75g assorted salad leaves
1 perfectly ripe avocado, sliced

Cook the lobster in boiling salted water, as per the guide above, then drain and dissect. Retain the empty shell and legs and cut the flesh into 1¼in/3cm (ish) cubes. Place the reserved lobster detritus in a small pan with the water and bring to a boil. Bubble away until the stock has reduced by about three-quarters (so you have about scant ¼ cup/50ml left), then strain it into another pan. Add the spices and mustard to the liquid over low heat, then beat in the butter, a couple of cubes at a time. Add the herbs, lime juice, and finally the cubed lobster meat, stirring it gently so that it heats through and becomes coated in the buttery sauce.

Arrange the leaves and avocado on a pair of pretty plates (large ice-cream coupes do very well), and spoon the warm lobster on top. Dribble the hot spiced dressing on top. Serve with casual flair, nice brown bread, and lashings of the aforementioned champagne.

CRAB LOUIE SALAD

This is another American classic. Legend has it first served at a San Franciscan restaurant called Solari's in 1914, but it was almost certainly created before then. It is, frankly, hard to better as crab combos go, as it packs in all of the natural accompaniments and counterparts to the sweet/*umami* flavor of the seafood.

LUNCH FOR 6

1 fresh crab (2lb/900g), or 1lb 10oz/750g
    frozen crab meat, light and dark

5 eggs

1 bunch of asparagus

1 medium iceberg lettuce

1 fat avocado, pitted and prettily sliced

4 lovely tomatoes, sliced

½ cup/3½oz/100g green olives, sliced

paprika, to garnish

FOR THE FAMOUS CRAB LOUIE
DRESSING:

1¼ cups/300ml good mayonnaise

scant ½ cup/100ml ketchup

2 tbsp sweet pickle relish

1 tsp Tabasco (authentically this would be
    Worcestershire sauce, but crab works well
    with some extra heat)

Okay, so go catch your crab… If you are using frozen, clearly you will need to defrost it. If you are using fresh, well, there is no great magic to it. First, always remember to handle the critter from behind. I once had to cook 200 giant crabs in an afternoon (long story)—let it suffice to say that I learned how to handle crabs the painful way. Myths are rife about the humane way to do this—some would have you stroking its head to lull it to sleep first, others suggest that you put it in the freezer for a couple of hours first to stun it a little before using a large knife or cleaver to crack the crustacean open lengthways (this dispatches the creature humanely). Then bring a pan of water to a boil and plop your crab in: a large one such as ours requires about 15 minutes to cook (the shell will turn a pretty orange when it is cooked). Once it is done, remove from the water and plunge it into a bowl of cold water briefly (it will otherwise continue to cook in its shell). When it is cool enough to handle, pull away and dispose of the yucky bits, carefully detach the claws and legs, and pull the brown meat out of the shell (if you are careful you can retain the shell to use for serving, and any residual juices can go into the mayo dressing). Finally, crack the claws and legs and draw out that prime white meat.

    Hard-boil the eggs (9 minutes from cold should do), then refresh and peel them. Mash 2 of them and reserve. Cook the asparagus in boiling salted water for 5 minutes, then drain and refresh.

    When you are ready to assemble the dish, arrange the lettuce on a platter. Crab Louie should be presented as a composed salad, and much as I hate symmetry, I will go with it on this occasion. Slice the remaining 3 eggs and arrange them around the outside of the plate. Follow with the avocado, tomato, and asparagus. Pile the crab, loosely shredded, in the center and stud with the chopped olives.

    Beat the dressing ingredients together, adding the mashed eggs, and present in a bowl on the side. Sprinkle both the sauce and the salad with paprika, and serve with brown bread and butter.

CRISPY CHILI WHITEBAIT SALAD WITH SALT AND VINEGAR "CHIPS"

Whitebait has to be one of the world's great novelty foods—toy fish that you can chow down, head, tail, and all.*

This recipe is proper fusion stuff: part British pub grub, part Levantine cuisine.

A LIGHT LUNCH OR
APPETIZER FOR 4

FOR THE SALAD:
3 small pita breads
5 tbsp/75ml non-extra-virgin
    olive oil
½ cup/125ml malt vinegar
1½ tbsp sea salt
5½oz/150g white cabbage, finely shredded
2 fat carrots, coarse grated
⅓ cucumber, cut into matchsticks
4 pickled onions, sliced
big handful of arugula
big handful of fresh parsley, chopped

2–3 sprigs of fresh tarragon, chopped
3 tbsp extra-virgin olive oil
juice of 2 lemons
1 heaped tsp English mustard
salt and freshly ground black pepper

FOR THE FISHY BIT:
2 heaped tbsp flour
1 tsp sumac
½ tsp ground cumin
½ tsp chili powder (less if you're a wuss)
½ tsp salt
9oz/250g fresh whitebait (or frozen**)
canola or sunflower oil, for frying
lemon wedges

Preheat the oven to 375°F/190°C.

Carefully split the pita bread slices so that you have 6 sheets, and spread them inner-side up on a baking sheet. Whisk the oil and vinegar together and brush the slices with the mixture before sprinkling them generously with sea salt. Bake in the oven for 6–8 minutes, or until they are good and crispy and starting to brown (they will continue to crisp once out of the oven, so don't worry if they are still a little soft at first). Set aside.

Toss the vegetables, pickled onions, and herbs together for the salad, and whisk together the oil, lemon juice, mustard, salt, and pepper.

When you are ready to serve, mix together the flour, spices, and salt. Carefully toss the whitebait in the flour. Now heat about ¾in/2cm oil in a pan until it reaches sizzle point. Shake each fish to remove any excess flour and lower them into the fat (you will probably need to cook them in 2 batches). Fry until golden brown and floating on the surface before removing with a spatula and draining on paper towel.

Pour the dressing over the salad, breaking the pita chips into pieces and mixing them in. Scatter the fried whitebait on top and serve immediately with extra lemon wedges. And maybe some nice bread and butter and a glass of ale.

*

I'm from a place called Southend-on-Sea, and while I wasn't quite raised on the stuff, along with cockles (of which more on p.183) and cotton candy, whitebait is more or less the civic dish—they even have a whitebait festival every year. So I was intrigued to learn that it is pretty much consumed all over the world and equally surprised when I learned (embarrassingly recently) that whitebait isn't actually one fish at all, but rather the collective term for the baby ("fry") fish of 20 or more different species. You live, eat, and learn, eh?

* *

If you use frozen whitebait, make sure that they are defrosted naturally: they are very delicate and will not brook much messing.

KIPPER SALAD WITH WATERCRESS AND DRIED LIME

Kippers. Well, I'm allowed to eat them as long as Mr. Shopkeeper isn't expected to kiss me within three hours of the partaking thereof, and preferably only in the store's backroom or outdoors. Eating them at home is strictly taboo. It's the smell you see.* So I often end up having this as a shopkeeper's lunch/treat.

Crazy but true kipper factoid: there is a kipper museum on the Isle of Man. Add it to your bucket list.

LUNCH FOR 2

2 kipper fillets, preferably uncolored
1 big bunch of watercress
1 small but perfectly formed leek, very finely sliced
½ orange, peeled, deseeded, and segmented
3 tbsp walnut oil (or extra-virgin olive oil)
1 generous tsp creamed horseradish
½ tsp lime powder**
salt and freshly ground black pepper

Grill, fry, or microwave the kipper fillets for a few minutes, then remove any skin together with any obvious bones, and set aside.

Toss the watercress, leek, and orange together on a platter, and whisk the oil, horseradish, and lime powder together, seasoning to taste.

When you are ready to eat, layer the still-warm kipper fillets on top of the salad and pour the dressing over them. Serve with some very elegant triangles of lightly toasted brown bread.

* Handy household hint

A slice or two of (stale will do) bread placed over cooking fish serves to absorb a lot of the smell. A wee bowl of vinegar next to your cooking area will also help to mask it. Both help, although neither is enough to get Mr. Shopkeeper to accept my kipper habit.

** Lime powder

Lime powder = ground *limoo omani*, aka dried limes, a particular variety of the citrus fruit that grows in Iran and the Gulf. They are used in Iraqi and Iranian cuisine—the Iranians prefer to use them while they are still pale, while Iraqis tend to leave them to mature longer. You can use the dried fruit whole, just by pricking it and dropping it into soups and stews, or ground, wherein you can use it like any other spice. If you can't find it, just use a teaspoon of fresh lime juice in its place.

SMOKED MACKEREL SALAD WITH *DUKKAH*-SPICED OATY SPRINKLES *HEALTHY*

A nice simple salad with real fancy accessories. Master Shopcat and I often have this for lunch—although needless to say he prefers it unadorned.

SUPPER FOR 2

FOR THE SPRINKLES:

1¼ cups/3½oz/100g rolled oats
2 tbsp *dukkah*
½ tsp red pepper flakes (either chili or hot
   Turkish pepper flakes)
½ tsp sea salt
3 tbsp olive oil
1 large egg white
1 tsp Worcestershire sauce

FOR THE SALAD:

2 sides of skinless smoked mackerel fillets
3oz/80g mixed green salad leaves and herbs
1 small onion, sliced

FOR THE DRESSING:

2 tsp lemon curd
1½ tsp English mustard
juice and grated zest of 1 lime
juice and grated zest of ½ orange
3 tbsp pumpkin seed oil (or olive oil)
sea salt and freshly ground black pepper

Preheat the oven to 340°F/170°C.

Mix the oats with the spices and seasoning, and whisk the oil with the egg white and the Worcestershire sauce. Pour the latter over the former and mix well with a wooden spoon before spreading out on a lightly oiled baking sheet. Cook for about 30 minutes, turning the "sprinkles" halfway through, before removing from the oven and allowing to cool.

When you are ready to serve, slice the mackerel diagonally into strips. Mix the leaves, onion, and mackerel in a bowl. Beat the dressing ingredients together and pour over the salad, tossing well. Dot the sprinkles on top. A nice crusty sourdough bread would go well with this.

SMOKED SALMON AND DILL SALAD STACKS

A vertical salad. What fun, eh? And simple, because the last thing you want is to start playing salad Buckaroo when you've got last-minute guests to feed.

A QUICK APPETIZER FOR 4
2 small pita breads
non-extra-virgin olive oil, for brushing
2 baby cucumbers (or ½ a small regular one)
1½ tbsp dill pesto (see below—but if you are in
  a hurry, any old pesto will do)
1½ heaped tbsp mascarpone

1 bunch of watercress
5½oz/150g smoked salmon, thinly sliced

TO SERVE
few sprigs of fresh dill
slices of lime

Toast the pitas lightly, split each piece open into 2 separate halves, and cut each of these halves both lengthways and across the middle. You should end up with 16 almost miter-shaped pieces of pita.

Preheat the oven to 375°F/190°C.

Arrange the pita slices on a baking tray, brush them with olive oil, and bake for around 10 minutes, or until starting to crisp (they will crisp still further once they are out of the oven). Allow to cool. Peel and slice the cucumbers lengthways (a mandolin would help here as you want the slices so thin that they curl).

Ready to rock and roll? Lightly coat each pita slice with a little pesto, followed by the mascarpone (again spread very thinly). Place 2 of the pita pieces across each other on a plate and top with watercress, cucumber strips, and salmon. Place another pita finger on top, and arrange a little more 'cress and salmon over it before topping with one more pita slice, this one with the pesto/mascarpone facing down. Repeat with the remaining ingredients until you have 4 very pretty salmon stacks. With a bit of imagination and a following wind they should look like a sloop in full sail. Garnish with a few sprigs of dill and slices of lime and serve.

BONUS RECIPE: DILL PESTO

Whisk scant ½ cup/100ml olive oil with 3 tablespoons apple or cide vinegar. Crumble 3 rye crackers into the mixture and leave to soak for around 5 minutes. Blend or whisk vigorously along with 1 heaped tablespoon fresh dill, 2 garlic cloves, ⅓ teaspoon sea salt, and some freshly ground black pepper. Store in a wee jar in the fridge until needed.

BONUS BONUS RECIPE: MR. SHOPKEEPER'S BELGIAN SMOKED SALMON SALAD

Jamshid did a bit of his growing up in Belgium, where a simple salad of onion, parsley, and smoked salmon is a popular snack to accompany a few beers. Simply macerate a very big handful of chopped fresh curly parsley and a small chopped onion in some lemon juice seasoned with sea salt and plenty of freshly ground black pepper. Leave for an hour, turning once or twice, then toss with strips of salmon. Serve with bread.

ALIVE, ALIVE-OH! — COCKLE AND MUSSEL SALAD

Can't be doing a chapter about fish and leave cockles out. This is clearly more of my East-Coast-of-England heritage coming out, but when it comes to English shellfish at least, the only way is Essex... all the way down to Old Leigh on the banks of the Thames estuary. There are few finer ways to spend a summer evening than supping fine ale at the Crooked Billet pub on the quay while partaking of freshly-caught shellfish from the adjacent kiosk. And cockles and mussels are, of course, good for you: they're one of the best natural sources of iodine.

This salad recognizes the cockle's humble heartland, but raises the stakes a little. The saffron is, by the way, authentic: Essex had a thriving saffron trade (ever been to Saffron Walden?). My home county isn't all white handbags, perma-tans, and fake bling, you know...

AN APPETIZER FOR 4
10½oz/300g live cockles (or other other small hard-shelled clams)
handful of rolled oats
10½oz/300g live mussels
¾ cup/175ml strong real ale
1 teaspoon sugar
1 onion, chopped
2 garlic cloves, chopped
½ tsp ground black pepper
big knob of butter
9oz/250g sea beans (use bok choi if you really can't find it), roughly chopped
1 level tsp fresh dill
½ tsp ground saffron steeped in a splash of boiling water
1 tbsp balsamic vinegar
3oz/80g lamb's lettuce

Wash the cockles and place them in a bowl of water. Add the oats and leave for a couple of hours. Bet that's got you intrigued, eh? Cockles are rather sandy critters: getting them to eat the oats will purge them of the dregs of the Thames Estuary, rendering them more palatable/less gritty. At the end of this time, scoop them out of the water and rinse again.

Clean the mussels by removing their "beards." If any of them are already open, tap them on your chopping board (if they remain open they are good only for the trash).

Place the ale, sugar, onion, garlic, and pepper in a saucepan. Add the cockles and mussels and bring to a boil. Turn down the heat and simmer for 4–5 minutes, or until all the shells are open, then scoop the shellfish out onto a plate. Bring the stock back to a boil and leave to reduce by two-thirds. Remove the fish from the shells and reserve.

Melt the butter in a frying pan and toss in the sea beans and dill. Sauté for around 3 minutes before adding the shellfish, saffron water, and balsamic vinegar, then turn off the heat.

Arrange the lamb's lettuce on a platter then use tongs to arrange the sea beans, cockles, and mussels in the middle. Tip the saffrony butter into the reduced beer stock, and boil a little bit more before tipping over the salad.

Serve with gourmet chips (like the celeriac chips in the bonus recipe, left).

BONUS RECIPE: CELERIAC CHIPS
Actually not a recipe at all, as it's such a snap. Peel half a small celeriac (celery root), and slice it very finely (with a mandolin if possible). Fry in non-extra-virgin olive oil until golden brown before draining on paper towel and sprinkling with celery salt. Serve sooner rather than later, as they will soften the longer they are left. The sweet nuttiness is a perfect foil for this salad.

SEARED MONKFISH AND CELERY SALAD WITH A PERNOD DRESSING

A LIGHT DINNER
FOR 4

1 large tail of monkfish (around
    1lb/450g), cut on the bias
    into about 8 medallions
juice and grated zest of 1 lime
1–2 tbsp extra-virgin olive oil
2 garlic cloves
salt and ground black pepper

FOR THE CELERY:

2 celery hearts, halved
    lengthways
2–3 tbsp olive oil
1 onion, sliced
2–3 garlic cloves, sliced
½ cup/125ml vegetable stock
2 tsp nigella seeds
salt and ground black pepper

TO ASSEMBLE:

3½oz/100g snow peas, trimmed
    and cut into strips
½ fat head of Chinese (Napa)
    cabbage, chopped
3–4 scallions, chopped
big handful of fresh cilantro,
    finely chopped
3 tbsp olive oil
juice and grated zest of 1 lime
1½ tbsp sour cream
½ tsp Tabasco sauce
sea salt
3 tbsp Pernod (or Ouzo/Raki)
pat of butter

Monkfish is a funny dude. Not quite like any other fish in the pond. He's ugly when he's fully dressed, and once he's undressed he doesn't even look like a fish. He's kind of rubbery if not cooked properly, and very rich. But he shines in salads, as he is wondrously boneless (at least, the part that you generally buy to cook is). This is based on a dish I used to cook when I worked as a sous sous sous chef in a highfalutin fish restaurant.

Place the monkfish tail in a tub or bowl and add the lime, oil, garlic, and some seasoning. Roll it around to ensure that it gets thoroughly coated, then cover and chill for an hour, or until you are about ready to serve.

Preheat the oven to 375°F/190°C.

Bring a pan of salted water to a boil and blanch the celery for around 2½ minutes. Drain thoroughly (patting dry). Heat the oil in a pan and add the onion, followed a couple of minutes later by the garlic. Once the onion has softened, add the stock, bring to a boil, and take off the heat. Lay the celery hearts in an oven dish and pour on the stock. Sprinkle with the nigella seeds, season liberally, cover with foil, and bake for around 35 minutes, or until the celery is tender without being mushy. Cool a little.

Mix the snow peas, cabbage, scallions, and cilantro on a big platter, and arrange the celery hearts in the middle. Whisk the oil, lime, sour cream, Tabasco, and salt to taste together with half the Pernod.

When you are ready to cook, heat a pat of butter in a pan, and add the monkfish tail. Sear it on both sides (you need to cook it for around 6 minutes altogether). At the last minute throw in the other half of the Pernod, shaking the pan to flame it (use a match if you have an electric stove).

Spoon the fish on top of the celery, and drizzle the salad and fish with the dressing. Serve with warm bread.

KHTAPODI VRASTO: GREEK OCTOPUS SALAD

MEZZE OR *TAPAS*
FOR 6–8

1 regular octopus (around
        2¼lb/1kg in weight)
    or 4–5 baby ones
1 glass of dry white wine
2–3 bay leaves
1 lemon
5 tbsp/75ml extra-virgin olive oil
2 tsp dried (or fresh) oregano
2 garlic cloves, minced
salt and coarsely ground
        black pepper
few sprigs of fresh dill

✳ Note

Believe it or not, this is the
correctest plural version thereof.
Octopusses just seems silly,
although it is used in the
vernacular. "Octopi" is all
wrong, as it teams a Greek word
with a Latin plural declension.

BONUS RECIPE: PICKLED OCTOPUS SALAD

Instead of dressing the
cooked octopus in oil, pack it
into sterilized jars and add
2 tablespoons crushed capers
and 2 tablespoons pitted
sliced olives, along with the
oregano, garlic, salt, and
pepper as above. Fill the jars
with white wine vinegar, seal,
and refrigerate. This will be
ready after a few days.

This is barely deserving of the salad moniker, as it is basically just dressed octopus, but it is regarded as such in Greece. It is one of the most famous *mezze* dishes of all: a platter of marinated octopus is the classic accompaniment to a glass of ouzo or wine… preferably consumed overlooking an idyllic, white-painted, salt-scented fishing harbor, where barefooted children play among the nets and wily stray cats weave in and out of all the taverna tables. Although your deck will do just as well, and I'm sure the neighbor's kids/cats will improvise for you.

Fun eight-legged facts: the octopus is scary-intelligent (scary if you're familiar with the legend of the kraken), famously able to use tools, navigate mazes, and break out of tanks in search of fields anew and better food. If you are ever trapped by a giant cephalopod, just bite or poke the lump between their eyes—this paralyzes them instantly. Read it in a Modesty Blaise novel I think, so it must be true.

First catch your octopus. Well, defrost it at least if you are using frozen. Frozen octopodes* are usually already cleaned, but if you are using fresh, you will need to remove the "beak" by turning the critter inside out and pulling the sharp plasticky rod out of its "mouth" (the white ring). Baby octopodes can be cooked whole, but if you are using a big boy you should also cut the head away from the body just under the eyes. Discard the head, since you only eat the legs. Again, if you are using a regular octopus you will need to tenderize it a little: traditionally fishermen do this by bashing it against the rocks of the harbor, but as your nearest harbor may be some way away, just beat the tentacles with a meat tenderizer a few times and remove any tough-looking suckers. Finally, soak the tentacles (or the whole baby octopodes) in a basin of water for 20 minutes or so to allow any sand residue to sink to the bottom. Fish out of the water and rinse well.

Next, bring some water to a boil in a saucepan and add the octopus: blanch for 3 minutes then drain, rinse, and return to the pan. Add a generous 1 cup (250ml) water, together with the wine and bay leaves, then cover and bring the contents of the pan back to a very gentle simmer. Baby octopodes will only need about 20 minutes to cook, but regular ones will need the best part of an hour to become tender enough. Once it is cooked, take off the heat and place the octopus in a colander to drain: a thrifty Greek housewife would retain the stock to make all manner of fish soups, but if you are not in tune with your inner Aphrodite, throw it away.

When your pet kraken is cool enough to handle, peel it (but only if the skin is tough, I nearly always leave it on), wrap it in plastic wrap, and refrigerate it for an hour or so. Once it is chilled and firm, slice it into ½in/1.5cm pieces (roughly) and put them in a bowl. Juice the lemon and add the juice to the oil, oregano, and garlic, seasoning the mixture to taste (octopus likes salt: it has just come out of the sea, remember). Pour the dressing over the octopus, mixing well, then chill some more. Enjoy cold or at room temperature, garnished with dill sprigs. Your *khtapodi vrasto* will keep for 3 days in the fridge.

CHAPTER NINE
Meat

If, like me, you are married to a rampant and unrepentant carnivore, this chapter will be the first to which you turn. You can use it to trick loved ones into eating healthier stuff while cleverly deploying other *viands* to stretch just a modicum of meat quite a long way. There is also the fact that the richness of meat is perfectly offset by salady surroundings: they simply go very well together.

FIAMBRE: A GUATEMALAN SALMAGUNDI

Fiambre (literally "cold meat") is perhaps the most elaborate and ingredient-heavy salad in the world. It's more of an event than a salad. It is made once a year to celebrate the Day of the Dead (All Saints Day—Nov. 1st), and was originally prepared as a (largely pickled) offering to the dead; the word is still used as a metaphor for a corpse. It comprises a blend of ancient Mayan beliefs in the afterlife, Catholic superstition, and imported Spanish ingredients. In Guatemala to this day November 1st is a public holiday, and even those who don't fancy feasting in a cemetery prepare *fiambre* and head off on a picnic. Truly some of the best food in the world is borne out of superstition and tradition.

Like many such dishes, it is impossible to declare any one recipe more authentic than others. It was probably originally made on a shoestring and composed of leftovers. Every family has their own system of preparation, secret sauce, list of ingredients, and ritual in the assemblage and the resultant salad rivalry is legendary. Some prefer to serve all the ingredients separately (to make a "divorced *fiambre*"); some Guatemalans make a sweeter, "white" version of the dish. This, hopefully, is a user-friendly Western version, but feel free to add and subtract as you see fit.

TO FEED 13–14, HANDSOMELY
10½oz/300g waxy potatoes,
    thickly sliced and boiled
3½oz/100g green beans,
    cut into 2in/5cm lengths, boiled
1 cauliflower, cut into florets, blanched
4 sticks of celery, cut into 2in/5cm lengths,
    blanched
1 bunch of asparagus, blanched (or canned)
2 carrots, peeled, finely sliced, blanched
12 baby corn, blanched
2 medium beets, peeled, sliced, and boiled
1 can (14oz/400g) chickpeas, drained
1 can (14oz/400g) kidney beans, drained
12 pickles, thickly sliced lengthways
generous 1 cup/7oz/200g olives (any color)
1 can (14oz/400g) palm hearts (or artichokes)
12 pickled onions, quartered
2 large romaine lettuces, roughly chopped
5–6 slices smoked ham
5–6 slices prosciutto (or *Serrano* ham)
7–8 slices salami
7–8 slices Spanish chorizo
7oz/200g shredded cooked chicken
7oz/200g cooked roast beef or tongue
1 can anchovies, drained, each fillet split in
    half lengthways
around 10 large cooked shrimp, shell-on

1 small can tuna steak, divided into chunks
3½oz/100g Cheddar-ish cheese, cubed
3½oz/100g crumbly white cheese (such as
    Caerphilly), duly crumbled
5 perfectly hard-boiled eggs, quartered
12 radishes, cut into crinkly little crowns
1 bell pepper (red or yellow—fiesta colored),
    cut into thin rings
2 onions, sliced
generous ¾ cup/200ml extra-virgin olive oil
2 tsp mustard

FOR THE DRESSING:
1¼ cups/300ml vinegar
½ bunch of fresh flat-leaf parsley
1 tbsp (drained) capers, chopped
1 level tsp dried oregano
1 level tsp thyme
3–4 cloves
6 garlic cloves, minced
2 red chilies, minced (optional)
2 tsp sugar
salt and freshly ground black pepper
2–3 bay leaves

Having got all that ready, perhaps you should have a little nap before we start…. When you're ready, blend all of the ingredients (except the bay leaves) for the dressing together, then check the seasoning and add the bay leaves. Place the potatoes, beans, cauliflower, celery, asparagus, carrots, and corn in a bowl, cover with three-quarters of the dressing, and refrigerate overnight. Use the remaining quarter for the beets (which we are keeping separate for now to avoid too much color leaching).

The next day, drain these marinated veg, retaining the dressing (but discard the bay leaves), and mix them with the chickpeas, kidney beans, pickles, olives, palm hearts, and pickled onions. Strew the lettuce across a massive platter, and pile the vegetable mixture on top. Next, arrange the meat, fish, cheese, egg, radishes, pepper, and onions on top, as artistically as the mood takes you.

Finally, whisk the olive oil and mustard into the dressing, check the seasoning once again, and drizzle across the top of your creation. Be impressed. Be very impressed.

LARB: FIERY PORK SALAD

My best beloved selected something like this on one of our first dates. Why do men do that? Order really spicy stuff to impress, I mean. It results at best in an unnaturally glowing complexion, and taken to its extreme can kill all possibility of romance. I'm sure you don't need me to expound on that any further.

This is, heat notwithstanding, an utterly addictive salad—and as you are making it, you can, of course, make it as hot or as mild as you like (use any meat you like—duck or beef both work equally well). The dish is generally known as a Thai specialty, but it does in fact come from neighboring Laos. Out East it is often served raw, but raw pork (and chicken) is potentially a killer, so if you don't mind, out West we will cook it thoroughly.

Larb is often served with sticky rice and *Bok l'Hong*: Papaya Salad (p.222).

A QUICK, ALBEIT EYE-WATERING, SUPPER FOR 2

½ sheet of pork skin (optional: cheat and use ready-made artisan pork rind)

sea salt

¼ tsp chili powder

10½oz/300g ground pork

2 garlic cloves, minced

½ tsp dried red pepper flakes (or more if you're up to the challenge)

2–3 scallions, finely chopped

around 2 tbsp cold water

2 tbsp fish sauce

3 limes, 2 juiced and 1 to garnish

salt

1–2 tbsp ground roasted rice (*khao kua*)*

big handful of fresh cilantro, chopped

big handful of fresh mint, shredded

First, let's make some pork rind. The authentic ingredient in Laos is boiled pork skin, but I couldn't quite get my head or my teeth around that. And who doesn't like pork rinds? Preheat the oven to 475°F/240°C.

Next, place the pork skin (outer skin uppermost) in a colander and pour a kettle of boiling water all over it. Shake the water off, rub the skin with sea salt and chili, and set it to dry (by an open window is ideal if there aren't any obvious natural predators in the area). After 15–20 minutes, score through the skin in a criss-cross pattern, place it on a baking sheet, and roast for about 20 minutes, or until golden and bubbling. Allow to cool by the aforementioned open window. Once cool, break into ¼in/5mm-ish cubes and set aside until ready.

Mix the ground meat with the garlic, red pepper flakes, and scallions, pounding well. Next, heat a wok to smoking point, and throw in the cold water, marveling at the lovely sizzle it makes. Add the pork mixture, stirring vigorously to stop it sticking, and cook until it is no longer pink (around 5 minutes should do). Take off the heat and allow to cool slightly.

Meanwhile, whisk the fish sauce and lime juice together. When the pork is no longer piping hot, stir the sauce through the meat and season it to taste. Add most of the ground rice, together with the chopped cilantro. Serve the still-warm salad garnished with the pork rinds, some lime wedges, the rest of the ground rice, and the shredded mint.

* Ground roasted rice (*khao kua*)

This is available in Chinese/Thai stores, but it is easy to make your own at home. Just dry-fry a few tablespoons of either jasmine or classic Thai sticky rice in a wok until it assumes a dark brown color, around 10–15 minutes, stirring constantly. Then grind it into a fine-ish powder in a mortar and pestle or spice grinder. Cool thoroughly and store in an airtight jar until needed.

DUCK SALAD WITH PUY LENTILS, SNOW PEAS, AND KIWI CHUTNEY

Potential vegetarian that I am, I have to confess that duck is one of those rare treats that I would find hard to renounce. It's all about the skin—the salt-crispy chin-dribbling naughtiness of it all. This light and piquant salad is the perfect foil for such indulgence (it would also work well with leftover lamb or shredded roast pork). Although lean duck meat is actually super-low calorie, and duck fat itself is surprisingly low in saturates (try cooking potatoes in duck dripping—it's healthier than butter), so maybe one needn't feel so guilty after all?

AN ELEGANT LUNCHEON
FOR 4

2 duck breasts
2 tbsp brown sauce (like HP, or use steak sauce)
1 tsp mustard
dash of olive oil

FOR THE CHUTNEY:

3–4 perfectly ripe kiwis, peeled
3 pickled onions
juice of 1 lime
2 tsp date syrup
1¼in/3cm knob fresh ginger, peeled
2 green chilies, destalked
pinch of ground cloves
½ tsp ground cardamom

big handful of fresh mint
big handful of mixed fresh parsley
    and cilantro
salt

FOR THE SALAD:

½ cup/3½oz/100g Puy (French) lentils
1 (3oz/80g) bag watercress
3½oz/100g Chinese (Napa) cabbage
3½oz/100g snow peas,
    cut into strips
2–3 scallions, chopped
3 tbsp extra-virgin olive oil
1 tbsp raspberry vinegar
½ tsp cracked black peppercorns
salt

First, marinate the duck. Score through the skin/fat of the duck in a criss-cross pattern. Mix the brown sauce, mustard, and oil in a tub or large bowl and add the duck, turning to thoroughly coat it. Cover and refrigerate for 2 hours, or until you're ready to cook.

Next the chutney: whack all the ingredients in your blender and whizz together. Or chop all the dry ingredients real fine then mix them with the wet stuff: chutney is better if it is a bit lumpy. Add salt to taste, and if you find it too sharp, add more date syrup.

Cook the lentils by placing them in a pan of cold unsalted water and boiling them for 35 minutes, or until just cooked. Drain thoroughly, refresh, then mix with the watercress, cabbage, snow peas, and onions. Whisk the oil, vinegar, and seasoning in readiness.

When you're ready to eat, heat a frying pan over low heat. Shake the marinade off the duck breasts and place them skin-side down in the pan. After 6 minutes, turn them over and allow to cook for a further 2 minutes, or until the flesh inside is just a teensy bit pink in the middle. Remove the duck from the pan and slice it on the diagonal into strips.

Arrange the salad on a plate and dot the still-warm duck on top. Coat with the dressing and serve with some warm crusty bread and the chutney in a bowl on the side.

A PAIR OF HAM SALADS

Because in word association trials 7/10 respondents paired the word "ham" with "salad"...

I may have invented the statistic, but 'tis true—of all the cold cuts that you can strew across or bury in a salad, ham is the most popular by far. According to both one's husband and one's cat, the food universe actually revolves around the stuff and so this section is for them: they were certainly avid taste testers (thieves).

Most recipes for ham salad from the last century seem to involve dicing leftovers and binding it all with mayonnaise. This concept didn't tickle my fancy, so I thought we'd do something different.

BLACK FOREST HAM WITH SOUR CHERRIES AND BLACKBERRY VINAIGRETTE

A ham-related fact with which to dazzle your lunchtime guests: in Black Forest speak (i.e. German), this ham is known as *Schwarzwälder Schinken*, which I am sure you will agree sounds a lot more appetizing than "ham." This is a real looker of a salad. Add some warm pumpernickel and it's a meal already. I just dare you to serve it in lederhosen and follow it up with Black Forest cake...

AN AUTUMN LUNCH FOR 6

FOR THE VINAIGRETTE:
scant ½ cup/1¾oz/50g blackberries
   (wild ones always taste better)
4–5 juniper berries
2 tbsp orange juice
1 tbsp balsamic vinegar
4 tbsp pumpkin seed oil
   (or extra virgin olive oil)
1 sprig of fresh thyme
salt, freshly ground black pepper,
   and sugar

FOR THE SALAD:
5½oz/150g mixed green salad leaves
   (heavy on the arugula)
15 slices proper Black Forest ham (you could
   substitute prosciutto or *Serrano*)
3 medium cooked beets, halved and thinly
   sliced into half moons
2 carrots, peeled, halved lengthways
   and thinly sliced
1 small red onion, finely sliced
½ cucumber, halved lengthways and thinly
   sliced into half moons
3½oz/100g pitted, dried sour cherries*
⅔ cup/2¾oz/75g pumpkin seeds

* *Dried sour cherries*
These are an Iranian speciality, and are usually lightly salted. If using these, add a little less salt when seasoning your dressing. If you can't find them, use unsweetened cranberries.

Blend (or crush) the berries with the juniper, orange juice, and vinegar, trickling the oil in at the end so it forms an emulsion of sorts. Add the thyme and season to taste, then set aside for at least an hour (better still, overnight).

When you're ready to serve, scatter the salad greens on a big platter. Tear the ham into strips and scatter it over the salad along with the beet, carrot, onion, and cucumber. Add the cherries and pumpkin seeds. Shake up the dressing (removing the thyme sprig) and dribble it over the salad. *Mahlzeit* (elsewhere in Europe they might say "*bon appetit*")!

HAM AND PEA SALAD

Peas and ham do well together as soup, so I thought I'd see how they get along as a salad. This is a wonderfully comforting repast, perfect for a blustery evening watching repeats of *Downton* or whatever your current favorite box set may be.

A SUNDAY EVENING SUPPER
FOR 2

6 waxy baby or fingerling potatoes, scrubbed

2 free-range eggs

4½oz/125g podded peas (frozen will be fine)

1¾oz/50g baby spinach leaves, roughly chopped

4 sun-dried tomatoes, chopped

12 pitted olives (black tend to look better in salads)

2 scallions, chopped

7oz/200g proper ham (non-slippery, nicely textured, preferably home-cooked), roughly chopped

scant ¼ cup/1¾oz/50g fromage frais (or use plain yogurt mixed with marscapone)

2 tsp green tapenade

1 level tsp *herbes de Provence* (or fudge it with a mixture of thyme and rosemary)

2 tbsp olive oil

1 tbsp wine vinegar

sea salt and freshly ground black pepper

Put the potatoes in a saucepan and bring to a boil. After 2–3 minutes add the eggs, and after a further 5 minutes, add the peas. Bubble for 3 minutes more, then drain. Slice the potatoes thickly, then cool the eggs slightly under running water before peeling and slicing them as well.

Mix the spinach, tomatoes, olives, scallions, and ham in a bowl. Whisk the fromage frais or quark together with the remaining ingredients, seasoning to taste. At the last minute add the still-warm potatoes, egg, and peas to the salad, and stir the dressing through it. Serve on trays in front of the TV/fireplace/fish tank.

VALERIE BERRY'S FANCY FRENCH BEEF SALAD WITH *RAVIGOTE* DRESSING

DÎNER POUR 4

1 large carrot

2 marrow bones (about 5in/12cm
    each)

2¼lb/900g brisket

1 onion, peeled and
    studded with 2 cloves

1 stick of celery

4 medium leeks, trimmed
    (reserve 1 of the green tops
    for the stock), cut into
    ¾in/2cm slices

salt

FOR THE *RAVIGOTE* DRESSING:

1 shallot, finely chopped

2 tsp wholegrain mustard

generous ⅓ cup/80ml red wine
    vinegar

freshly ground black pepper

generous ¾ cup/200ml canola
    oil

1½ tbsp salted capers, soaked for
    10 minutes and drained

3 small pickles, finely chopped

1½ tbsp fresh tarragon,
    finely chopped

1½ tbsp fresh chives,
    finely sliced

1½ tbsp fresh parsley,
    finely chopped

1 large hard-boiled egg,
    finely chopped

TO SERVE:

small toasted sourdough
    bread slices

4oz/120g watercress

Valerie is the talented lady who styled all the food for *The New Middle Eastern Vegetarian*, *New Middle Eastern Street Food*, and this book. An author herself, she possesses an encyclopaedic knowledge of food and I have come to regard her as a bit of a mentor. Her most enviable quality, however, is her sheer unflappability.

As she is from over the Channel, it seemed only right to turn to her to inject a soupçon of French flair into the proceedings. This salad is very wholesome; she writes thus of it:

What I mainly remember of the monthly gargantuesque pot-au-feu lovingly cooked by my grandmother were the marrowbones of which I could never get enough, and the leftover beef salad with which she would send us home. No one ever left her house without food. Today I nostalgically cook brisket for the sole purpose of a beef salad. I serve the marrow on toasted sourdough as a side treat.

Ravigote comes from *ravigoter*, an old French word which means "to invigorate," referring to the kick this aromatic vinegary sauce gives to boiled meat.

Cut the carrot into 1½in/4cm chunks then cut 4 slices lengthways off one of the carrot chunks. Place 1 slice at each end of the marrow bones and tie with a string to secure. This clever trick will prevent the marrow from slipping out into the stock.

Place the brisket and bones into a heavy-based pot and cover with 6⅓ cups/1.5 liters cold water. Slowly bring to a simmer.

Add the onion, remaining carrot chunks, celery, and the green leek tops. Bring to a bare simmer and cook for 2½ hours (this will ensure that the beef is very tender). Halfway through, add 1 teaspoon salt. Salt draws out the juice and flavor from meat, so your meat will taste better if you add it once the meat is partly cooked and the flavors are locked in.

Leave the meat to cool for an hour in its stock. You can also cook it in advance and simply reheat it in its stock for 30 minutes. If you cook it in advance, remove the vegetables from the stock or they will spoil it (within 24 hours).

Place the leeks in a frying pan, cover with some of the beef stock, and simmer for 3–4 minutes. The leeks should be "al dente." Allow to cool while you prepare the sauce.

Mix the shallot, mustard, and vinegar in a jar. Season with pepper but don't use salt (the capers will add the saltiness). Add the oil, seal the top of the jar so that nothing spills out, and shake vigorously. Add the capers, pickles, herbs, and hard-boiled egg and shake again. Set aside.

Cut off the string around the marrow bones and remove the carrot slices. With a knife, dig out the marrow from inside the bones and delicately divide between the toasts.

Roughly slice or chop the meat. Arrange the leek slices and watercress on a plate, top with the meat, spoon the *ravigote* dressing over the top, and don't forget to serve the marrow toasts on the side. *Bon appétit*!

As for the leftover stock, Valerie suggests enjoying it as a hot drink or boiling potatoes in it.

KAREN RESTA'S BROOKLYN DELI SALAD

Karen is one of that new genre of friends that we are all slowly cultivating: the Facebook friend. The really good friend that you've never met; the one that lives on the other side of the world; the one whose social media posts are so very fascinating and different from yours that you feel inexorably drawn into their circle; the one whose impartial, long-distance advice often makes more sense than that of your nearest and dearest. She's a funny lady, a great writer, and an erstwhile catering pro, but before any of that she's a New Yorker through and through—so for my New York Deli Salad it seemed only right and proper to ask for her guidance. She writes:

The inspiration for this salad is the most New York City of all places to eat in New York City—the Jewish Deli. These places are dying out, but for many years they've been one of the faces of the city representing "who we are." And these delis do not exist in the form they exist here anywhere else on earth. They are famous for their overstuffed sandwiches, towering high above the plate... .

What we've done with this is to unpack the aforementioned sammie and render it into a composed salad.

SALAD ART FOR 6

oil, for frying
2 slices seeded rye bread,
　　cut into ⅝in/1.5cm cubes
3½oz/100g sliced turkey, julienned
3½oz/100g sliced tongue, julienned
3½oz/100g sliced corned beef, julienned
2 fat pickled beet, cut into matchsticks
3 half-sour pickles,* sliced
1 small tub (around 3 tbsp) coleslaw
sprigs of fresh dill

FOR THE "RUSSIAN" DRESSING:

4 tbsp mayonnaise
2 tbsp ketchup
¼ onion, finely chopped
1 tsp freshly grated horseradish (in an ideal
　　world: if your world, like mine, is less than
　　ideal, use 1 tsp horseradish sauce instead)
1 tsp Worcestershire sauce
salt and freshly ground black pepper

Heat a glug of oil in a frying pan and toss in the rye bread. Cook for about 3 minutes, turning regularly, then drain on paper towel.

Meanwhile, whisk all the ingredients for the Russian dressing together.

Ready to roll? Arrange the meat, pickles, and coleslaw as symmetrically or asymmetrically as you will, lined up in a row, or fanned out in a circle. Top with croutons, drizzle with the dressing, and garnish with dill sprigs.

Serve with chocolate egg cream.**

* Half-sour pickles
New Yorkers have turned the art of pickling cucumbers into a real science. Half-sour pickles are those that have been preserved in brine but are still immature enough to retain their crunch and color.

* * Chocolate egg cream
Ah. Yes. Karen's idea not mine—a real Brooklyn speciality. It is soda water, milk, and chocolate sauce or syrup. Gotta be done, I guess.

MUSTARD DOG SALAD

The husband could possibly live on hotdogs. This has, I am told, something to do with a misspent youth in Belgium, where sausage culture is pretty big. But I suspect he is not alone in this passion: I know quite a few otherwise self-respecting folk who only visit Ikea so that they can loiter round the register area at the end stuffing themselves with Swedish dogs. So this salad is a sure-fire hit with frankfurter fans.

FOR 4

2½ tbsp sour cream	12 cherry tomatoes, halved
1½ tbsp ketchup	3½ oz/100g white cabbage, finely shredded
1 tbsp lemon juice	2 carrots, grated
½ tsp cayenne	2 tsp dried dill
1 tsp Worcestershire sauce	canola oil, for frying
salt	1 fat onion, sliced
1 small frisée (curly endive) lettuce,	4 pieces of thinly sliced white bread
roughly shredded	2–3 tsp English mustard
	6 frankfurters

Heat the broiler or grill. Whisk the sour cream, ketchup, lemon juice, cayenne, and Worcestershire sauce together and season to taste.

Next, toss the lettuce, tomatoes, cabbage, carrots, and dill together in a bowl.

Heat a sloosh of oil in a pan and fry the onion until it is brown. Scoop out of the pan. Toast one side of the bread on the grill (or under the broiler). Spread the toasted side with mustard. Spoon the onions on to 2 of the slices of bread, and press the other 2 slices on top very firmly (with the untoasted side outermost), so that you effectively have 2 rounds of compressed onion sandwiches. Add a little more oil to the pan in which you have fried the onions, then cut each of the sandwiches into around 8 squares, before frying them until they are golden brown. Scoop these too out and drain on paper towel.

Finally, grill the hotdogs, turning regularly (they will need around 6–7 minutes) before cutting them into thick slices on the bias.

To assemble, pour the dressing over the salad and toss well. Strew the naughty onion croutons and sliced sausage over the top and serve immediately.

CORONATION CHICKEN SALAD

How are the mighty recipe ideas fallen? What started life in this instance as an exotic salad creation to celebrate the coronation of HM the Queen of England has become a rather dreary and misunderstood sandwich filling all through the country. Coronation Chicken was invented by Rosemary Hume of the Cordon Bleu Cookery School: little could she have known what she had started. My mother (like, I suspect, many housewives of that era) still has a flimsy snippet of a recipe from *Good Housekeeping* or some such: the recipe below is based on that but is a bit lighter and has a pinch of the Middle East thrown in for good measure.

A BUFFET SALAD FOR 10 OR SO

1 fat chicken (3¼–4½lb/1.5–2kg), skinned
    and jointed
1 small onion, chunked
1 level tsp ground turmeric
3–4 dried limes (or cut 1 lemon in half and
    throw that in)
2–3 bay leaves
salt and freshly ground black pepper
1 fat onion, finely chopped

oil, for frying
1 good tsp curry powder
1 heaped tsp tomato purée
2 tbsp good mango chutney
scant ¼ cup/50ml red wine
1¼ cups/300ml mayonnaise
3 tbsp plain yogurt
1 small bunch of fresh cilantro, chopped
handful of romaine lettuce leaves
1 cup/3½oz/100g slivered almonds, toasted
    (dry-fried)

Place the chicken in a saucepan, add the small onion, turmeric, dried limes, bay leaves, and seasoning and cover with water. Bring to a boil, turn down the heat, and simmer for around 45 minutes, or until the chicken is just cooked. Drain (retaining the stock to use for something else, like the Good Housekeeper that you are) and allow the chicken to cool before stripping it away from the bones and chopping it.

Fry the second onion in a little oil. As it begins to brown, add the curry powder, stirring well, followed a minute later by the tomato paste and the mango chutney. Cook for 2 further minutes, then add the wine, bubble for 2 minutes more, and take off the heat. Allow to cool completely.

Once the curry concoction is cold, stir in the mayonnaise and yogurt, then fold the chicken and cilantro through it. Arrange on a party platter surrounded by lettuce, and garnish with the almonds. The salad is often served with a platter of rice. Union Jack napkins are optional.

"STEAK AND FRIES" SALAD

Just to prove to your carnivorous best beloved that salad never means having to say you're sorry. There are, of course, some unswayable types for whom steak is only steak if it comes in sizzling slab format, but for the rest of the world this is a slightly healthier/funkier option.

SATURDAY NIGHT DINNER
FOR 2

2 medium russet potatoes

1 small beet

4 tbsp canola or sunflower oil

2 heaped tsp Dijon mustard

1 level tsp paprika

pinch of garlic sea salt

3½oz/100g mixture of arugula, watercress, and
    baby spinach

6 small mushrooms, finely sliced

6 cherry tomatoes, sliced

1 small onion, cut into rings

2 (6oz/175g) prime sirloin steaks, fat removed
    (although a paltry 6oz/175g would never
    suffice for Mr. Shopkeeper)

sea salt

freshly ground black pepper

FOR THE DRESSING:

2 tbsp extra-virgin olive oil

1 tsp horseradish sauce

1 tbsp cider vinegar

salt

Peel the potatoes and beet, cut them into thin fries, and place them in a bowl of cold water for about 10 minutes.

Meanwhile, preheat the oven to 425°F/220°C and line a baking sheet with some oiled parchment paper.

Drain the tubers and pat them dry with paper towel. Mix the canola oil with the mustard, paprika, and garlic salt and toss the "frites" in this mustardy coating before spreading them out across the parchment paper. Bake for 10 minutes, then turn the oven down to 375°F/190°C; turn the fries over and bake for another 10 minutes, or until they are crispy and cooked.

While they are cooking, mix the salad greens with the mushrooms, tomatoes, and onion. Time too to whisk the dressing ingredients together.

Ready for your steak dinner? Season your steaks with salt and pepper and griddle them for a few minutes on each side or until cooked to your liking (please say this is not "well done"…). Put them on a chopping board and cut the meat into thin strips.

Assembly time. Dot the salad with the French fries, arrange the steak strips on top, and dribble with the dressing. Eat with gusto while watching whatever passes for Saturday night entertainment down your way.

BAJAN CHICKEN SALAD

Sometimes a shopkeeper has to go to great lengths to get proper time off, to get their little emporium covered. Mr. Shopkeeper and I decided we really needed a vacation, but the only way that we could bully the stand-in to, well, stand in for us was to come up with something truly dramatic. Which is how we ended up getting married, for who can deny a couple's right to have a fab honeymoon? This is a roundabout way of explaining how we came to fall a little bit in love with Barbados.

Bajan food is a beguiling mix of Africa and India and the Caribbean. This recipe is a similar jumble—of all the lovely flavors that we sampled on our trip.

A TOTALLY TROPICAL SUPPER FOR 2

2 skinless, boneless chicken breasts
1 garlic clove, minced
¼ tsp ground cumin
½ tsp paprika
½ tsp ground allspice
1 red chili, finely chopped (or use green for less heat)
½ tsp dried oregano
juice and grated zest of 1 lime
1 tbsp peanut oil
salt

FOR THE SALAD PART:

scant ½ cup/2¾oz/75g dried pigeon peas*
    (or 1 can/14oz/400g), soaked for 6 hours
1 small jicama** or white (daikon) radish,
    peeled and diced
1 red onion, diced
1 mango, carefully peeled and diced
big handful of fresh parsley, chopped
1 bunch of fresh chives, chopped
1 lime
2 tbsp extra-virgin olive oil
dash of hot sauce
salt

* Pigeon peas
Also known as gungo peas, these tasty legumes are a feature of Caribbean cuisine. All beans make me happy, but pigeon peas are particularly full of tryptophan, which is a mildly mood-enhancing amino acid. If you can't source them, black beans also work well in this recipe.

** Hmm. Jicama
This is such a commonplace vegetable in half of the world, especially Central America, where they pop up in all sorts of recipes (unfortunately I live in the other half of the world). You can find this turnip-like veggie in Latin American and sometimes Asian grocery stores. Radish makes an acceptable sub.

Slice the chicken breasts into thin strips of 2in/5cm in length. Mix the garlic, spices, chili, oregano, lime juice and zest, and oil together in a bowl. Add a little salt and toss the chicken strips in, turning them over so they become well coated in marinade. Cover and leave in the fridge for an hour or so (or marinate for just 30 minutes at room temperature).

Meanwhile, drain the soaked beans, bring to a boil, then turn down the heat and simmer in unsalted water for about 45 minutes, or until cooked without being mushy. Drain and allow to cool.

When you are ready-ish to assemble your salad, preheat the broiler or grill. Shake the chicken so that any surplus marinade slides off, then broil or grill the strips for around 6 minutes, turning once or twice. Keep warmish.

Mix the peas with the jicama, onion, and mango, then stir the herbs through the mixture. Next, use a sharp knife to remove the skin and pith from half of the lime. Discard any seeds and chop the rest of the flesh into the salad (if you don't like things too sharp, you can omit this part and just use the juice in the dressing instead).

Squeeze the other half of the lime into a bowl, and whisk in the olive oil, hot sauce, and salt to taste before trickling it over the beans. Serve the still-warm chicken on top. Steamed white rice or some good bread would render this dinner rather than supper.

CHAPTER TEN
Fruity salads

I've got a bit of a thing about cooking savory dishes with fruit. I sneak fruitiness into the most unexpected nooks and crannies: I love the unexpected kick and contrast it gives to dishes (and the curious-but-too-proud-to-ask look on the faces of dinner guests). We have a long history of cooking with fruit: Victorian cooking tomes are full of rich meat dishes containing hidden fruit, and the use of chutneys and conserves with meat and fish dishes goes back centuries. But the practice originated in the Middle East and was honed in the great courts of Shah Abbas and the Ottomans.

THE WALDORF STORY

This is a real crowd pleaser of a salad (unless you belong to the small percentage of the population that truly detests celery)—creaminess, crunchiness, sweetness—a perfect combo really.

The dish was famously created in 1896 by a guy called Oscar Tschirky, the *maître d'* of New York's Waldorf Hotel (later to become the Waldorf Astoria), for a society dinner. The original was a simple affair recorded thus in Tschirky's cookbook:

Peel two raw apples and cut them into small pieces, say about half an inch square, also cut some celery the same way and mix it with the apple. Be very careful not to let any seeds of the apples be mixed with it. The salad must be dressed with a good mayonnaise.

The walnuts got added in the 1920s, and since then all manner of bastardizations have appeared. Waldorf with peanuts, or carrot, or pear, or grapes, or yogurt, or pecans, or raisins, or celeriac, or cheese… It is a resilient recipe, however—the Waldorf Salad is one of the world's very few salad design classics. Hell, the great Cole Porter gave it a mention in his classic crooner-ville number *You're the Top*, and *Fawlty Towers* had a whole episode hinging around Basil's ignorance of what it involved.

For what it's worth I respectfully offer my rendition… along with a very Persian version on p.208.

WALDORF-ISH SALAD

TO SERVE 4

2 red apples

2 green apples

½ lemon

4 sticks of celery

⅓ cup/1¾oz/50g shelled walnut quarters

2 tbsp nice mayonnaise

1 tbsp crème fraîche (or use sour cream in a pinch)

salt and freshly ground black pepper

8 romaine lettuce leaves

Cut the apples around the "waists" of the fruit in crenelated (well, zigzag really—I just like the word crenellated) fashion so that you end up with 8 pointy apple halves. Core the fruit carefully with a pointy knife and excavate as much flesh as you can without damaging the apple shells. Rub the hollowed-out fruit and the reserved apple flesh with lemon juice to prevent discoloration.

Roughly dice the reserved apple with the celery and mix with the walnuts. Beat the mayo with the crème fraîche and season to taste before stirring through the apple/celery mixture.

Arrange the lettuce leaves on a platter or individual side plates then wedge the apple bases on top, using the lettuce to stabilize them. Spoon a quarter of the Waldorf filling into each apple, then cover each one with an apple top of the reverse color (so a green base gets a red lid and vice versa). Kitsch but fun, no?

SALAD-E-SHAH ABBASI:
A PERSIAN WALDORF

The Iranian equivalent of the Waldorf Astoria would probably be the Shah Abbas hotel in Isfahan: it's really fancy and very old.

TO SERVE 4–6

2 quinces
2 cloves
2 cardamom pods, cracked
1 tbsp sugar
3 tbsp apple vinegar
2 tbsp water
2 tbsp creamed *labneh* (or use cream cheese)

pinch of ground saffron steeped in
    2–3 tsp boiling water
salt and freshly ground black pepper
2 sticks of celery
2 pickled Iranian cucumbers (or use regular
    pickles but not sweet ones)
½ cup/2¾oz/75g shelled walnut quarters
2 tsp dried dill

Peel and quarter the quinces (leaving the core in) and place them in a small saucepan. Add the spices, sugar, and vinegar together with the water and bring the liquid to a boil. Poach/steam the fruit for about 15 minutes (you are looking merely to soften the quince, not to poach it to oblivion). Using a knife and a fork, remove the fruit quarters from the stock, slice out the cores, and lower them (seeds and all) back into the bubbling stock. Set the semi-cooked quince aside to cool.

Reduce the liquid by simmering it for another 10 minutes (during which time it should start to acquire a pretty pink color) then strain the resultant syrup into a jug. Beat in the *labneh* and saffron water and season to taste.

Next, chop the reserved quince roughly along with the celery and cucumber. Tip them into a bowl with the walnuts and dill, and stir in the creamy dressing. Serve with warm flatbread. And make a mental note of how fabulous quinces are and vow to use them more often.

DATE AND FETA SALAD

Dates and cheese are common plate-fellows, found at breakfast tables all over the Middle East, providing a simple lunch for desert nomads, or offering a nutritious repast for Ramadan sunsets. This is quite a rich salad, but is a winsome accompaniment to sharp or tomato-ey dishes. It is also a winner for *mezze*-style eating.

AS A SIDE DISH FOR 4
½ stale *barberi* bread, OR 1 stale *pide*
   (OR 2 slices of stale ordinary white bread)
pure olive oil, for frying
½ bunch of fresh cilantro
1 bunch (bag) of fresh arugula
12 fresh (or dried) dates
5½oz/150g real feta, cubed
about ½ cup/2¾oz/75g toasted hazelnut
   halves (or walnuts if, like me, you get a
   tingly tongue with hazelnuts)

1 sweet white onion (use a red onion if you
   can't find a white one), finely sliced

FOR THE DRESSING:
4 tbsp olive oil
2 tsp date syrup
3 tsp balsamic vinegar
handful of shredded fresh mint
salt and freshly ground black pepper

Cube your stale bread, then fry it with a little oil in a pan, turning regularly, until it is a pleasingly golden color. Set the croutons on paper towel to drain and cool.

Break the stalky bits off the cilantro and separate the rest into pretty, curly fronds. Mix it with the arugula leaves, and pile them into your favorite salad bowl.

Next, halve and pit the dates, then mix them gently with the cheese, nuts, onion slices, and croutons. Arrange the nutty cheese over the salad leaves, then whisk the dressing together and drizzle it over the top. *Bah bah!* (Which is what Persians say when they like the look of something.)

HARISSA SPICED FIG, *MERGUEZ*, AND ALMOND SALAD

This is a rather special salad. Actually, figs have the capacity to render pretty much anything special: their appearance is lush for starters—they have but to lie down on a plate or pose in a fruit bowl and they steal the show. They are also feted for their aphrodisiac properties: yup—they are the all-round floozy of the fruit world.

Fun fig fact: they would not have survived as a species if it wasn't for a tiny critter known as the fig wasp, *Blastophaga grossorum* (a name straight out of the *Hitchhikers Guide to the Galaxy*, surely), pollinating them. This must be the only useful recorded function of any wasp, anywhere.

BONUS RECIPE

This started off as a fig, prosciutto, and pistachio salad, but I decided that that was too predictable: if something weathers the storm of culinary cliché it becomes a classic, but fig and prosciutto ain't there yet. It is, however, undeniably delicious, so here's a quick summary. Prepare the figs in the same way, but instead of spices, just top them with a little brown sugar. Mix the grilled figs with some strips of prosciutto, sliced pistachios, and salad greens, then drizzle with a dressing of olive oil, raspberry vinegar, fresh mint, salt, and pepper. Add crumbled ricotta or goat cheese as optional extras.

FOR 2
½ tsp ground coriander
½ tsp ground cumin
¼ tsp smoked paprika
pinch of caraway seeds
pinch of red pepper flakes
½ tsp dried mint
pinch of salt
3 tsp runny honey
6 fresh figs
6 *merguez* sausages (or spicy Spanish chorizo)

smidge of oil
⅓ cup/1¼oz/35g slivered almonds
1¾oz/50g dark green salad leaves
handful of frisée (curly endive) lettuce

FOR THE DRESSING:
2 tbsp olive oil
1 tsp orange flower water
½ tsp harissa paste (optional: it is HOT)
1 tbsp balsamic vinegar
salt

Preheat the broiler. Mix the spices, mint, and salt with the honey. Make a cut through each fig from the top to within a few millimeters of the base, followed by another at right angles to the first cut, so that you effectively end up with a cross cut through the top of the fruit. Pinch the 4 quarters created by the incisions so that the fig opens up a bit like a flower, and divide the spiced honey between the figs. Broil them for around 1½ minutes until the fruit starts to sizzle. Turn the oven off, but leave the figs sitting there to retain their heat.

Slice the *merguez* on the diagonal into ½in/1cm thick oval slices. Heat a teeny bit of oil in a pan and cook the sausage for around 3 minutes, then remove with a slotted spoon. Toast the almonds in the same pan for a minute or so until they start to color.

Toss the greens in a bowl. Whisk the ingredients for the dressing together. Arrange the figs on top of the salad, and scatter with the *merguez* and almonds. Drizzle with the dressing and serve with crusty bread.

PRUNE AND BACON SALAD

This is based on Devils on Horseback, the classic Victorian dish of bacon-wrapped prunes.

A FUN STARTER FOR 2

12 fat pitted prunes

1 cup of Earl Grey tea

1 fat tbsp cream cheese

1 tbsp broken walnut pieces

1 tsp *za'atar**

4 rashers (slices) smoked Canadian back bacon

good handful of mustard leaves, watercress, batavia, escarole, and arugula—you choose the mix

1 bunch of fresh chives, snipped

2 tbsp olive oil

1 tbsp balsamic vinegar

1 tsp chutney

salt and freshly ground black pepper

Soak the prunes in the tea for about 1 hour. Meanwhile, preheat the broiler. Beat the cream cheese with the walnut and *za'atar*, and broil the bacon until it is pleasingly crispy.

When you are ready to assemble, drain the prunes and wipe dry. Make a small incision along the side of each one, and use a teaspoon to stuff them with the nutty spiced cheese. Chop the bacon into bite-sized pieces.

Mix the lettuce and the chives in a bowl. Whisk the oil, vinegar, chutney, and seasoning together (not forgetting that the cheese and bacon are both salty) and stir through the salad greens. Top with the prunes and bacon, and serve with sourdough (or some other fancy) bread.

* *Za'atar*

The classic Arabic seasoning of sumac, ground wild thyme, sesame seeds, and salt.

A SALMAGUNDI SALSA CLASS

A salsa is basically just a salad so finely chopped it resembles a chunky sauce. It is a lot easier to learn the art than it is to master the dance of the same name. Although dancing/cooking classes may indeed be the way forward.

The original concept evolved in Mexico, and (as with the word salad, in fact) the word is derived from the Spanish word for salt (*sal*), as at its simplest a salsa is micro-cubed anything seasoned with salt (salt draws the liquid out of most food, naturally creating a kind of sauce). The classic versions are *salsa rojo* (red salsa), which uses red tomatoes, garlic, and onion, and

salsa verde (green), which uses tomatillos and onion and cilantro. Usually the veggies or fruit in question are also seasoned with chili and lime juice, but there are a squillion variations and I rarely make the same combo twice. This style of salad creation is a conveniently quick way of using up mushy, bruised, less-than-perfect fresh fruit and veggies: you can chop more or less anything up into a salsa and serve it as a sandwich filler or a side dish or a relish. It is also a good number for dieters, since authentically salsas don't feature oil. I have included three in this chapter as my favorite salsas always seem to involve fruit.

PERSIAN CUCUMBER AND POMEGRANATE SALSA

FOR A BOWLFUL— SALAD FOR 6

1 luscious, large pomegranate
    (in summer you could use
    redcurrants)
1 medium cucumber, finely diced
2–3 tomatoes, finely diced
1 green pepper, finely diced
1 hot chili, chopped
½ bunch each of fresh mint
    and cilantro, chopped
1 bunch of scallions, finely diced
salt and freshly ground
    black pepper
drizzle of olive oil
juice of 1 lime

This is just knockout as accompaniments go—a really lovely salad, appetizer, or relish depending on your requirements. It's a looker and it takes nanoseconds to make.

First, make sure that you are wearing pomegranate-colored clothes (or perhaps put an apron on). Cut the pomegranate in half with a sharp knife, and with your fingers gently prize free the seeds, pulling off any pith as you go. Mix them together with all the other ingredients, stir well, cover, and chill until needed.

HOT KIWI SALSA *SUPER-HEALTHY*

TO SERVE 2 AS
A SIDE DISH

3 ripe kiwi fruits, peeled
    and diced
1 small red onion,
    finely chopped
1 small ripe avocado, peeled,
    pitted, and diced
2 green chilies, chopped
big handful of fresh cilantro,
    chopped
juice of 1 lime
dash of olive oil
sea salt

Kiwis are great in salads; their sharpness and juiciness mean that they need little extra dressing.

Just shake it all together baby. But gently so, otherwise you'll end up mashing the avocado. This salsa is a perfect pal for smoked meat and fish.

KASHMIRI-STYLE SALSA

A SIDE DISH FOR 4

8 tamarind pods (or use around
    2¾oz/75g pressed deseeded
    tamarind)
2 ripe mangoes, peeled, pitted,
    and diced
8 small florets cauliflower,
    broken into tiny pieces
¾in/2cm knob fresh ginger,
    peeled and minced
1 level tsp hot curry powder
    crushed with a little sea salt
2 tsp tamarind concentrate
    mixed with 3 tbsp cold water
dash of oil

Mango and tamarind are lifelong plate-fellows: the ineffable sweetness of one perfectly complimented by the crabby sharpness of the other. Bit like Mr. Shopkeeper and I.*

Remove the hard outer casing of the pods, then pull away the stringy bits encasing the fruit. Prise out and discard the stones and chop the remaining tamarind flesh (if you are using the pressed stuff, just chop it).

Mix the tamarind, mango, cauliflower, and ginger together. Mix the curry into the tamarind liquid, add a little oil, check the seasoning, and stir it through the salsa. This works well with cheese or poultry.

*This is a joke. I am really not that sharp or crabby.

POACHED PLUM SALAD WITH PECANS

AN EARLY FALL
TREAT FOR 2–3

¾ cup /5½oz/150g sugar

⅔ cup/150ml water

1¼ cups/300ml dry hard cider

¾in/2cm knob fresh ginger,
    peeled and diced

3–4 allspice berries,
    lightly crushed

⅓ tsp red pepper flakes

just over 1lb/500g plums, halved

⅓ cup/1¾oz/50g shelled pecan
    pieces (or walnuts)

3oz/80g mixed salad greens

1 red onion, sliced

¼ cucumber, peeled and sliced
    into half moon shapes

5½oz/150g Roquefort cheese,
    crumbled

1 tbsp balsamic vinegar

2–3 tbsp extra-virgin olive oil

⅓ tsp ground black pepper

salt

* BONUS COCKTAIL
RECIPE:

Rub the rims of 2 glasses with
a slice of lime, then dunk
them into sugar to achieve that
pro-frosted look. Fill the
glasses with crushed ice and
to each add a scant ½ cup/
100ml tonic water, followed
by the remaining plum syrup,
small shot of Calvados, ½
small shot Triple Sec, and the
juice of ½ lime. Garnish
further with lime, cucumber,
and mint. A prize for whoever
comes up with the best name
for this little creation…

One of our customers is from Bulgaria and recounted this rather fun plum-related Bulgarian folk tale to us one day. I do feel that plum-related Bulgarian folk tales are probably best shared, so if you're sitting comfortably…

Once upon a sugar plum, in old Plovdiv (which those who can pronounce it may know as Philippopolis), there lived a wily market farmer and his five sons. The farmer was anxious to find a wife for the eldest boy; but he wanted a girl as virtuous as she was beautiful, and pondered how he could find such a maiden.

It was late summer and his plum trees were groaning with fruit. This gave our farmer an idea, and he set about boxing up all the plums. On market day he set off with a tower of fruit and a determined look on his face. He set up stall, but when his regular customers demanded the price, he requested that they pay in household dust. The women assumed the old boy had lost his marbles, but eagerly rushed home to sweep up whatever dust they could find. The farmer kept his word and measure for measure exchanged his crop for dust: he soon had a big pile of dust… and a crestfallen expression. There had been plenty of pretty girls buying his fruit but he knew that none of them matched his requirements.

Just as he was clearing up, an attractive, thoughtful-looking lass with raven locks and deep, velvety eyes came to hover by the stall. "How much are your plums, sir?" she asked. "I've heard that today you are charging in dust: I couldn't find much I am afraid. Do you have any left? I couldn't get here earlier as my folks are sickly and I had to run their errands before I could think of my own."

At this the old man noticed that she was clutching the smallest bag of dust. "Well if that's all you've got, my dear…" he said, smiling enigmatically, "You'd better take the rest of my load." And with that he gave the astonished girl two whole boxes of juicy red plums. "Just one thing: I would love to see what you make of the fruit. My son and I are heading this way tomorrow: may we call on you?" The girl happily showed the farmer where she lived, and set off with her load. And the farmer for his part did a little ancient Bulgarian happy dance…

Rumor has it that she prepared this lovely salad for them. But I wouldn't be listening to rumors if I were you.

Put the sugar, water, cider, and spices into a little saucepan and bring to a boil. Carefully lower in the plum halves and poach them for 10–15 minutes, or until just cooked (watch them carefully otherwise you will end up making jam). Remove the fruit with a slotted spoon, but leave the poaching liquid simmering so that it reduces by three-quarters.

Toast the pecan pieces in a frying pan for around 2 minutes, stirring constantly.

When you are ready to serve, toss the salad leaves, onion, cucumber, cheese, and pecans in a bowl. Place the remaining ingredients in a jug and strain a scant ¼ cup/50ml of the remaining syrup into it (keep the rest to add to your evening cocktail*); whisk well and adjust the seasoning to taste. Arrange the still-warm plums on top of the salad and cover with the dressing. Serve with warm bread and try not to drool.

HERBED GRAPEFRUIT SALAD WITH SMOKED SALMON

This lovely if odd salad works as a foil for more or less any smoked or rich fish and meat dishes.

One tends to forget about grapefruit, no? It was one of the original slimming super-foods, then it became one of the most hackneyed appetizers of all time, then it got a bad press for not being very helpful for those on certain types of medication. Nowadays it seems mostly to be the preserve of boarding house breakfast buffets. But you know, it's a corker in salad. It can give savory dishes some real oomph.

This recipe evolved out of an uncharacteristic moment of weakness one day when I entrusted the mister with my grocery list. Men are quite shocking at shopping, no? All those little extras that fall into their baskets... and the essentials that they just somehow "forget" to buy. I never have any trouble eating smoked salmon, but presented with a fridge of largely random ingredients, rather than scowl at aforementioned spouse ungraciously, I decided to do something a bit different with them...

A FUNKY STARTER FOR 4
2 medium grapefruits
1 lime
½ sweet (mild, white) onion, finely sliced
big handful of fresh cilantro, chopped
few sprigs of fresh basil, shredded
few sprigs of fresh dill (or use ½ tsp dried)
2½ tbsp olive oil

½ small stick of fresh lemongrass
  (or use 1 tsp dried)
salt and coarsely ground black pepper
7oz/200g package smoked salmon (it may be a
  little too much, but you're going to pick
  at it, obviously, then there's the cat)

✳ Melba Toast: *easy peasy to make your own.*

Toast 2–3 pieces of regular (stale if you like) sliced bread, then put it flat on a chopping board and cut through it horizontally so you end up with very thin squares of bread. Preheat the broiler and spread the squares out, untoasted side up, on your grill rack. Cook until the bread just starts to color, then leave for 5–10 minutes for the bread to crisp up. Perfect, thrifty, useful, and great with salads. Pat yourself on the back.

Using a narrow, sharp knife, remove the top and bottom of the grapefruits so that you remove most of the pith. Sit them flat on your chopping board and slice down around the fruit carefully, removing the peel and pith; chop the fruit firstly into thin slices, before cutting each slice into half so you end up with semi-circular pieces. Remove any obvious seeds, then place them in a bowl, tipping any surplus juice into a smaller separate bowl.

Grate the zest of the lime and add it to the smaller bowl, then cut the lime in half and squeeze the juice of one half into the small bowl as well. Remove the skin from the second lime half and dice the flesh, discarding any seeds, before adding it to the slice grapefruit. Add the sliced onion and fresh herbs and mix gently.

Whisk the olive oil into the citrus juice. Purée the lemongrass (whether using fresh or dried) and add this to the dressing along with a little salt and pepper.

When you are ready to serve, add the salmon to the grapefruit salad and drizzle with the dressing. Serve with bread and butter, or better still, Melba toast* (to get another 70s food fad out of the closet).

DODO (PLANTAIN) SALAD

This is a lot of fun since it is served on a plantain (or banana) leaf. Plantain leaves are big (in every sense) in the East, where they are used for wrapping and steaming and baking food, as well as on which to serve stuff. The leaves are full of phytonutrients, which it is believed are imparted on to foodstuffs served thereon. Any which way, it will make a change from your finest Limoges or discount store platters (although clearly these will have to suffice if you cannot source the real thing), and what's not to like about biodegradable crockery?

Plantains are just not-very-sweet bananas but they still have lots of flavor. The green ones can be quite cloying and are better incorporated into hot, more complex dishes: the blacker ones are much sweeter and can be enjoyed butter-fried on their own (another favorite shopkeeper lunch: especially good with some sneaky bacon added). If you can't find plantains, use sweet potatoes.

A BARBECUE/BUFFET SALAD
FOR 6 (ISH)

1 cup/5½oz/150g raw shelled peanuts
splash of peanut (or non-extra-virgin olive) oil
1 tsp smoked paprika
sea salt
4 black-ish plantains, peeled and cut into
    ¾in/2cm chunks
1 tbsp butter for frying, and a splash of oil to
    stop the butter burning
2 bunches of scallions, chopped
4–5 garlic cloves, finely sliced
1 red bell pepper, diced
1 green bell pepper, diced

1 small bunch of fresh cilantro
1 large plantain/banana leaf, rinsed and
    thoroughly dried, to serve

FOR THE CHILI DRESSING:
4 tomatoes
scant ¼ cup/50ml extra-virgin
    olive oil
1 tbsp peanut butter
1 tsp hot sauce (although strengths
    and tastes vary, so add to taste)
juice of 1–2 limes
salt

* Heads-up on plantain leaf table etiquette

In India and parts of the Far East, leaves are always served with the pointy end pointing towards a diner's left hand. Furthermore, it is customary, if you have enjoyed your food, to fold the leaf in towards you: conversely, if you think your food was a bit lousy, you can fold the side furthest away from you outwards and the chef will get the message.

Preheat the oven to 375°F/190°C.

Coat the peanuts in a little oil and sprinkle with smoked paprika and salt before spreading them out on a baking tray and roasting them for around 10 minutes; allow to cool (hot peanuts will burn your tongue, so no picking).

Fry the plantain cubes in melted butter/oil until they are pleasantly browned, before draining them on paper towel.

Toss the scallions, garlic, peppers, and cilantro together, then stir in the plantain.

Plunge the tomatoes into boiling water then peel and chop them finely before beating them together with the other dressing ingredients.

Arrange the salad on the plantain leaf,* sprinkle with the peanuts, and serve the dressing in a bowl on the side.

ENSALADA DE AVOCADO AND PINEAPPLE: A POSTCARD FROM CUBA

I used to make this Cuban classic regularly when I was going through my South American phase. This consisted mostly of eating *fajitas*, hanging around at Ronnie Scott's Jazz Club, and listening to lots of Arturo Sandoval, so we're not talking very radical here.

The two prime ingredients are not obvious salad *compadres*, but bound together with chili, lime, and mint they become a sort of salad *mojito*. Add a scattering of nice shrimp and the dish becomes an appetizer already.

AN UNUSUAL SIDE
SALAD FOR 4

FOR THE DRESSING:
3 tbsp extra-virgin olive oil
juice and grated zest of 1 lime
1 green chili, minced
big handful of fresh mint, shredded
½ tsp Angostura bitters* (optional but great)
salt

FOR THE SALAD PROPER:
1 small pineapple, skinned and cubed
2 firm, just-ripe avocados, peeled,
    pitted, and chunked
1 red onion, sliced

TO SERVE:
4 cocktail glasses or ice-cream coupes
1 lime, halved
sprinkle of superfine sugar
wee shake of salt
1 big bunch of watercress

Shake all the dressing ingredients together in a cocktail shaker (yes: an empty jar will do). If you can, leave it for at least 30 minutes for the flavors to mingle. Mix the salad ingredients together gently in a bowl.

When you are ready to serve, rub one half of the lime around the rims of your chosen serving vessels. Mix a little sugar and salt together on a plate and roll the wet glass rims in the mixture to frost them. Next, arrange the watercress carefully in the base of each dish, topped with the pineapple mixture. Drizzle with the dressing, then slice the rest of the lime and put a slice atop each salad. Serve your salad cocktails alongside barbecued fish or chicken, accompanied of course by some real *mojitos*.

*Useless bitters
factoid:
This is one of the world's quickest home cures for diarrhoea: to quote somebody's aunt, "it'll have you passing concrete in no time." It is also a quick remedy for hiccups. Not a lot of people know that.

BOK L'HONG: SOUR GREEN PAPAYA SALAD

There's a lot going on in this salad: the first time I made it and plonked it in front of my mostly unappreciative guinea pigs,* they were hard put to identify what they were eating—but they did finish it with relish, which is always a relief. It's got sweet, sour, salty, crunchy, bitter, *umami*—and for this reason I like to serve it as an appetizer rather than an accompaniment, but it is most often eaten as street food in Laos and Cambodia (usually as a sidekick to *Larb*, see p.190). If you want to make a meal of it, you could add crayfish or shredded chicken.

A TONGUE-TICKLING SIDE DISH OR STARTER FOR 4

3½oz/100g green beans, topped and tailed and cut into 2–2½in/5–6cm pieces

1 medium green papaya (use an unripe mango if you really can't find papaya), peeled

1 fat carrot, peeled

4 garlic cloves, peeled

1–2 red (bird's eye) chilies, destalked

4–5 anchovies (authentically shrimp paste, but anchovies make a fine substitute)**

1 tbsp fish sauce

2 tsp soft brown sugar

juice of 2 limes

1 tbsp toasted sesame oil

big handful of fresh cilantro, chopped

½ cup/2¾oz/75g unsalted but roasted peanuts, roughly chopped

Bring a small pan of water to a boil and blanch the green beans for 2 minutes before refreshing and leaving them to drain.

Deseed the papaya and grate it*** along with the carrot. Toss them together with the green beans in a bowl.

Place the garlic, chilies, and anchovies in a mortar and pound with a pestle (or improvise in a small bowl using the handle of a knife) before adding the fish sauce, sugar, lime juice, and oil. Spoon the sauce over the salad, mixing well, then top with the cilantro and peanuts. Serve with crisp bread or shrimp chips.

* Notes

One's nearest and dearest are always one's sternest critics, which is good news for you as they are not afraid to speak up if they think something is inedible/tasteless/weird/unmitigated rubbish.

** Vegetarians and vegans can get around the whole fish sauce/paste thing by deploying miso paste mixed with soy sauce.

*** Handy papaya grating hint of the day. Either wear gloves or oil your hands: this is one sticky fruit and you could otherwise end up washing your hands obsessively for the rest of the day.

CHAPTER ELEVEN
Salads for dessert

Can't write a book without a dessert section! Fruit salad as we know and (may or may not) love it has been around since the nineteenth century, but the idea of mixing fruit and nuts by way of a repast has been around for millennia. I grew up in a time (OK—the 1970s—I admit it) when fruit salad mostly came out of a can and consisted of rather dire, oversweet mini cubes of often unidentifiable slimy fruit broken up with bits of candied cherry for added excitement. Fresh fruit salad was mostly of the orange, apple, pear, and banana variety, with grapes providing the highlight. So I would like to think that with this chapter I will be able to expunge all thoughts of that canned past: please find here below spiced creams, cake croutons, and all manner of naughty add-ons to raise that erstwhile "healthy option" into the dessert of choice rather than the dieter's punishment.

KHOSHAB/HAFT MEWA: CENTRAL ASIAN DRIED FRUIT SALAD

This may well be the first ever recipe for fruit salad, although the dish is prized as much for the fruit juice produced as for the fruit "salad" itself.

In Afghanistan and across Central Asia, *Nowrooz*, or the New Year, is one of the biggest holidays of the year. The origins of the festival (which falls on the Spring equinox) are almost certainly as old as the human race itself, as it pertains to the seasons, and the miraculous rebirth of spring, and the banishment of wicked winter. The traditions attached to it are equally archaic and earthy, none more so than the business of each house arranging a spread of seven items representing thanks for the year gone by and wishes for the year ahead. For Iranians this is done in the form of the *haft sin*, or seven items beginning with the letter "s" (in Farsi, naturally), but in Afghanistan and the other "istans" it is more common to present seven plates of fruit and nuts (or *haft mewa*), which are subsequently soaked and made into a salad. The traditional ingredients are apricots, large raisins, small and large golden raisins, pistachios, *senjed* (or wild Russian olive—aka the fruit of the oleaster), and almonds, but nowadays there are probably as many recipes for it as there are valleys in the Hindu Kush. The following is a Westernized user-friendly version based on the way my store customers make it.

AN ANCIENT TREAT FOR 4

generous ½ cup/3½oz/100g (preferably organic) dried apricots
generous ¼ cup/1¾oz/50g golden raisins
1¾oz/50g dried figs
scant ⅔ cup/3½oz/100g plump raisins
2–3 cloves

2–3 cinnamon sticks
⅔ cup/3½oz/100g raw almonds
⅓ cup/1¾oz/50g walnuts
⅓ cup/1¾oz/50g pistachios
2 tbsp rose water

Wash the fruit well, place it in a bowl, and cover it with cold water (allowing 1½–2in/ 4–5 cm extra above the surface of the fruit). Add the cloves and cinnamon and allow to soak for about 2 days.

When the 2 days are up, put the nuts into a different bowl and pour boiling water over them. Leave to soak for 2 hours then drain them, at which point you should be able to peel the skin off the nuts. Add them to the fruit and its soaking water, along with the rose water.

The juice thus produced is known as *khoshab* (literally "happy water") and is sometimes drained off and enjoyed separately. The fruit itself is served chilled: I particularly like it with a blob of honey-sweetened yogurt on the side, because that's the sort of devil-may-care kind of girl that I am.

RUJAK: SPICY SUMATRAN FRUIT SALAD

This is a taste sensation: a nutty, spicy, and yet undeniably sweet fruit salad. It is ubiquitous in the streets and markets of Malaysia and Indonesia, although every vendor seems to make it differently. It is a kind of sweet, Asian version of salmagundi. This is my (user-friendly, slightly Westernized) take on the dish.

STREET FOOD FOR 4–6
flesh of ½ medium coconut

1 green apple, cored

¼ medium pineapple, peeled

½ cucumber

1 guava (or pear), peeled and cored

1 small mango, peeled and pitted

1 (pink-fleshed) sweet potato

juice of 1 lime

1 (7oz/200g) block of firm tofu

toasted sesame oil, for frying

FOR THE SAUCE:
1 tbsp tamarind concentrate

1 tbsp peanut butter

1 tbsp rice vinegar (or just use white wine vinegar)

1 tbsp honey

2 tsp palm sugar (or soft brown sugar)

¼ tsp shrimp paste (it is worth the effort to source this)

1 tsp chili paste (less if it just seems too weird for you)

Retaining a little of the coconut, cut all the "fruit" except the sweet potato into ½–¾ in/ 1–2cm cubes and mix in a bowl. Dress with the lime juice and set aside.

Grind the tamarind, peanut butter, vinegar, honey, sugar, and pastes together in a mortar and pestle, then add just enough water to render it almost pourable.

Cut the tofu into ½–¾ in/1–2cm cubes and fry it in hot sesame oil until golden all over. Drain on paper towel.

Now peel and cube the sweet potato and add it to the fruit salad (yes, you can eat them raw in small quantities) along with the fried tofu, then spoon the dressing over it, mixing well. Spoon into little bowls and grate the reserved coconut over each portion by way of a decoration. Stand back and watch your guests' faces turn from expressions of disbelief to delight.

TROPICAL FRUIT BOWL WITH FRIED CAKE CROUTONS

Tropical fruit salad used to mean that the dish had been shown a slice of pineapple. This number is a little more exotic than that. If you do happen to live somewhere where the arrival of a mango in the village is a matter of parish-wide wonderment, well, you'll have to improvise.

A FUNSTER DESSERT FOR 6
FOR THE SYRUP:

⅔ cup/150ml cup water

⅔ cup/150ml orange juice

¾ cup/5½oz/150g brown sugar

3 cinnamon sticks

2 star anise

¼ tsp grated nutmeg

juice and grated zest of 2 limes

5 tbsp/75ml dark rum (optional but mighty fine)

FOR THE SALAD:

1 papaya, peeled, deseeded, and cubed

1 mango, peeled and cut into chunks as best as possible

3 kiwis, peeled and cubed

½ medium pineapple, cubed

roughly 9oz/250g cubed melon—any variety will do, including watermelon

3 fat passion fruit

big pat of butter plus a little oil to prevent burning

5½oz/150g spongy cake (stale is fine, brioche works well), cubed

scant 1 cup/2¾oz/75g dry unsweetened coconut

First, make the syrup. Place the water, orange juice, sugar, spices, and lime zest in a pan, bring to a boil, turn down the heat, and simmer for around 10 minutes, or until the sugar is dissolved. Add the lime juice and rum, simmer for a few minutes more, then take off the heat and allow to cool.

Mix the prepared fruit in a bowl. Halve the passion fruits and scoop the contents into the bowl as well. Strain the cooled syrup over the fruit and mix gently.

When you are ready to serve, melt the butter/oil in a small pan and toss in the cake. Just as it starts to brown, add the coconut, stirring well so it doesn't catch. Take off the heat and drain the coconutty croutons on paper towel before sprinkling over the fruit salad. Serve as it is or with crème fraîche or whipped cream for added naughtiness.

BOOZY VINE FRUIT SALAD

Alcoholic fruit salad? It's a no-brainer and of course they'll love it. This one is rich and unusual, since it only uses grapes. It is also dangerously addictive. It is easy to assemble, but the fruit needs 4–6 hours to macerate, so start early.

AN ENDLESSLY POPULAR PUD FOR 4

generous 1 cup/250ml water

½ cup/3½oz/100g soft dark brown sugar

2½ tbsp Amaretto

9oz/250g green grapes, halved and deseeded

7oz/200g red grapes, halved and deseeded

2 cardamom pods, lightly crushed

generous ¾ cup/200ml black tea

scant ⅔ cup/3½oz/100g raisins*

generous ½ cup/3½oz/100g golden raisins*

⅔ cup/150ml white wine (use "leftovers" if you like)

⅔ cup/3½oz/100g raw almonds

2 tsp butter

2 tsp brown sugar

around 1½ cups/350ml crème fraîche

Put the water and sugar in a little saucepan and bring to a boil. Turn down the heat and simmer for about 10 minutes, or until all the sugar has dissolved, then add 2 tablespoons of the Amaretto. Bubble for just a minute more then take off the heat and allow to cool a little before pouring over the halved grapes. Cover and chill for 4–6 hours.

Add the cardamoms to the tea in a small bowl, then tip the raisins in, stirring well. Again, cover and set aside for 2–3 hours. Likewise with the golden raisins; cover them with the wine and chill.

Shortly before you are ready to serve, sizzle the almonds in the butter in a frying pan. Add the sugar and the reserved Amaretto, stirring well, and cook for about a minute longer or until the nuts start to caramelize.

Drain a little of the macerating liquid from the fruits: you want to use some of it for flavor, but if you add too much you will end up with fruit soup (albeit nice, alcoholic fruit soup). You will need 4 pretty sundae or cocktail glasses. Place a spoonful of crème fraîche in the base of each dish, followed by a layer of the grapes, a layer of the raisins, and a layer of the golden raisins. Repeat until the fruit is all used up, then top with the caramelized nuts and another spoonful of the crème fraîche. Serve immediately, perhaps with some biscotti and a fancy dessert wine.

*Note on currants

Haha! Bet at least half of you are really quite hazy as to the difference between types of raisins. I conducted a mini-poll in my store, and only 2 out of 20 customers asked knew what was what on the vine fruit front. Raisin is a general term for dried grapes. Sultanas (or golden raisins) are a smaller, rounder, sweeter, seedless type (unless you buy Iranian green sultanas, which are huge). Currants are also raisins (and quite unrelated to blackcurrants and redcurrants—who knew?), originally from Corinth, whence they get their name.

MINTED LETTUCE AND STRAWBERRY SALAD

This is a delightfully simple salad. Let's face it: strawberries have to work less hard than other fruits to get the oohs and aahs and curtain calls—and so we will let them do most of the talking in this recipe. It is a great little number to prepare if you are, um, trying to ~~get lucky~~ impress. The dish goes particularly well with a cheeseboard chaser.

Random strawberry lore: in Bavaria lucky cattle get little baskets of strawberries tied to their horns as an offering to the region's elves. Seems the little green folk are inordinately fond of berries, and it is believed that in return the elves will promote healthy calving across the herd.

A SASSY LITTLE PUD FOR 2

¼ small iceberg lettuce

1 container (around 16) really juicy strawberries, hulled

½ cup/2¾oz/75g pumpkin seed kernels (an aphrodisiac, by all accounts), toasted

big handful of fresh mint, julienned

1 tsp maple syrup (or golden syrup/ dark corn syrup)

2 tsp balsamic vinegar

pinch of salt

½ tsp ground black pepper

1 tube candy powder (like Pixy Stix)

Shred the lettuce roughly and quarter the berries. Toss them gently in a bowl along with the seeds and mint, then arrange the salad in a couple of fancy glasses—wide champagne flutes or sundae coupes will do. Whisk the dressing ingredients together and trickle over the salads. Top with the powder. Good luck and all that…

PEACH SALAD WITH CHILIED GINGER CREAM DRESSING

I love peaches and I love spices. Which makes this dessert a creation of pure self indulgence.*

A LUSCIOUS TREAT FOR 4

1 red bird's eye chili, roughly chopped (add more or less according to your tolerance levels/level of chili addiction)

1½in/4cm knob fresh ginger, peeled and chopped

3–4 brown cardamom pods, "bruised"

2 cloves

5 tbsp soft brown sugar

scant ¼ cup/50ml water

3 tsp raspberry vinegar

8 tbsp/4½oz/125g softened butter

2 tbsp heavy cream

4 practically perfect peaches

1 cup/5½oz/150g blueberries

1¼ cups/5½oz/150g pert-looking raspberries

handful of fresh basil leaves, shredded

First, wrap the spices in a piece of cheesecloth and tie it with (pristine) string (as opposed to the bit that's been knocking around at the back of the kitchen drawer for 3 years). Or do what I do and shove them inside a tea infuser.

Next, put the sugar, water, and vinegar into a pan and heat slowly until the sugar dissolves. Add the butter, cream, and spice bag and leave to bubble very gently for around 2 minutes. Remove the spices and keep the sauce warmish until you are ready to serve.

Pit the peaches and cut them into thin slices, then mix them carefully with the berries and basil. Dress with the still-warm sauce.

* Note

The fact that I have developed a wee dairy intolerance in the last year or so doesn't cramp my style in the slightest, as oat cream is tastier than real cream (soy cream ain't bad either)—although it is always possible that as a cock-eyed optimist I might just have convinced myself that this is the case.

WATERMELON BOAT SALAD WITH FENNEL

Little melon boats with candied cherry pennants and prociutto sails. Hands up who remembers those? They probably still exist somewhere, but when I grew up they were the height of exotic on menus up and down the land. The thing is, melons are kind of destined to be made into little boats: it's all in the shape. Similarly, watermelons are just asking to be made into big boats and punch bowls.

This salad is a great party dessert—light and yet fun, great for sharing. I will leave it up to you as to whether you fashion a dinky sail and adorn it with silly cocktail paraphernalia.

A PALATE CLEANSING DESSERT FOR 6

1 large bulb fennel
scant ½ cup/100ml water
⅔ cup/150ml orange juice
juice and grated zest of 1 lime
1 tbsp honey
¾in/2cm knob fresh ginger, peeled and minced
2 tsp orange flower water
2 tbsp Cointreau (optional)
1 small cucumber
½ medium round watermelon
2 oranges
few sprigs of fresh mint

Trim the fennel (retaining any pretty fronds) and slice it fairly thinly lengthways, then halve the slices crossways—you are aiming for 2in/5cm strips. Place it in a little pan with the water, juices, zest, honey, ginger, flower water, and Cointreau, if using. Bring to a boil, then turn down the heat to simmer for 20 minutes.

Meanwhile, halve the cucumber lengthways, scrape out the seeds, then cut it crossways into quarters (again, you are aiming for 2in/5cm strips). Cut the flesh lengthways into thin strips (a mandolin would be handy). After the first 20 minutes of poaching time, add the cucumber to the pan, and cook for around 10 minutes more until both the fennel and cucumber are tender. Remove the vegetables from the pan (retaining the poaching liquid) and allow to cool.

Halve the watermelon and cut the fruit out carefully, discarding as many of the seeds as possible. Cube the flesh and place it in a bowl. Use a small sharp knife to remove the peel and pith from the oranges, and remove the seeds. Pull them into segments then cut these in half and add them to the melon, along with the cooled fennel and cucumber. Spoon the salad into the empty melon shell, drizzle any remaining poaching liquid on top, and decorate with mint together with any retained fennel fronds.

POACHED AUTUMN FRUIT SALAD WITH ELDERFLOWER CUSTARD

Autumn is generous in her bounty, as she brings us the most fragrant of produce with which to play. Quince and elderflowers are both imbued with the headiest of scents: this combined with the cinnamon, cardamom, and nutmeg in the recipe below will have them drooling at your kitchen window.

In fact in the Middle East quinces are oft times purchased purely for the fragrance they emit just hanging around in the fruit bowl (they certainly aren't bought for their looks, as they are the knobbliest of fruits).

A FRAGRANT TREAT FOR 5–6
FOR THE COMPOTE:
2 medium quinces*
scant ¼ cup/50ml water
1 tbsp honey
2 cinnamon sticks
2 cardamom pods, bashed a bit
6 damsons** (or use regular plums), halved
    and pitted
generous 1⅓ cups/7oz/200g blackberries

FOR THE CUSTARD***:
6 egg yolks
2 tbsp superfine sugar
1 tsp all-purpose flour
½ vanilla bean
generous 2 cups/550ml whole milk
4 tbsp elderflower syrup

Peel the quinces (if they are very fluffy you may wish to wear gloves, as the fluff can cause mild irritation) and core them, retaining the seeds (see note). Place them in a small pan with the water, honey, and spices and bring to a gentle boil. Simmer for around 15 minutes before adding the plums. Cook for another 5 minutes, stir, then carefully add the blackberries. Simmer for a final 5 minutes then take off the heat.

Next, whisk the egg yolks, sugar, and flour together until they are quite creamed and pale. Put the vanilla and milk in a saucepan and slowly bring them to a boil before taking them off the heat. Leave the vanilla to infuse for around 15 minutes before removing it. Add the syrup to the milk and bring it back to just under boiling point, before adding a little to the creamed egg mixture, stirring well. Keep adding and stirring until all the milk has been incorporated. Now, in theory you are supposed to cook the custard in a double boiler (i.e. a bowl set over a pan of boiling water), but if you have a heat infuser or a gas stove with super-low settings, you can dispense with this: just pour the custard back into the milk pan and heat over a low flame very slowly, stirring with a wooden spoon, until it thickens and coats the back of the spoon. Pour into a jug. It is actually a crime NOT to lick out the pan at this stage.

Serve the fruit compote warm or chilled with warm or chilled custard.

* A note on quinces

The quince is one of nature's best cough remedies. Keep the seeds and steep them in a little boiling water. Drink the resultant mucilaginous gloop. Curse the food writer who made you do it, but trust her anyway. They are a demulcent, and will help clear your chest. If you are stewing quinces on their own, leave the seeds in, as these are what give the cooked fruit its famous pink hue.

* *

A note on damsons

Damsons are super-plummy plums and it is well worth the effort of trying to source them. You can even find them growing wild in some regions. A word of warning, though: when raw, they are cheek-suckingly sour. You should also know that they were once used as a dye for clothes: meaning you should totally wear an apron when handling them.

* * *

A note on custard

My mother is a domestic goddess in my eyes but I don't remember her ever making real custard, and I was thus raised on a diet including plenty of Birds instant custard. It is good stuff, so if you are in a hurry, cheat. Canned custard, however, is an abomination.

MOROCCAN DATE AND ORANGE PLATTER

Versions of this are ubiquitous by way of dessert in Morocco and after a rich meal there is nothing finer. I also like serving this at breakfast when I am showing off: little, thoughtful gestures like this allow me, albeit fleetingly, to appear more Martha Stewart than Ma Kettle.

A PALATE CLEANSING
DESSERT FOR 4

3 oranges

around 16 dates, pitted and
    quartered lengthways

½ cup/1¾oz/50g slivered almonds, lightly
    toasted

1½ tbsp rose water

1 level tsp ground cinnamon

handful of fresh mint, chopped

Use a thin-bladed sharp knife to remove the skin and pith from the oranges; slice them into thin circles, removing any seeds as you go. Arrange them on 4 plates (or a big platter) and arrange the dates and almonds on top. Sprinkle with the rose water, cinnamon, and mint and serve.

RICOTTA WITH HONEY
AND PAPAYA

I have never figured the strangely addictive nature of ricotta: it is to all intents and purposes tasteless, and yet one spoon is never enough. Because of its capacity to swing both ways (sweet or savory), not to mention the fact that as cheeses go it is very low fat, it is a useful ingredient to have in your fridge for last-minute creations. This composed dessert salad takes 5 minutes tops to make.

A SUPER-SIMPLE SWEET
SALAD FOR 2
1 tbsp honey, slightly warmed
2 tsp fresh orange juice
1 sprig of fresh thyme

1 small papaya, cut into elegant thin slices
(or use mango, kiwi, or nectarine...)
2/3 cup/5½oz/150g ricotta, cut into thin slices
pinch of sea salt
fresh mint leaves, to decorate

Whisk the honey, orange juice, and thyme together and set aside for the flavors to marry. Arrange alternating slices of the papaya and ricotta on 2 side plates, sprinkling the latter with the teensiest pinch of sea salt as you go. Drizzle with the honey and decorate with the mint.

CHAPTER TWELVE

Dips: the not-quite-salad salad

Now I had a bit of dilemma with this: are dips salads? The Greek certainly
think so: *taramasalata, melitzanosalat...* . They do comprise ingredients with
a sauce, and are usually served in the same manner. Well, I love dips: they are
versatile enough to be vamped up into a meal, thinned down to make a dressing,
and enjoyed as an anytime snack. So I have given them their own
chapter anyway.

CACIK, TSATSIKI, JAJIK, MUST-O-KHIAR:
YOGURT WITH CUCUMBER

TO SERVE 6–8
AS AN APPETIZER

½ regular cucumber (or about
    5 baby ones)
generous 2 cups /500ml plain
    yogurt
3–4 garlic cloves, crushed
1 small onion, diced
2 tsp dried mint
2 tbsp olive oil
salt and freshly ground
    black pepper

You have all had a version of this dish I am sure. Every nation in the lands east of Athens and west of Tokyo makes something like it. The combo of cooling yogurt and even more cooling cucumber is a natural for mopping the sweat of summer heat and soothing spice-scorched taste buds.

Central Asia prepares a more soupy version, sometimes with dill or sumac, while in Iran, raisins, walnuts, and rose petals are sometimes added. Indian cuisine, of course, offers you *raitha*. This is your basic Greek or Turkish taverna recipe.

Most Middle Eastern chefs would have you peel your cucumber first. I don't: the skin is such a pretty color. They would also suggest that you grate it, which I also don't do: grating bruises a vegetable so (which means that the end product will become watery or "go bad" more quickly). Instead (I suggest that you) dice the cucumber very finely, then stir it into the yogurt. Add the garlic, onion, and mint, beat in the olive oil (which helps to thicken the yogurt and gives it a lovely sheen), and season to taste.

BORANI-YE-BADEMJUN

FOR A SMALL
BOWLFUL

2 medium eggplants
2 medium onions, peeled
3–4 garlic cloves, peeled
sunflower oil, for frying
1 tsp garam masala
1¾ cups/14oz/400g thick
    plain yogurt
salt and freshly ground
    black pepper

Borani in Farsi refers to a dish of cooked anything with yogurt. It gets its name from one Queen Pourandokht, who seemingly had a serious yogurt habit. This recipe, with eggplants, is one of the most popular versions thereof.

Preheat the oven to 375°F/190°C.

Prick the eggplants and put them in the oven for around 15 minutes, or until soft, then allow to cool a little.

Reserving half an onion, chop the rest, along with the garlic. Fry them in a little oil until the onion soften; at this stage add the garam masala. Cook a little more before allowing these too to cool.

Remove the eggplant calyces and peel some but not all of the skin away (it's good to leave a little on as it gives dishes a chunky homemade feel to them). Scoop the eggplant, together with the cooled onion mixture, into a blender and give it all a quick whizz (or chop thoroughly with a knife) before stirring the mixture into the yogurt. Season to taste.

Chop and fry the other half of the onion until it becomes quite crispy and brown, then when it is cool use it to garnish the *borani*.

This makes a good sammie filler and a great *mezze* item.

MIRZA GHASSEMI: EGGPLANTS, GARLIC, TOMATO, AND EGG

TO SERVE 4

3 eggplants

4 garlic cloves, chopped

salt

dash of olive oil

1 tsp ground turmeric

freshly ground black pepper

4 medium tomatoes

4 perfectly boiled eggs (a bit
    more than soft, but not as
    hard as hard, if you see what
    I mean), roughly chopped

This recipe is to be found across the whole of Iran (although it comes from the north), and is one of those dishes in which it is easy to overindulge. It can be served hot—in which case you may serve the eggs fried on top. But since this is a salad book I suggest serving it warm or cold, with the egg as garnish.

Preheat the oven to 400°F/200°C.

    Prick the eggplants and bake them in the oven for 20–30 minutes. Remove and allow to cool a bit (else you will burn your fingers). Chop off the eggplant "hats," and semi-peel (in Iran they would do it properly, but as this dish is about flavor and not finesse, I think a little skin enhances it), then chop or mash roughly. Blend the garlic in a pinch of salt and fry in a dash of oil. Just as it starts to cook, sprinkle in the turmeric and a sprinkle of black pepper, followed by the tomatoes, and finally the eggplant. Continue to fry for a few more minutes, then take off the heat. Serve sprinkled with the chopped egg and accompanied by warm *lavash* (Iranian flatbread).

MAMA GHANOUSH

FOR A PARTY
BOWLFUL

6 zucchini, trimmed

olive oil (a splash, followed by a
    splash further on)

6 garlic cloves, sliced

2 tsp roughly cracked coriander
    seeds

salt and coarse ground
    black pepper

3–4 large tomatoes (squishy
    ones will do)

2 tbsp *tahina*

juice and grated zest of 1 large
    lemon

handful of fresh cilantro

½ tsp ground cumin

½ tsp smoked paprika

Because Baba shouldn't get all the credit. Yep, OK, so there is no such thing as *Mama Ghanoush*, and I'm just being silly. But if *Baba Ghanoush* translates as "beloved of Baba," then the title is apt, since this recipe is much beloved by my own dear Mama. And the two recipes ARE pretty similar: smoky mashed vegetables with *tahina* and garlic...

So all you do is... preheat the oven to 350°F/180°C. Halve the zucchinis lengthways, place them in a roasting pan, and drizzle them with a little olive oil. Sprinkle the garlic, coriander seeds, salt, and pepper over the top, then bake uncovered for around 30 minutes, or until the corgis* are tender. Allow them to cool a modicum.

    Once the vegetables are cool enough to handle, pop them in a blender (or chop them if making this by hand), garlic and all, and blend along with the tomatoes, *tahina*, lemon, cilantro, and spices. After a couple of minutes drizzle in some olive oil so that the mixture emulsifies a little. You will probably need to do this in 2 batches if you wish to avoid oily overflow mayhem. Season to taste, and serve with warm dippy bread or crunchy croutons.

*Note

No, not an auto-correct classic, but rather British greengrocer slang for courgettes (i.e. zucchini). In the hope that adding the odd bit of vernacular will enhance one's street cred.

MEXICAN-ISH REFRIED BEANS

This is one of those dishes that totally steals the thunder in a meal: it is addictive to the extent that it is all too easy to fill up on it and eschew the main feature. It is, of course, the secret ingredient of many a more complex ensemble (think tacos, fajitas). My version is a real Mexican salmagundi, since I have thrown all the classic ingredients of Mexican food into one dish: corn, avocado, tortilla chips, sour cream...

Original *muchachos* would use pinto beans, but you can improvise with borlotti, red kidney, or turtle (black) beans. By the way, because I am sure that you have always wondered about this, the "refried" bit is a case of culinary misinterpretation—it is a corrupted translation of *refritos* which means "well cooked."

* A note on beans

If you're like me, you're always confusing borlotti and pinto beans. They're real similar, after all: stripy show-off legumes that lose most of their markings when you cook them. Pinto beans, which are used mostly in South American food, are pale salmon pink, with red markings, and have a soft creamy flavor, which is ideal for mashing. Borlotti (also known as cranberry beans) are used more in Mediterranean and Middle Eastern food, and they are beige with rusty brown markings. They are a little firmer than pinto, and so are better for salads/casseroles. They are both, like most common beans, known as *Phaseolus vulgaris* in botanical circles, which is a fancy way of saying "common beans": they probably all originated from one basic species.

A RATHER DISTRACTING SIDE DISH FOR 4

scant 1½ cups/9oz/250g dried pinto beans,*
   soaked overnight (or use 2 cans/14oz/400g)
1 red onion, chopped
sunflower oil, for frying
4 garlic cloves, minced
1 level tsp ground cumin
1 tsp ground coriander
½ tsp chili powder
1 can (14oz/400g) corn, drained
⅔ cup/2¾oz/75g grated Monterey jack-type
   cheese (optional)

salt
3 large firm tomatoes, finely diced
⅓ cucumber, finely diced
½ avocado, diced
4 scallions, chopped
1 green chili (like jalapeño), chopped
   (optional)
big handful of fresh cilantro, chopped
juice of 1 lime

TO SERVE:

nachos or plain tortilla chips
sour cream or plain yogurt

Drain the beans and put them in a pan of unsalted water. Bring to a boil, turn down the heat, and simmer for about 1 hour, or until cooked, before draining. If you are using canned of course you have but to open the things and drain them.

Fry the onion in a little oil. Once it starts to soften, add the garlic and spices, followed a minute or so later by the corn and the drained beans. Cook for few minutes more, mashing and pounding and stirring: at this stage you could put the whole thing in your blender, although I favor the chunky, less homogenized approach. Take off the heat, mix in the cheese, if using, season to taste, and set aside.

Mix the tomatoes, cucumber, avocado, onions, chili, and cilantro together, dress with the lime juice, and add salt to taste.

Spread the still-warm bean mixture onto a serving dish and pile the salsa on top. Serve with nachos (or plain tortilla chips) and sour cream on the side.

SPICED YAM AND *LABNEH*

I suppose I take yams for granted, living in such a wonderfully mixed part of London. But it is impossible to overstate their importance in some parts of the world where they are a staple crop. In his wonderful book *Things Fall Apart* Chinua Achebe writes "Yam stood for manliness, and he who could feed his family on yams from one harvest to another was a very great man indeed."

This is one of those great little dishes that live a double life posing as something else when you're not looking. It works not only as a dip, but also as a rather nice puréed "salad" to go with hot food and as a sandwich spread. Strictly speaking it is a double dip, as I serve the yam and the *labneh* separately: I started doing this originally to cater for vegans, but to be honest the two distinctive layers of flavor are more interesting (and a lot prettier) than if I had just lobbed it all in together.

If you can't find yam, sweet potato makes a dandy stand-in (and in fact little distinction is made in the US).

TO PROVIDE A GOOD PARTY
BOWLFUL

FOR THE YAM:
10½oz/300g water yam
5½oz/150g carrots
2 garlic cloves, chopped
¾in/2cm knob fresh ginger, peeled
     and minced
½ tsp cayenne pepper
1 tsp paprika
1 level tsp ground coriander
½ tsp ground cumin

salt
2 tbsp carrot juice
juice of 1 orange
2 tbsp rice milk (or you can use the regular
     cow-shaped stuff)
1 tbsp peanut oil

FOR THE *LABNEH*:
generous 1 cup/9oz/250g creamed *labneh*
     (or use thick, salted Greek yogurt)
juice and grated zest of ½ lime
1 tsp sumac and an extra pinch to garnish
1 tsp *za'atar*

Peel the yam, cut it into small pieces, and plunge it immediately into a pan of cold water (to stop discoloration). Peel the carrots and add them to the pan. Bring the water to a boil and cook the tubers for around 35 minutes, or until tender. Drain and mash them with the garlic, spices, seasoning, juices, milk, and oil: I do this in a blender, adding the liquid elements while the machine is running.

Next, mix the *labneh* with the lime juice, zest, and spices.

Serve the yam purée in a bowl with the *labneh* dolloped on top. Sprinkle with sumac and serve with warm bread.

MUHAMMARA: PEPPER AND WALNUT PURÉE

**FOR A BIG BOWL
(1½ PINT/750G JAR)**

1lb 2oz/500g *biber salçasi*
    (see bonus recipe)
2 tbsp pomegranate molasses
scant 1 cup/4½oz/125g shelled
    walnuts, crushed but
    not powdered
½ tsp ground cumin
1 tsp ground coriander
1 tsp red pepper flakes
2 tbsp dried breadcrumbs
3 garlic cloves, minced
scant ¼ cup/50ml or so extra-
    virgin olive oil

Muhammara is a bit of a super-star in the Turkish *mezze* kitchen. It works well with warm bread or crudités, or try using it as a dip for a platter of assorted lettuce leaves. *Pictured on far left, opposite.*

I usually mix this by hand since it is better if it has got some chunk and texture to it. Mix all the ingredients, trickling the olive oil in last until the paste is smooth and fairly stiff. It keeps for a week in the fridge.

BONUS RECIPE: *BIBER SALÇASI*

1lb 2oz/500g sweet red peppers
1 tsp salt
2 red chilies, deseeded

Roast the sweet peppers in a hot oven for 20 mins, then cool, peel the skins off, and remove stalks and seeds. Place in a blender with the other ingredients. Scoop the resulting purée onto an oven tray and put back in the oven on a low heat for about 30 minutes, so that any excess water can evaporate. Can be used/stored like tomato paste.

BESARA: FAVA BEAN MASH

**TO MAKE A BOWLFUL
(WILL FEED 4 AS A
GENEROUS SIDE DISH)**

generous 1 cup/7oz/200g dried
    split fava beans, soaked for 6
    hours, or overnight
splash of olive oil
1 large onion, chopped
1 tsp green cumin seeds
    (optional)
1 level tsp smoked paprika
juice of 1 lemon
salt and freshly ground
    black pepper

TO GARNISH:
olive oil, for frying
extra-virgin olive oil, for drizzling
a smidge of paprika

A versatile purée from the Maghreb—and a top comfort food to boot. Enjoy hot or cold. Again, it is rather good with a platter of raw vegetables. *Pictured at bottom, opposite.*

Drain the fava beans. Next, heat a little oil in a saucepan and fry the onion and cumin seeds together for a few minutes, followed by the smoked paprika and most of the drained beans (keep a handful back). Stir well before adding a generous 2 cups/500ml water. Bring to a boil then turn down the heat and simmer for about 1 hour, or until the beans are mushy and most of the water has been absorbed (do check during the cooking process that the liquid has not dried out—if it looks dry, just add another glass of water). Once the beans are cooked, blend or mash them together with the lemon juice and season to taste.

    Finally, heat a little olive oil in a pan and fry the remaining beans until they are browned and crispy. Spoon the *besara* into a bowl, scatter the fried beans on top, then swirl the surface with extra-virgin olive oil and paprika. This is a dish that is best enjoyed fresh and still warm. Serve with crusty bread, extra lemon wedges, and perchance some crudités.

CAULIFLOWER AND TAPENADE DIP

FOR A SMALL
BOWLFUL

1 cauliflower, broken into florets

1 onion, sliced

4–5 garlic cloves

dash of pumpkin seed oil or
    olive oil

3 tbsp herby tapenade (see
    below)

olive oil, to taste

lemon juice, to taste

Tapenade is a classic blend of black olives, anchovies, capers, and olive oil. As a spread or part of another dish it's a corker, but you could no more eat it as a dip (i.e. unaccompanied or in quantity) than you could pesto or wasabi. So we're going to add some puréed cauliflower to spread the flavor.

Preheat the oven to 375°F/190°C.

Spread the cauliflower florets out in an oven tray along with the sliced onion and garlic cloves and drizzle with some pumpkin seed (or olive) oil. Cover with foil and bake for around 25 minutes, or until the veggies are soft. Allow to cool slightly then blend all the veg with the tapenade, olive oil, and lemon juice to taste. Speaking of which…

HERBY BLACK OLIVE TAPENADE

TO MAKE AROUND
7OZ/200G

¾ cup/4½oz/125g pitted black
    olives

3–4 anchovies

2 tbsp olive oil

2 tsp capers

1 tsp herbes de Provence*

Pictured at top, on p.246.

Simply pound or coarsely blend all the ingredients together. This will keep in the fridge for up to a month.

* Make your own herb mix

Been a while since you've been to the South of France? Make your own herb mix by crushing 2 tablespoons dried thyme with 1 teaspoon dried rosemary. Add 1 teaspoon dried lavender, 1 tablespoon dried marjoram, and 1 teaspoon dried savory. Store in an airtight container.
In case of deep stress, open jar and inhale: *you are walking barefoot through a Provençale olive grove; all you can hear is the chirruping of cicadas and the distant sound of goats bleating. There is a gentle breeze but the sky is cloudless. You seek out the shade of one of the larger trees and lie down in the whispering grasses at its base…* Well, you get my drift, yes?

GUACAMOLE

**FOR A MEDIUM
BOWLFUL**

2 ripe avocados

2 large tomatoes, chopped

1 large handful of cilantro,
    chopped

1–2 green chilies, minced

lime juice

salt

The world's favorite green gloop.

Everyone knows how to make guacamole, so I'll keep it brief. This wondrous concoction was being enjoyed by the Aztecs hundreds of years ago in Mexico, but is now pretty much a staple in every Tex-Mex burger joint across the globe. Mash the ripe avocados with the tomatoes, cilantro, chilies, plenty of lime juice, and some salt to taste: resist the temptation to use a blender, as guacamole should be slightly chunky. Serve with tortilla chips, or make it runny and use as a salad dressing.

Handy avocado hint: retain the stone of the fruit and plop it into the dip if you don't eat it all at one sitting—this helps prevent discoloration, which is cool, since guacamole quickly turns sludge-brown when left unattended.

SAFFRON AIOLI

**TO MAKE JUST
A WEE BIT**

¼ tsp ground saffron, steeped in a
    splash of boiling water

juice of ½ lemon

1 egg yolk

4 garlic cloves

pinch of freshly ground
    black pepper

scant ½ cup/100ml light
    (e.g. Spanish or Moroccan)
    extra-virgin olive oil

scant ½ cup/100ml canola or
    sunflower oil

1 cooked, mashed waxy potato
    (cooled)

a big handful of chopped fresh
    dill and cilantro

salt, to taste

Aioli is basically mayonnaise but without the mustard. Another "but" is that it's made with some olive oil instead of just vegetable oil. The Spaniards' secret ingredient for a thick end product is… mashed potato. *Pictured on far right, on p.246.*

To the steeped saffron, add the lemon juice, then either use a whisk or your blender to mix in the egg yolk, garlic cloves, and black pepper. Slowly add the oils, while continuing to blend: you're aiming for a glossy, thick emulsion. Finally, stir in the mashed potato, beating well, and mix in the herbs and salt to taste.

A MARMITE DIP

FOR A WEE BOWLFUL
scant ½ cup/3½oz/100g
    mascarpone
scant ½ cup/3½oz/100g ricotta
1 big tsp Marmite (yeast extract
    paste—check the world foods
    aisle of your supermarket)
1 bunch of watercress
freshly ground black pepper

With the rising popularity of Middle Eastern food, it seems the Middle West has gone dip crazy. Of course we have guacamole, and cream cheese with chives, and *aïoli*, but the genre really belongs to the Eastern end of the Mediterranean. This is my attempt at balancing things out. It doesn't get more British than Marmite and 'cress. (Ignore the fact that I've bulked it out with Italian cheese.)

Marmite and cream cheese go together well, and Marmite and cress are also a celebrity sandwich coupling. So I've hedged my salad bets and lobbed all of these into one recipe.

Whisk it all together. Share if you must. Serve with fancy toast and celery crudités.

CREAM CHEESE, CHIVES, AND BACON

**FOR A LITTLE
BOWLFUL**
2–3 rashers streaky bacon
1 cup/9oz/250g cream cheese
a bunch of chives
    (or scallion tops)
a squeeze of lime juice
cracked black pepper.

This comprises crumbled salad ingredients bound together with cream cheese. A tub of this in your fridge will see you effortlessly through lunchtime sandwiches to cocktail nibbles. And it ain't bad as a midnight snack either.

Broil the rashers of bacon until super-crisp, allow them to cool, then crumble them (I use a rolling pin). Mix them with the cream cheese, chives, lime juice, and black pepper. Stud with chicory leaf "spoons"—or use as a spread.

WHITE BEAN AND ARTICHOKE DIP

**ENOUGH FOR A
SMALL BOWL**
1 can (14oz/400g) cannellini
    beans (drained)
1 can artichoke hearts (drained)
2–3 garlic cloves
a big handful of parsley
1 tsp paprika
½ tsp smoked paprika
sea salt and freshly ground black
    pepper, to taste
lemon juice, to taste
olive oil, to taste

A subtle blend: this is a doddle and can be made in minutes entirely out of store cupboard staples.

Just blend the cannellini beans with the artichoke hearts. Add the garlic cloves, parsley, paprikas, salt and pepper, lemon juice, and olive oil, to taste. Serve with warm bread.

CHAPTER THIRTEEN
The dressing room

Ou pantos andros estin artusai kalos
It is not for every man to season well…
Cratinus

Salads can rise or fall on their dressing: sauce brings the rest of a salad's ingredients together. Simple salad greens can be rendered quite special just by the addition of suitable seasoning and some good oil. And so in this chapter I look at a few basic rules for power dressing. I will also investigate some more unusual (ancient) recipes and some fun dressings that weren't covered in the rest of the book. Mostly it is a question of balance, as Evelyn observes below:

We have said how necessary it is that in the composure of a sallet, every plant should come in to bear its part, without being overpower'd by some herb of a stronger taste, so as to endanger the native sapor and virtue of the rest; but fall into their places, like the notes in music, in which there should be nothing harsh or grating: And though admitting some discords (to distinguish and illustrate the rest) striking in all the more sprightly, and sometimes gentler notes, reconcile all dissonances, and melt them into an agreeable composition.
John Evelyn, *Acetaria: A Discourse of Sallets* (1699)

Although the truth is that you can add herbs or spices to any kind of wet stuff and something kind of oily and you have a dressing already. Notwithstanding the fact a sallet can be as simple as some salted herbs (see p.11), it is pretty much the case that most salads are dressed, and that most of these dressings comprise a combination of oil, seasoning, and a souring agent.

Time for an Oil Change?

Choice of oil is important: the stuff may look innocuous, but some oils are strong and can kill a salad at 30 paces, and some oils are better for you than others. Most of the oil mentioned in this volume is only suitable for salad and cold use, as it is unrefined and has a low cracking point (i.e. it starts smoking when you heat it), which is potentially carcinogenic (these include most nut and seed oils, together with extra-virgin olive oil). Other oil is highly refined (and quite tasteless) and should perhaps be reserved for deep-frying. Here's a mini-salad guide to all things oleaginous:

Argan oil: fancy and very *a la mode*, this stuff is one of the original fairtrade products as all proceeds go back to the Berber women who make it (see p.114). It is quite delish but pricey. Nice with lemon or lime or sour orange, and enjoys the company of fresh herbs and spices.

Avocado oil: wonderful for cooking and salads. A pretty shade of green and great for the skin when used either internally or externally. In dressings it blends well with citrusy souring agents and herbs, but as it is a shade on the pricey side, I have avoided specifying its use here.

Blackseed oil (aka Nigella seed oil): strongly cuminy, as you might imagine. This oil has been used as a panacea in the Middle East for millennia, and is often consumed for medicinal purposes by the spoonful. Use very sparingly in spicy dressings, or in fruity salads.

Canola oil: great for cooking and good for you. Unfortunately, like that over-achiever at work whom you cannot fault, it is in final analysis, rather characterless. A pantry stand-by rather than essential.

Coconut oil: not the easiest to use in salads since it is a solid at room temperature. But use it in a warm dressing in Asian or tropical salads. Your synaptic pathways (or whatever) will thank you (see p.148).

Corn oil: not at all nice for salads, but works well in some dips such as *Taramasalata*.

Grapeseed oil: light and not too expensive, this blends well with fragrant additives such as lavender and herbs. It is another oil which promotes "good" cholesterol.

Linseed oil: linseed produces another super-healthy oil, but it is expensive, strongly flavored, and goes rancid a bit sharpish after opening. One to buy if you're on a health kick maybe. Works well with balsamic vinegar and mustard.

Olive oil:

The soul is olive oil, enamored of fire; it seeks fire as the lover seeks the beloved. (Rumi)

Please tell me you have some of this in your cupboard: it will be hard to use *Salmagundi* without a nice olive oil. There is now pretty much overwhelming evidence that the Mediterranean diet is GOOD FOR YOU, and the lynchpin of this cuisine is olive oil. Olive culture began in ancient Crete, and spread across the region from there. Such was the importance of the commodity to the ancient Greeks that none other than Athena was given the job of being goddess of olives (her gift of an olive tree to the people of Athens can still be seen by the temple of Dionysus at the Acropolis): the fruit thence became a symbol of peace, achievement, and immortality, for it was noted that the olive tree lived for centuries. The Romans loved the stuff too: Cato wrote extensively about early methods of extraction and uses.

As I have mentioned elsewhere, there are two types of olive oil: pure—which you can use for cooking—and extra-virgin—which doesn't like high temperatures and should be reserved for your salad bowl.

The oil is made by crushing black olives in a press: the resultant paste is spun, centrifugal force causing the oil and water components of the product to split. The bitterer (younger) the olives, the finer the oil produced.

Competition among oil-producing nations is fierce. For what it's worth, I rate Cretan (*Kolymvari*) oil but we have recently had some astonishingly tasty oils in from Morocco.

Peanut oil: tastes surprisingly peanutty, and is lovely in Asian-ish salads, not to mention for cooking. It is available in an extra-virgin version, and this is well worth seeking out if, like me, you are a bit of a peanut fan. Mix with rice or apple cider vinegar and aim for a sweet-sour combo. Pals with hot spices too.

Pomace oil: this is the highly refined cheap by-product of real olive oil manufacture. It is tasteless on the whole: not bad for cooking, and good for mixing with olive oil if you want to "stretch" the dressing but not something I recommend, not least because it has experienced a fair share of bad press and related health scares over the years.

Pumpkin seed oil: another luxury oil (i.e. not one for everyday use unless you are heir to a pumpkin plantation). It has such a distinctively nutty flavor that it is worth splashing out on once in a while—the thrifty can stretch it by blending it with olive oil.

Sunflower oil: ditto the bit about canola oil—OK-ish, but only use out of desperation in salads.

Tahina: can be used instead of oil in salads although you will need to thin it with water and lemon juice. It is very rich, and likes citrusy things with which to contrast. Fresh herbs and garlic go well with it too. It doesn't like vinegar.

Toasted sesame oil: has a rich nutty flavor and is best used sparingly—blending with another oil (such as the lighter peanut oil) is always a good option. It is best with vinegar or sweet-sour pastes such as pomegranate molasses.

Truffle oil: needs a wee mortgage add-on to finance, but should you acquire some, use it very sparingly. This is not because of the cost alone, but rather because it is very strong. It works well with carbs—potato, rice, and pasta salads—and blends with vinegar or lemon.

Untoasted sesame oil: use just as you would toasted sesame oil, but you can splash it around a bit more since it is less in-your-face nutty. Mixes well with spices and citrusy souring agents.

Vegetable oil: does anyone use this to make salads? It would be better to make an oil-less dressing than to use this, to be honest—it mostly comprises what I call "empty calories" (i.e. it neither tastes good nor has any nutritional benefits). Keep it for when you are bulk-frying anything.

Walnut oil: another pricey one—but worth having for its pleasantly bitter undertones. Mix with canola or olive oil to make it go further. It goes well with sweet, fruity salads: blend with sour orange or a good vinegar.

Pimp Your Oil!

It is really easy to make your own flavored oil for salad dressing: just take a good (but not the best) extra virgin olive oil and add stuff to it. In order for this to work, you need to wash and thoroughly dry your extra ingredients, as you may otherwise add unwanted foreign bodies and increase the risk of bacterial growth. Bottle and store in the fridge (or freezer for longer-term storage).

Things to add include fresh herbs (rosemary, thyme and tarragon are the best), dried herbs, spices—especially dried chilies and peppercorns—and garlic (obvs).

Have fun with this: at worst it might bring out the domestic-god/goddess wannabe in you, and flavored oils do make great thrifty gifts. Just make sure you read up on the USDA food preservation guidelines and store safely to avoid the risk of harmful bacteria.

A Bit of Sour

Once you've chosen your oil, you'll need something to blend and contrast with it. For most dressings this means a souring agent.

The two most common souring agents are citrus juice (lemon, lime, sour orange, grapefruit) and vinegar. When you should use one and not the other is largely a matter of taste, but they lend such different things to salads that they should in no way be regarded as interchangeable.

For years I was guided by an old Cypriot maxim that salads with tomatoes should be dressed with vinegar, and anything else gets lemon. This works up to a point—and yet in the Middle East salads rarely get shown a bottle of vinegar (it is believed that vinegar is too "cold" and makes you choke), but are mostly dressed simply with lemon, salt, and pepper. Conversely the majority of delicious Far Eastern salads are dressed with vinegar.

As a hopelessly general guide, use citrus with the more savory salads, and vinegar with those that are either sweet or contain a mega-rich ingredient such as cheese. Lemon/lime juice love chili and fresh herbs and spices. Vinegar's best pals are mustard, honey,* soy sauce, and fish sauce. They both love garlic (who doesn't?).

If you decide to go citrus, fresh is ALWAYS better than bottled. But if you do go for bottled, please never ever buy "lemon dressing"—it is vile, chemical-ish, and mostly water. Another word of warning: if you buy Middle Eastern lime or lemon juice, it is usually eye-wateringly strong, so use in small quantities (one can only surmise that Western versions are in some way diluted).

There are many vinegars from which to choose: you can leave anything that contains natural sugars to ferment and you will end up with some sort of vinegar. The stuff has been used for thousands of years but was originally used to preserve food, and then later as a medicine. It was only those gourmandizing French who started producing it specifically for culinary purposes around the sixteenth century. Evelyn refers to making raisin vinegar in his *Acetaria*.

The most common vinegars are wine derived, but in the Middle East grape and apple are more popular, while in the Far East rice vinegar is the thing. Oak-aged balsamic vinegar is another matter entirely: rich and syrupy and wonderful, it should nevertheless be used with caution as it can overpower your salad.

A note on Rumi

I'm a bit besotted with Rumi (who isn't?), and so you'll forgive me the inclusion of another quote thereof:
Tribulation is like vinegar. And kindness is like honey; the two form the basis of sekanjebin... (see p.14—aka salad dressing).

Other fun vinegars for which to watch out include:

Apple cider: all the rage currently, since it is being touted as being most efficacious in the treatment of arthritis. Some diet gurus also recommend it for weight loss, as it "burns fat." It is very good for reducing catarrh. More importantly for us, it adds a lovely fruity flavor to salads. Mixes well with mustard, ginger, and horseradish.

Champagne: light in flavor, but such a fun idea. Blends well with nutty oils and *beaucoup de moutarde*.

Date: thick and delicious, and hard to find outside Iran/Iraq. We are working on it, trust me.

Malt/distilled: put these on your fries. Clean your windows with them, but please only use them on your salads in dire emergencies as they are way too heavy.

Raspberry: this has real wow factor for me, since it works well on sweets as well as salads. I always have a small bottle in my cupboard. Fresh mint and ginger are good companions for it.

Sherry: quite heavy. Tone down with horseradish or something creamy like mascarpone.

Tarragon: so easy to make your own. But lovely in salads, so, if you have to, buy it, otherwise (see below)...

Pimp Your Vinegar!
This is real easy. Boil your chosen vinegar, pour it over your chosen added extras, cool, and set aside (fridge is good) for about a week. Then strain the vinegar and pour it into sterilized* bottles. For max Susie Homemaker effect, insert a few (freshly washed and dried) sprigs of herbs/peppercorns/whatever to the bottle to add color/character. (Check out the USDA's guidelines for safe food preservation and storage.)

Things that work well with vinegar include:
* fresh herb sprigs (thyme, rosemary, tarragon)
* spices: chili, turmeric root, ginger, coriander, cumin…
* berries: blueberries, raspberries, blackberries
* lemon or orange

A note on sterilizing bottles/jars
Sterilizing for this kind of thing is simple. Just pour a little boiling water into your chosen vessels, empty out, and leave to dry thoroughly. (Or you can place in a large pot, cover with water, and simmer for about 10 minutes.)

Other Sour Things

Since oranges are not the only fruit—and so vinegar and lemon don't get all the salad action.

If you fancy a change or want to keep your dinner guests guessing, try one of the following to add sharpness to your salad.

Fruit purée: kiwis, green mangoes, unripe plums, cooking apples, tart berries: all of these can be stewed or blended to add to dressings to make your salads a little bit fabulous.

Pekmez: made from boiled grape (or sometimes mulberry) must, this is a famous Turkish ingredient. Use in stocks and stews and marinades but it works best of all in salad dressings.

Pomegranate molasses: for a sweet sour zing. Blend with oils and spices or use all on its own as a curiously fruity drizzle. Turkish and Arabic versions are best for salad—the much thicker, sharper Iranian variety is just a bit too heavy.

Tamarind paste: very dark and gloopy, so mix judiciously with other ingredients. Tamarind loves ginger and vice versa.

Verjuice (aka sour grape juice): used extensively in the Middle East, and again in seventeenth-century Britain and France. It is like wine vinegar, but is less acidic than vinegar and less, well, winey than wine. Many verjuices are slightly salty, so you will have to adjust your dressing accordingly.

Yogurt: a good sharp yogurt blended with herbs and oil makes a splendid dressing (see Chapter 10).

The Emulsion Principle

The easiest way to make a dressing is to whisk it into an emulsion of sorts. This ensures homogeneity.

My father was a paint chemist — I spent many a happy afternoon watching him mess around with colors and resins in his shed. The principles of salad dressing are very similar: a liquid and an oil are blended at speed until these two normally immiscible* substances bond into a thick paste.

Mayonnaise is the most notable example of this. Its creation in the 1750s following a victorious sea battle at Mahon (whence it gets its name) in Menorca changed salad history.

Mayo in minutes: blend 1 egg yolk with a splash of vinegar and some salt and pepper. Slowly trickle in your oil of choosing (sunflower or a light olive oil are best in this context), whisking constantly (or with the motor of your blender running). Continue until the mayo reaches the required thickness. If it curdles don't despair: just empty the blender (retaining the contents), wash it, and run it under cold water to cool it, and then start a new batch using the curdled gunk in place of oil. Dress up as you wish with garlic, herbs, spices. Check out the Saffron Aioli recipe on p.249.

But mayonnaise aside, most dressings use the same handy rule of physics. You can just shake oil and vinegar or lemon together and you will notice that the sauce thickens and pales in color. If you leave the dressing lying around for a while, it will slowly separate back into its constituent layers (oil on top). But if you add a bonding agent, such as mustard or ketchup or chopped egg yolk, you will create a "permanent" emulsion, which will only separate under extreme pressure (heat usually does it).

The quickest way to make a perfect dressing is to shake everything together in a jar. A whisk and some good wrist action will also achieve the same result. If you have chunky stuff to add in, or are making lots of dressing, then clearly a blender is your best option. Ideally you should always add oil slowly to your other ingredients rather than the other way round.

* Note

Excellent paint vocab for non-blendable: try rolling the word around your tongue a few times—it's a good one, no?

Fatless Dressings

All this talk of oils being good for you and making perfect emulsions is probably rather irritating if you happen to be on a super-low-fat diet. But salad making is just as fun without oil. And some "salads" are better without it (look at the salsa section on pp.213–214).

To be honest you can't go wrong with salt, pepper, and lemon juice on most salads, but you can make a dressing out of practically anything in your pantry, so get it all out and have a play around. Anything you make yourself will be a hundred times better than one of those dire, chemical infused and strangely gelatinous store-bought concoctions. Here are a few of my favorites:

* blend low-fat yogurt with barbecue sauce, chives, and garlic;
* try a mixture of orange juice, lemon juice, mustard, soy sauce, and honey;
* pomegranate molasses, mint, ginger, and vinegar are great on a green salad;
* add harissa paste, chopped cilantro, and flower water to some tomato juice for a great *Maghrebi* dressing;
* add anything to blended silken tofu for a nice creamy low-fat dressing: carrot juice and soy sauce and rice vinegar work well;
* Use any of the lower fat dips in Chapter 10—just make them a whole lot runnier.

Pantry Dressings

In which I clear your cupboards out.

Sometimes, when I don't have much in the way of tangible salad ingredients, I'll get all of my toys out of the cupboard or pantry and make a dressing first. After that I'll rummage around and assemble stuff to go with it. Thus a simple lettuce or some leftover beans can become quite special.

Obviously I can't see inside your cupboards, but these are just a few of my favorite dressing components:

Anchovy paste/crushed anchovies: instantly takes your salad to somewhere warm and happy (unless you don't like fish). It goes without saying that you should only use a teensy amount as it will otherwise be mega-salty and -fishy.

Barbecue/brown/steak sauce: Now don't pooh-pooh this: we've all seen you sneak these into your bacon sandwich. Water down a little, whisk with oil and a little lime juice, and you have a very hearty dressing indeed. Just be warned that the dressing will be rather dark in color.

Chutney/pickle: chop up any chunky pickle or chutney, blend it with oil, check the seasoning, and you have instant salad dressing. I do it all the time in the store—don't tell anyone, now will you?

Essential oils: these are lots of fun to play with but please check with the producer that the oils are food-grade. Lavender, rose, geranium, peppermint, and lemon oil are the best. Just 2–3 drops will suffice.

Jam: yes, jam. Just a little though. Sharper fruit such as sour cherry and plum work best. Add pungent herbs such as thyme or savory, together with some oil and vinegar, and you get a tongue-tinglingly intriguing dressing.

Flower water: just a smidge in a spicy or citrusy dressing adds an extra dimension to your salad.

Ketchup: adds instant sweet-sharpness to dressings. Obviously buddies with mayonnaise but you can slip a little bit in all over the place. See the Queen of Sheba dressing below.

Mint sauce: binds dressings very well. Mix with oil, vinegar, honey, and black pepper, or add as a "cooling agent" to spicy dressings.

Nut butters: for that naughty-but-nice dimension to a dressing. I often mix with soy sauce and rice vinegar. Nut butters will take a bit of extra blending but it is so worth it.

Sun-dried tomatoes: Purée or chop, and mix with garlic and balsamic vinegar. Instant Mediterranean.

Tapenade (or pesto): Ditto the sun-dried tomatoes. Just loosen with some oil and vinegar. Job done.

Secret Seasonings

These are a few of my favorite things to sneak into salad dressings and wow my guests/ungrateful family. Most of these things need a good 30 minutes or so to macerate/marry.

Garlic: hardly secret—half the recipes in this book must contain garlic. Apologies if I've accidentally ruined any dates or business meetings. Anyway, there is a secret to using garlic in dressings, which is to let it sit and infuse for a while. It makes a world of difference.

Ginger: chopped ginger is one of my favorite salad add-ins, and one of the easiest ways to include more in your diet.

Herbs: if using fresh, bruise them first to release the flavor. If using dried, leave for an hour or so for the flavors to infuse.

Lavender: simply lush. Best to buy organic but if you are picking your own, like any foraged food, pick stuff that's away from busy roads/out of dogs' "reach."

Tea: for a touch of hidden class, really fragrant teas such as Earl Grey and Lapsang Souchong and even Rooibos can be infused in warm vinegar, which is then allowed to cool and strained. I often cheat by using the contents of a fragrant teabag.

Toasted spices: adding raw ground or whole spices to your dressing may add texture, but for the flavor to come through, you should toast the spices first. Or use a blend such as harissa seasoning which comprises pre-toasted ingredients.

Five Golden Rules

The very essence of salmagundi is that of a kind of free-for-all salad jamboree, but there are one or two general principles the adhering to which will make your dressing routine that much the easier.

* Always leave your salad ingredients to dry/drain properly: an oily dressing will be repelled by wet leaves, etc.

* When using dried herbs, garlic, ginger, spices—anything that is solid rather than liquid, in fact—always give your dressing as long as possible to infuse.

* Dressing rarely improve for being refrigerated (a lot of good oil solidifies in the fridge for starters), so try and make/serve them at room temperature. If you do need to refrigerate them, bring them back to room temperature before using.

* If your salad dressing is particularly heavy or dark in color, do consider serving it separately or dressing your salad in front of guests: it may otherwise resemble a lumpy slurry.

* With very few exceptions, salads are always best dressed at the last possible minute. This applies particularly to leafy salads, which sink fast once they are dressed. Only grainy salads or those that require time to marinate are best sauced up in advance.

Some Famous Dressings

I have tried in the pages of this book to globe trot and pootle through history, but there are, inevitably, a few omissions. So here are a few of the more important dressings that didn't make it into an actual recipe.

A Modern Oenogarum

Seeing as the Romans more or less invented salads, it seems only fair that I offer you a typical Roman dressing. As I mentioned previously, the reason we know so much about Roman cuisine is because of Apicius, one of the earliest food writers. And thanks to Sally Grainger's excellent book *Cooking Apicius*, we can, with a reasonable degree of tenacity, recreate many of the more unusual recipes at home. The single most important ingredient is fish sauce. For real. It came in two forms: *garum*, which frankly sounds disgusting and was composed of rotted fish blood; and *liquamen*, which was made of fermented, salted, pressed fish (often anchovy) and resembles the fish sauce so beloved of Thai and Far Eastern chefs. It is the ultimate *umami* flavoring. Grainger suggests boiling grape juice and Asian fish sauce to a thick paste to replicate the taste of *liquamen*. She also refers to *defrutum*, which is a thick grape paste a bit like *pekmez*, and *passum*—a sweet, strong dessert wine. So our dressing here has elements of those.

To dress a salad for 4, blend 1 tablespoon bottled Asian fish sauce with 1 tablespoon *pekmez* and 1 tablespoon port. Whisk in 2 tablespoons olive oil together with 1 teaspoon summer savory. Use on a salad composed of mixed leaves, capers, eggs, and pine nuts (pignolias). Eat while wearing togas, reclined and quaffing copious quantities of wine. Dancing women are optional. But be warned: vomiting in the back room is strictly not allowed.

He also "wrote" (a term used advisedly, as much of his work comes down to us through second-hand writings) of a salad dressing used as a remedy for indigestion and flatulence: *for* ad digestionem, *mash cumin, ginger, black pepper, and rue leaves with some dates and honey. Add vinegar and use to dress lettuce or sup after a heavy meal.*

A Homage to Evelyn

As mentioned in the introduction, John Evelyn wrote the first ever treatise on salad preparation. The dude was well ahead of his time in most every respect, and also sets a fine precedent for books going off on a (albeit fascinating) tangent. Ahem. He would have you prepare your leafy salad, preferably home-grown and carefully washed, in an earthenware bowl (not metal).

To make the dressing, work to a ratio of three parts olive oyl [sic] to one part vinegar (he would have used home-made raisin vinegar). Steep some grated horseradish root and a "bruised pod of Guinny pepper" (this is actually cayenne, so use a pinch of grated cayenne) in the vinegar, followed by "as much grated Tewkesbury mustard* as will lie upon a half crown piece." Mix the oil and vinegar at the last moment before you wish to serve your salad, mashing them together with the yolks of two boiled eggs. Garnish with "sprinklings of aromaticks" and flowers, and horseradish (this would be one eye-watering salad methinks), and red beet and berberries. This is, as referenced in the intro to this chapter, a "warm" dressing designed to offset the typically "cold" ingredients which it is destined to coat: Evelyn, like most of his contemporaries, strongly adhered to the theory of the four humors, and sought balance in all things.

*Tewkesbury mustard was a famous in the seventeenth century: it was blend of mustard and horseradish, which was then dried in balls ready for reconstitution as required. I was greatly cheered to see that the tradition has recently been revived as a cottage industry, and you can once again buy mustard in this way.

On French Dressing

This is the classic, simple dressing for leafy salads: the one with which we are most familiar. It is clearly related to Evelyn's dressing above: the French were just as busy on the gastronomic front in the seventeenth century as the Brits were—and Evelyn had visited France.

A proper French dressing requires three parts (olive, *bien sûr*) oil to one part (red wine, obvs) vinegar. Any seasoning is first mixed with the vinegar, then blended or shaken with the oil. And the classic vinaigrette recipe stops there: the only flavoring is salt and pepper. In practice most French chefs add a bit of Dijon mustard to bind the dressing, and many add garlic and herbs.

The dressing should be applied at the last minute, otherwise your salad will sink, and it should only ever be applied to dry leaves: the best technique is to pour the dressing into a bowl and toss the leaves in by hand. *Et voila*!

The Origins of Thousand Island Dressing: The Pink Stuff!

This is another classic. There are a million variations, and I have certainly made use of mayonnaise mixtures in this book.

Like a lot of American recipes, it is hard to ascertain who devised the original recipe: our buddy Oscar Tschirky of the Waldorf is one possible, as is a dame called Sophia Lalonde, who ran an hotel in the Thousand Island area between NYC and Canada.

The earliest accounts refer to maynnaise being mixed with heavy cream, chives, tarragon vinegar, lemon juice, and various types of pepper. It seems to have become spicier (through the addition of hot sauce, mustard, or Worcestershire sauce) and pinker (through the addition of paprika, and, more recently, ketchup) as the years went by.

For what it's worth I make mine by beating 3 tablespoons mayonnaise with 1 tablespoon low-fat yogurt, 1½ tablespoons ketchup, the juice of 1 small lemon, 2 teaspoons mustard, 1 teaspoon Worcestershire sauce, and Tabasco to taste. Freshly chopped chives and tarragon get thrown in when I have them on hand.

Blue Cheese Salad Dressing

Everybody's favorite, yes? It's one of those dressings wherein you come to resent the actual salad; the kind you just want to shovel in by the spoonful. This is at its best served with a bacon-bit strewed salad of apple and celery and iceberg lettuce, but hey you can put it on your oatmeal, if you like.

FOR A SMALL SIDE SALAD FOR 4

4oz/120g blue cheese
5 tbsp/75ml sour cream
1 tbsp walnut oil (or use grapeseed, or canola)
1 tbsp apple cider vinegar
1 squeeze of lemon juice (i.e. to taste)
⅓ tsp freshly ground black pepper
celery salt

Mash the blue cheese then beat in the other ingredients. You can use a blender for a smoother end result. Don't stand and eat it with a spoon: you will make yourself sick.

Queen of Sheba Dressing

Just for a bit of fun…
This is a modern Ethiopian dressing that I sourced from one of my East African customers. Since it is quite different (and a bit of a crowd pleaser) I thought it should have a place in the book. It is (if you leave out the hotter spices) a fabulous (sneaky) way of getting reluctant small folk to eat vegetables.

FOR A SALAD FOR 4

scant ½ cup/100ml ketchup
scant ½ cup/100ml red wine vinegar
scant ¼ cup/50ml Marsala (or other sweet wine,
    but replace with grape juice if cooking for kiddies)
scant ¼ cup/50ml salad oil
1 tsp Tabasco
2 garlic cloves, minced
salt

Just beat all the ingredients together. In Ethiopia this dressing is poured over a salad of chunked tomatoes, red onions, and salami. An all-red salad—woop-di-doop.

CHAPTER FOURTEEN

The prop cupboard

So you've got your salad sitting there in the bowl waiting for you. And you realize that it just lacks something. Maybe it's color, crunch, or that *umami* something in flavor. Or maybe it's just boring.

A salad is just like a good outfit: it can be raised to something rather fancy by the addition of a bit of edible bling. A tired lettuce, tomato, and cucumber combo suddenly becomes a lot more attractive with the addition of a few basic croutons. Add in a few herbs, some flowers, or a handful of nuts and you'll have them fighting over the salad rather than shuffling it in lackluster fashion around the table. In this section we will take a look at all the little add-ons that can turn a good salad into a real fancy one.

Croutons

It should be obvious by now (if you have read any of the preceding pages) that I hate waste, and have picked up the Middle Eastern thing of believing that it is sinful to throw stale/surplus bread away. Croutons provide the perfect answer, are endlessly popular, can be made in advance, and give salads some bite.

Making them takes just minutes: cut your bread (flatbread, fat bread, rye bread, gluten-free bread…) into pieces or cubes of the desired size and fry in hot oil, flavored if you like with garlic, herbs, or spices. If your bread is still soft it is best to toast it lightly before frying it—this stops the bread soaking up all the oil. When frying the croutons, don't forget that they will continue to crisp once out of the pan, so do not wait until they resemble little lumps of charcoal. Drain on paper towel, then for goodness' sake hide them, otherwise everyone who wanders through the kitchen will be helping themselves.

Want croutons but you don't have the time to make your own (or you don't have any stale bread)? Just crumble some crackers over your salad at the last minute: rye crackers are particularly good for this since they hold their shape relatively well.

Sprinkles and Crunchies

These are the little extras that most kitchens have, knocking around somewhere that can be deployed to add a bit of fun to your salads.

In theory anything that is crunchy and comestible and not obviously designated for the dog bowl or dessert trolley can be lobbed into a salad. Here are a few ideas, but the list is not finite:

* savory granola (see p.180);
* fried legumes: when you soak beans or peas for cooking, retain a few uncooked ones, then drain them and fry them for salads and garnishes. Season with salt, paprika, etc. Works especially well with chickpeas and split fava beans;
* chips and other junky snacks—want to disguise your potato chip habit? Bury them in salads, but add them at the last minute, obviously, as they will otherwise go soggy;

* fried, dried vegetables—crispy-fry sliced onion, grated carrot, or zucchini, pat them with paper towel to remove excess oil, then bake them in an oven preheated to 300°F/150°C (ish) for about an hour to dry out any residual moisture;
* Punjabi mix—for the ultimate in taste bud titillation— it is small enough to vanish into the salad and keep everyone guessing, but man enough to hold its shape and flavor;
* some breakfast cereals—fried shredded wheat is quite fun. Or use any unsweetened crunchy wholegrain cereal.

And last but not least…

Make your own bacon bits. Oh yes.

Let's admit it: we've all had bacon bits on some cheap all-you-can-eat buffet somewhere. And we've all though, "Ew—I hate to think what's in these but aren't they wonderful." Well, you can make your own, and they keep. Wanna know how?

Just grill around 6 rashers of bacon until brown—as in just starting to be a bit too brown. Dab with paper towel to absorb any surplus fat, cool, then blitz in a blender. Preheat the oven to 375°F/190°C, spread your bacon bits out on a tray, and bake for around 5 minutes. Allow to cool then store in an airtight container in the fridge: they'll keep for up 4 days (and 3–4 months in the freezer).

Edible Flowers

Bring a little pizzazz to your salads with a handful of edible flowers. I get terribly over-excited by these—what could be better than having a whole bunch of flowers that you can eat? Having said that, Master Shopcat will eat any flowers, regardless of whether they are deemed suitable or not.

Now if you are an experienced gardener, apothecary, herbalist, or what-you-will, this business of grow stuff and eat stuff is just fine. But for most of us it is fraught with pitfalls. As in the vast majority of blooms that cannot be eaten, and the minority that are actually poisonous. So while I offer here a short list of flowers you can eat, please don't go cruising the neighborhood with your garden shears: do what I do and buy the stuff as an occasional treat. There are some which are common in gardens, unmistakable, and safe but even if you are sure of what you are picking, you still need to

be sure that it has not been sprayed with pesticides or peed on by the neighbor's dog.

It is a snap in this electronic age to source pretty, washed, organic, pert-looking flowers online.

The common or garden stuff which even this botanical ignoramus can identify include:

* arugula flowers, wild and cultivated—peppery, like the plant itself;
* borage—pretty blue, tastes like a peppery cucumber, good in tea and cocktails as well as salads;
* calendula (aka marigold)—only use the petals. Slightly citrusy in flavor;
* cilantro flowers—tastes much the same as the herb itself. Dainty and white;
* cornflower—as blue as blue can be. Once again, just use the petals;
* dahlia—not strong in flavor, but they offer a great range of colors to add to your salad palette;
* nasturtiums—perhaps the most notable edible flower of the bunch;
* violas—a boon to any salad for the variegated, bright colors.
* zucchini flowers—famously good for stuffing—try making little salad parcels with them or shred the petals into a salad.

Other suitable salad blooms include: anchusa, fava bean flowers, chicory flowers, chive flowers, some daisies, some types of geranium, gladioli, honeysuckle, pea flowers, primrose, primula, snapdragons, and tulips.

Fresh and Micro Herbs

A handful of freshly strewn or chopped herbs add instant depth and color to the flavor and appearance of any salad. I have already gone on about the importance of herbs in Chapter 1 (p.11): if you have a herb garden, or a bag of prepared, washed herbs in your fridge, your salad days will be a snap. Just mix a few herbs through a bowl of shredded lettuce and you have an instant and appealing salad.

Micro herbs are a bit of a culinary fad, but there is no great mystery to them: they are simply the young sprouts of regular herbs that have been picked before they reach maturity. They are easy to grow as they only take a few weeks to germinate and sprout: my micro green insider recommends that you plant them in lengths of guttering.

Why are they so popular? Because they pack such intense flavors into every bite: somehow micro parsley is more parsley-ish, and micro basil more basil-ish. And they are salad eye-candy. Micro stuff to look out for includes:

* red amaranth—sensational wherever it goes (check out the smoked salmon and grapefruit salad on p.218)
* fennel tops—wispy and ethereal
* purple basil—strong in color and flavor
* lemon balm—surely one of the happiest flavors around
* garlic chives—elegant, but with a great big butch taste
* baby chard leaves—peppery, earthy
* mustard and cress/micro watercress—more peppery
* celery leaf—curiously lemony.

Nuts and Seeds

This is a no-brainer: adding any kind of nuts, whether raw or roasted and salted, is going to get the family fighting over the salad bowl. They add crunch and protein and make a feature or what might otherwise be a drab side dish. Any nuts will do the job, so I will not waste space with a list.

Seeds do the same and offer a way of getting some healthy oils inside recalcitrant smalls: pumpkin, sunflower, linseed, hemp, sesame, chia, poppy… and again, you can go toasted or untoasted.

Toast nuts or seeds by dry-frying them. Or you can toss them in seasoned oil and bake or fry them until golden. They can also be microwaved for a few minutes. Alternatively, caramelize nuts by frying them with a dash of brown sugar.

It is a subtle but satisfying touch to use matching oils and nuts in your salad: thus pumpkin seed oil dressing gets some crunchy pumpkin seeds in the actual salad, and a salad with shelled walnuts is coated with a walnut oil-based dressing.

Things in Jars

Olives, chilies, pickles, capers, sun-dried tomatoes, pickled onions—everyone has some of these in their cabinets or pantries. There is a whole salad composed of things in jars on p.70, but this is just a quick, albeit quite unnecessary, reminder that you have a bunch of last minute salad props at your disposal. Use the contents of those jars, ladies and gentlemen: keep the stuff in your cabinets moving.

Most stuff in jars is pleasingly salty or piquant, and often brings a desirable *umami* flavor to salads: just make sure you adjust your dressing to take the extra vinegar/seasoning that such additives bring into account.

Showing Off: On Carved Stuff

An unfeasibly pretty girl with exquisitely manicured hands talks in an angel-like tinkle about food and aesthetics, while simultaneously whittling a carrot into the shape of the Eiffel Tower with a shiny mother-of-pearl knife, all the while beaming at the camera. YouTube is a wonderful thing, but it can be depressing at times. I can only dream of the manicure, the knife skills (Mr. Shopkeeper often hides sharp objects from me, I'm that clumsy), the patience…

Fruit and vegetable carving is a wondrous art, and one that takes time and dedication. The practice evolved in all likelihood in fourteenth-century Thailand, as a means of impressing the royal courts: it is also widespread in China and Japan (where it is known as *mukimono*). You may have seen watermelons carved into the features of famous peeps, and beautiful birds of paradise crafted from bits of radish and zucchini. Well, I'm not going to tell you how to do this: it is beyond me. The good news is that you don't have to resort to online tutorials: most Thai restaurants are proud to help spread their culinary culture, and the better chefs therein will happily give you a lesson or two (in return, perhaps, for doing the dishes?). Furthermore, there are formal classes across the country.

There are some simple tricks, however, that even I can manage: two-second twists that will make you salad look just that bit prettier/zanier. And who doesn't like to show off?

* Funky cucumber: wash your required length of cucumber, then take a fork and rake the sides of the cucumber firmly (taking care not to slip and prong yourself). When you slice the cucumber it will have pretty edges, like it's been cut with pinking shears.
* Citrus flowers: cut any citrus fruit in half, and remove a tiny bit from the bottom of one half so that it has a flat surface on which to sit. Using a sharp vegetable parer, carefully pare a thin ribbon of skin to nine-tenths of the way around the cut edge of the fruit without cutting through the ribbon (i.e. leave it attached to the fruit). Curl and tie the pared strand back on itself so it looks like a flower. So much better than a wedge of lemon as a garnish, no?
* Tomato flowers: you will need a firm tomato for this. Use a sharp knife to peel a thin continuous strip around the tomato from top to bottom. Chop the tomato flesh into your salad, then wind the loose strip of peel back in on itself to form a rose bud garnish. Cute, eh?
* Scallion/radish sprays: remove the rooty bits from the end of scallions or radishes, and cut through the vegetable lengthways—about 1¼in/3cm for the former, and ⅝in/1.5cm for the latter. Roll them over and do the same at right angles, so that the end of each veggie in effect has a cross-shaped incision in it. Leave to soak in cold water for about an hour, and watch them open out into real fancy sprays/fans. Dot on top of Asian salads.

* Zucchini leaves: cut a thin slice the length of a zucchini, then trim it into the basic shape of a long pointed leaf. Use a craft knife (best wash it first if you have just rescued it from the shed) to delineate the shape of the stalk of the leaf (engrave two parallel lines from top to bottom), then carve out triangular nicks all the way down this central stalk to represent the leaves. Make further triangular nicks along the outer edges of the "leaf." Clever stuff. Make several to go around the outside of a salad platter.
* Salad *banderillas*: use a mandolin to shave lengths of cucumber, zucchini, and carrot. Concertina them and poke on to cocktail sticks with cherry tomatoes, cocktail onions, and whatever else takes your fancy. Makes for an unusual salad garnish for a plate of whatever.
* Carrot flowers: cleverest of the bunch, this. There are two options here. The first requires a sharp and very small pastry cutter: slice a fat carrot thinly, then use the pastry cutter to stamp out flower (or whatever) shapes. You can further delineate the shape with a craft knife. The second method is a bit trickier. You will need a fairly straight carrot of medium thickness. We've recently started selling bio-dynamic* veggies, and our heritage carrots are purple, white, and orange, so look out for these if you see them since they make excellent garnishes. Cut thin flat slices—4–5 of them—from top to bottom of the carrot, so that if you held it on end it would seem to have a square (or pentagonal) shape, and the pointy end looks extra pointy and thin. Next, hold the carrot pointing away from you and use a sharp knife to cut from where the carrot begins to go pointy, under one of the edges created by your previous cuts: cut nearly all the way to the end.

Repeat with the other 3–4 angled edges: you should now be able to pinch the end of the carrot and pull off a perfect, partly opened flower. Repeat all the way up the carrot: you should get 5–6 flowers out of each carrot. Super impressive on a salad or you could wear them in your hair to confuse people.

*Useless info

Bio-dynamic is the term used to refer to a holistic approach to agriculture, where the properties of the soil, the farming methods, and the range of products/livestock cultivated on a farm are all seen to be interdependent, part of an ecological chain. It is kind of organic farming with extra-ethical bits, notwithstanding a helping of pixie dust. It is based on a system of rural practice evolved by Rudolph Steiner in the 1920s, and is governed by an international organization that rejoices under the splendidly James Bondian title of Demeter.

INDEX